"Seventeen Syllables"

Women Writers
Texts and Contexts

VOLUMES IN THE SERIES

"Seventeen Syllables"

□ HISAYE YAMAMOTO ■

Edited and with an introduction by
KING-KOK CHEUNG

Rutgers University Press

Library of Congress Cataloging-in-Publication Data

Yamamoto, Hisaye.
  Seventeen syllables / Hisaye Yamamoto ; King-Kok Cheung, editor.
    p.   cm. — (Women writers)
  Includes an authoritative text of the story, along with a
chronology, critical essays, and a bibliography.
  Includes bibliographical references (p.   ).
  ISBN 0-8135-2053-3 (pbk.)

  1. Mothers and daughters—United States—Fiction. 2. Japanese
Americans—Fiction. I. Cheung, King-Kok
  II. Title. III. Series: Women writers (New Brunswick, N.J.).
PS3575.A43S4   1994   93-31171
                                                              CIP

British Cataloging-in-Publication information available

To Hisaye Yamamoto

❏ Contents ∎

❏ Acknowledgments ■

Research grants from the UCLA Academic Senate and the Asian American Studies Center enabled me to undertake this project. I would like to thank Martha Banta, Leslie Mitchner, and Stuart Mitchner for their careful reading of the entire manuscript; Gerard Maré, Rosalind Melis, Kathryn Poethig, and Stan Yogi for their helpful suggestions; Kyungwon Grace Hong, Barbara Jung, and Rachel Lee for their valuable research assistance; and Marilyn Sanders for allowing me to use her portrait of Hisaye Yamamoto. Special thanks to Barbara Smith of Kitchen Table Press for making the work of Yamamoto available to a wide audience in America.

My deepest gratitude goes to Hisaye Yamamoto, who graciously put up with my importunate questions.

❑ Introduction

Introduction

I

Hisaye Yamamoto reveals that though all the details of "Seventeen Syllables" are invented, this "most reprinted" story of hers is about her mother: "Maybe she, wherever she is, guided the writing of it, and, even now, this propagation of it . . . so that her story would be known."[1] This story, which first appeared in *Partisan Review* in November 1949, has since been included in so many anthologies that the author has lost count.

Yamamoto was born in 1921 in Redondo Beach, California. Her parents were immigrants from Kumamoto, Japan. She studied at Excelsior Union High and Compton Junior College, majoring in French, Spanish, German, and Latin; she also attended Japanese schools for twelve years. She started writing as a teenager, for a time assuming the pseudonym Napoleon "as an apology for [her] little madness." Yamamoto says she "fell into writing" because she had "early contracted the disease of compulsive reading." But she also writes "to reaffirm certain basic truths which seem to get lost in the shuffle from generation to generation, so that we seem destined to go on making the same mistake over and over again." If readers are "entertained, wonderful"; if they learn something, "that's a bonus."[2]

During World War II Yamamoto was interned in a detention camp for Japanese Americans in Poston, Arizona. There she served variously as a columnist and an editor for the *Poston Chronicle* (the camp newspaper) and published "Death Rides the Rails to Poston," a serialized mystery. In response to the government's effort to resettle the nisei,*

---

* Nisei are second-generation Japanese Americans, children of the issei (Japanese immigrants). Authors handle the words "issei" and "nisei" differently:

Yamamoto worked briefly one summer as a cook in Springfield, Massachusetts. She returned to Poston upon receiving the news that her brother Johnny had been killed at the age of nineteen fighting with the American army in Italy. "After Johnny died," she recalls, "one kind soul insisted that now I had experienced all a Japanese in America could and that I must put it all down in a book for all the world to read." Instead, she gathered all the notes urging her to write about Johnny "into a nice pile and chucked them all in the wastebasket. They made a hauntingly lovely thud."[3]

After the war Yamamoto worked from 1945 to 1948 as a columnist and re-write person for the *Los Angeles Tribune,* a black weekly. We can get a sense of how strongly that experience affected her from "A Fire in Fontana" (1985), her memoir about reporting the death of a black family that had moved into a white neighborhood. Soon after the publication of her first story "The High-Heeled Shoes" in *Partisan Review* in 1948, she left the *Tribune* to try writing fiction full time, with the support of her brother Jemo and with "posthumous help"—an insurance bequest—from Johnny.

In 1950 she received a John Hay Whitney Foundation Opportunity Fellowship. She recalls how Paul, a child she adopted in 1948 when he was five months old, "used to pound on the door, demanding to be let in" or "would wedge himself between the typewriter and [Yamamoto] and, spreading out his arms, say, 'Don't type!'" She wrote stories and translated *L'Enfant à la Balustrade* by the turn-of-the-century novelist René Boylesve during this period of "subsidized writing," but for some reason concluded she "didn't contain enough information to be a writer." Though encouraged by Yvor Winters to accept a Stanford Writing Fellowship, she "regretfully said no" when an inquiry came as to whether she would consider accepting one.[4]

Drawn to the pacifist and selfless ideals advocated in the *Catholic Worker,* a monthly founded by Dorothy Day and Peter Maurin, Yamamoto volunteered in 1953 to work for a

---

some have them capitalized, others have them italicized. The variations have been left as they appeared in the various works reprinted in this volume.

Catholic Worker community farm on Staten Island and lived there with Paul for two years. She married Anthony DeSoto in 1955 and became mother to four more children after returning to Los Angeles. Though she did not stop writing completely, she confided that on questionnaires, she must "in all honesty list [her] occupation as housewife."

II

Knowledge of Japanese American history is conducive to our appreciation of "Seventeen Syllables" (and all Yamamoto's fiction) as well as her achievement as a writer.[5] Most Japanese immigrants came to the United States between 1885 (the year the Japanese government officially permitted the emigration of Japanese nationals) and 1924 (the year the Asian Exclusion Act was passed). The first waves of immigrants consisted mainly of single young men who saw America as a land of opportunity. Only after establishing themselves in the new country did they contemplate marriage and family. Many marriages were arranged by means of photographs exchanged across the Pacific. Hence a large number of Japanese "picture brides" came to America after the turn of the century to meet bridegrooms they had never seen in person. By 1930 the American-born nisei outnumbered the first generation issei. Roughly half the Japanese American population lived in rural areas in the western United States. The Alien Land Law Act of 1913 had, however, prohibited "aliens ineligible for citizenship" from buying or leasing land for more than three years, forcing many families like Yamamoto's to move constantly. As Japanese was the language generally spoken at home, many nisei (including Yamamoto) spoke only Japanese until they entered kindergarten.

Interest in literature was strong among Japanese Americans. Despite the hardscrabble life in the New World, many issei wrote poems. There were literary groups engaged in the traditional forms of haiku, tanka, and senryu, and numerous magazines devoted to issei poetry. Yamamoto's mother wrote senryu and published in Japanese-language papers. Nisei with a literary bent, on the other band, expressed themselves in the English sections of Japanese American newspapers such as

The New World in San Francisco and *Kashu Mainichi* in Los Angeles. Yamamoto contributed regularly to *Kashu Mainichi* as a teenager. In the 1930s and 1940s magazines such as *Reimei, Current Life,* and *Leaves* published fiction and poetry by nisei. In 1939, the League of Nisei Writers and Artists was founded, of which Yamamoto was a "peripheral associate."[6] This group met weekly at the house of journalist Mary Oyama to "promote their own culture," "organizing themselves like the League of American Writers."[7]

World War II drastically altered the Japanese community in America. Within four months of the bombing of Pearl Harbor over 110,000 Japanese Americans were forced to abandon homes, farms, and businesses all through the West Coast and were detained in various internment camps. Besides dislocating Japanese Americans physically and psychologically, the internment also disrupted their nascent literary tradition. Many issei destroyed their own writing in Japanese to avoid being suspected of disloyalty. But some issei and nisei persisted in their writing, even while in camp. Poems and short stories appeared in camp magazines such as *Poston Notes and Activities, Trek,* and *Tulean Dispatch Magazine.*

The experience of incarceration looms large in postwar writing, notably in the works of Jeanne Wakatsuki Houston, Lawson Inada, John Okada, Mine Okubo, Monica Sone, Yoshiko Uchida, Mitsuye Yamada, and Wakako Yamauchi. "Any extensive literary treatment of the Japanese in this country would be incomplete without some acknowledgment of the camp experience," Yamamoto observes in "'. . . I Still Carry It Around,'" an essay on literature about the internment. "It is an episode in our collective life which wounded us more painfully than we realize." "The Legend of Miss Sasagawara," a story about confinement and derangement, is set in the camp at Poston.

III

Yamamoto was one of the first Japanese American writers to gain national recognition after the war, at a time when anti-Japanese sentiment was still rampant. "The High-Heeled Shoes" (1948), "The Brown House" (1951), and "Epithalamium" (1960) appeared in Martha Foley's lists of "Distinctive Short Stories"; "Yoneko's Earthquake" (1951) was included in *Best American Short Stories: 1952*. The editors of *Aiiieeeee!* (1974), an influential anthology of Asian American writers, consider Yamamoto to be "Asian-America's most accomplished short story writer, as of this writing." These editors reiterate their assessment in *The Big Aiiieeeee!* (1991): "Technically and stylistically, [Yamamoto's] is among the most highly developed of Asian American writing."[8] Yet it was in Japan that a collection of her stories first appeared, in 1985. Entitled *Seventeen Syllables: 5 Stories of Japanese American Life*, it was edited by Robert Rolf and Norimitsu Ayuzawa. In 1986 Yamamoto received the American Book Award for Lifetime Achievement from the Before Columbus Foundation. Fifteen of her short stories can now be found in *Seventeen Syllables and Other Stories*, published by Kitchen Table Press in 1988. *Hot Summer Winds*, a film written and directed by Emiko Omori, is loosely based on "Seventeen Syllables" and "Yoneko's Earthquake"; it was first broadcast in May 1991 as part of PBS's *American Playhouse* series.

Yamamoto acknowledges the "great influence" of the Japanese tradition on her as a writer, but it is the "interaction of the Japanese tradition with the American experience" that quickens her fiction.[9] Rich in local color, her writing commands a wide range of subjects: sexual harassment in "The High-Heeled Shoes"; romance with a twist in "Epithalamium"; an issei odyssey that spans Japanese American history in "Las Vegas Charley"; prismatic interethnic and interracial encounters in "The Brown House," "Wilshire Bus," and "The Eskimo Connection." Nevertheless, Yamamoto has told an interviewer that she "didn't have any imagination" and that she "just *embroidered* on things that happened, or that people told [her] happened."[10] The statement—a reflection of her inordinate modesty—reveals the extent to which personal and historical circumstances form the grist for her fictional mill. Stories such as "The High-Heeled Shoes," "After Johnny Died," "A Fire in Fontana" are explicit memoirs. Many others are inspired by real people or events: the title character in "The Legend of Miss Sasagawara" is based on an actual dancer; "Yoneko's Earthquake" draws on the 1933 earthquake in

Long Beach; the brother remembered in "Florentine Gardens" is clearly Johnny.

In dramatizing the encounter between the New World and the Old, Yamamoto, who describes herself as an "anarchist Christian," does not shy away from religious and moral issues. She alludes frequently to both Buddhism and Christianity without ever being dogmatic or moralistic. She shows remarkable compassion toward putative deviants and sinners, be they illicit lovers, gamblers, alcoholics, or prisoners. Her characters tend to be caught in circumstances that render unqualified approval or condemnation difficult.

Perhaps her "anarchy" is best represented by her insistence on giving voice to the voiceless. Recurrent in many of her stories is the theme of repression and silence. "High-Heeled Shoes" describes the anger, frustration, and shame that overwhelm women who are victims of harassment and whose grievances fall on the deaf ears of male police. In "The Legend of Miss Sasagawara," a female dancer who fails to conform to patriarchal, communal, and racial norms is considered "mad" and is eventually institutionalized. "Wilshire Bus" (1950), "Life among the Oil Fields" (1979), and "A Fire in Fontana" (1985) depict the impotent rage of characters dumbfounded by racism. But Yamamoto seldom protests openly. She uses muted plot, symbolic scene, and understatement to evoke feelings that lie beneath the surface of language, compelling her readers to grapple with what is left unsaid. We experience through her characters the pain and frustration of silence; we learn through her narration its evocative power.

Yamamoto is most noted for depicting the muffled drama in Japanese American families: the cultural distance between immigrants and their children, the uneasy adjustment of issei in the New World and, above all, the constrictions experienced by Japanese American women. Because of the prevalence of arranged marriages among issei, compatibility between couples could hardly be assumed. Yamamoto saves her strongest sympathy for women married to dutiful but often oppressive husbands. Rural issei women were not only separated by the Pacific from their extended families but often cut off from one another. Fully occupied with the care of children and farm work alongside their husbands, they had little time and opportunity to cultivate friendships with other women.[11] The only females to whom they could disclose their thoughts were their own daughters, who all too often were engrossed with problems of their own. Yamamoto recalls with pain how her own mother "could have used a more understanding daughter at the time—but, of course, I was wrapped up in myself at that age."[12] The issei husbands in her fiction, though not vicious, are earthbound men oblivious to the artistic or romantic inclinations of their wives and daughters. Yet these men also suffer in trying to live up to a traditional code of manhood in their adopted country.

Two of her best-known stories, "Seventeen Syllables" and "Yoneko's Earthquake," describe sotto voce the precarious relationship between issei spouses and between issei parents and nisei children. Yamamoto presents the two stories from the perspectives of nisei daughters; only through their ingenuous observations do we catch troubling nuances of adult silence.[13]

In "Seventeen Syllables" Yamamoto deftly juggles a manifest and a latent plot and deploys symbolic objects to convey the unspeakable. By using Rosie's point of view, she suspends the story of Tome Hayashi, Rosie's mother. Rosie cannot appreciate Tome's haiku, though she pays lip service to its beauty. Her inability to understand her mother's poetry bespeaks her general incomprehension of her mother's experience. While we are informed of the poetic interest of Tome from the beginning and are reminded of it periodically, the manifest plot revolves around Rosie's adolescent concerns, especially her secret rendezvous with Jesus Carrasco, the son of the Mexican couple working for her family. Only at the end of the story do we learn the submerged tragedy of Tome, who, before her marriage, became pregnant by a lover in Japan who abandoned her.

This revelation is precipitated by an event that confounds both mother and daughter. Tome's obsession with poetry has caused a rift between her and her husband, a farmer who cannot share her interest. The conflict escalates when she wins a haiku contest sponsored by a Japanese American newspaper. The editor personally delivers her prize—a delicate woodblock print by Hiroshige (1797–1858), a *ukiyo-e* or "floating world" print artist. Annoyed by the editor's visit, which interrupts a pressing tomato harvest, her husband smashes and then sets fire to the award—an act that puts an end to Tome's creative life.

As Tome and Rosie watch the award burn—a scene that speaks for the father's fury and the mother's despair—the lives of mother and daughter intertwine.[14] Rosie, still in the flush of her first romance, is confronted with her mother's devastating love affair and troubled marriage. Yamamoto fuses their conflicting emotions in the dramatic last paragraph: with a desperate plea the mother pits her disenchantment against the daughter's hopes.

IV

Yamamoto's style matches the verbal economy of haiku, in which the poet "must pack all her meaning into seventeen syllables only." Thus the title story of her collections is open to many angles of interpretation, as is evident from the critical essays included in this volume. Robert T. Rolf, Elaine H. Kim, and Charles L. Crow discuss "Seventeen Syllables" alongside other major stories by Yamamoto. Rolf analyzes her disarming style (which he considers "quintessentially American"), her deft characterization of people from different ethnic and racial backgrounds, her depiction of cultural differences between issei and nisei, and her delineation of sexuality "from girlhood innocence to womanhood." Kim sees Yamamoto's fiction as "consummately women's stories." She believes that the men in the stories, however domineering, are weak in comparison with the women, who are "strengthened by a combination of madness and a thirst for beauty and meaning in their lives." Crow focuses specifically on Yamamoto's portrayal of issei fathers, against whose sway their wives and children must struggle. He views five of her stories as "an extended quarrel with or perhaps rite of exorcism against this generalized Issei male." According to Crow, only in "Las Vegas Charley," in which the issei father becomes totally helpless, does Yamamoto finally forgive the oppressive patriarch.

Dorothy Ritsuko McDonald and Katharine Newman trace the friendship between Yamamoto and Wakako Yamauchi, another accomplished nisei writer, and illuminate their lives and works against the backdrop of the internment. Their lasting friendship began in Oceanside and bloomed in Poston. (Yamauchi, at the time a painter and Yamamoto's co-worker on the camp newspaper, attributed her switch from painting to writing to Yamamoto's inspiration.) McDonald and Newman register several "hallmarks" in Yamamoto's fiction: the extensive literary allusions that attest to her wide reading, the references to actual people and events, her graphic sensory details, and her use of soliloquies and imaginary dialogues. They believe that a "love for all humanity"—especially for "all those who seek but lose"—pervades Yamamoto's work. Yamamoto, they observe, chooses as her main characters "those who are hurt, who have deviated from the norm, who are grasping for some bits of beauty in their desperation."

Stan Yogi and I bring out common themes and parallel narrative strategies in "Seventeen Syllables" and "Yoneko's Earthquake." Yogi demonstrates how Yamamoto uses "buried plots" to reveal the experience of issei women and the "legacy of disruption and pain that mother passes on to daughter," showing how the motifs of deception, volition, and thwarted desire are interwoven between the lives of Tome and Rosie in "Seventeen Syllables." He concludes that "by layering her stories . . . Yamamoto fully explores the tremendous psychological and emotional costs to Issei women who attempt to pursue their desires in a context hostile to their wishes." I explore how the multiple levels of silences embedded in Yamamoto's fiction complicate feminist discussions of narrative gaps in women's writing. Although patriarchy effectively stifles the women in the two stories, the issei fathers are also repressed, both by an ancestral culture that marks expression of feelings as a sign of weakness and by a dominant culture that erodes their traditional authority. Transforming cultural constraint into stylistic restraint, Yamamoto at once conceals and reveals the characters' hidden emotions through her sparse telling.

Donald C. Goellnicht and Zenobia Baxter Mistri offer entirely different interpretations of Yamamoto's use of the haiku as a structuring device. Goellnicht offers a class analysis of the haiku's significance in Yamamoto's story. Tome's obsession with the haiku—considered a high art traditionally—is symptomatic of the class conflicts between husband and wife. Tome's poetic pursuit, he argues, is tied to her failed love affair with a man of a higher social class in Japan. He believes that Mr. Hayashi, who is of a lower class than his wife, has reasons to resent her "class-conscious pretensions." For Mistri, the power of the story derives from the "collision of Eastern and Western values." She views the haiku as a "metaphor for Tome's separateness" from a husband who expects her to adhere to the traditional role of an issei wife and from an American-born daughter who can hardly understand Japanese. She also shows how the haiku resonates as poetic imagery in Tome Hayashi's pseudonym, in the duration of her career as a poet, and in the Hiroshige.

Robert M. Payne contrasts Yamamoto's narrative ambiguity with the cinematic closure of *Hot Summer Winds,* the film adaptation of "Seventeen Syllables" and "Yoneko's Earthquake." He believes that the ellipses in Yamamoto's stories provoke the reader to question what is censored in American discourse. By filling these gaps visually, the film works against the tenor of Yamamoto's narratives and accommodates itself to the perspective of the dominant culture. Payne especially takes issue with the character reversal of the father—a reversal that transforms the writing of haiku from a feminist bid for independence to a form of amusement approved by a benign patriarchy. Whereas Yamamoto's stories inaugurate an alternative Asian American discourse, *Hot Summer Winds,* in Payne's opinion, conveys the Asian American image within the confines of dominant discourse.

V

I am not always in agreement with the viewpoints expressed in this volume. While Crow rightly discerns a pattern of failure among the issei fathers in Yamamoto's fiction, I find his assessment of these men unmitigating. Despite Goellnicht's perceptive analysis of the multiple class differences in the story, I am unpersuaded by his contention that Tome's desire to excel in haiku is "in alliance with bourgeois power." Nevertheless, the array of interpretations presented attests to the open-endedness and suggestiveness of Yamamoto's fiction.

"Seventeen Syllables" stands alongside the best of Katherine Mansfield, Flannery O'Connor, Toshio Mori, Ann Petry, Grace Paley, and Tillie Olsen in its technical sophistication, its humor and poignancy, its awareness of classism, and its expression of ethnic and feminist sympathies.[15]

It is not surprising that Yamamoto's own favorite short story is "Tell Me a Riddle" by Tillie Olsen, also author of *Silences*. Both "Seventeen Syllables" and "Tell Me a Riddle" address the pain of "unnatural silences," of "the unnatural thwarting of what struggles to come into being, but cannot."[16] Yamamoto discloses that "Seventeen Syllables" is her mother's story because "like most women, she didn't fulfill her potential. She had us kids to look after, on top of all the housework and working alongside my father in the fields." Perhaps not only the spirit of Yamamoto's mother but the spirits of the many who have suffered aborted creativity have been guiding the writing and propagation of "Seventeen Syllables" in order that their stories be known.

As a woman who came of age during World War II in an internment camp and shares the nisei anxiety about "what others think of us," who once doubted that she had sufficient knowledge to be a writer and claims to possess "one of the most extensive collections of rejection slips extant," Yamamoto has contended with both external censorship and self-censorship. A mother of five herself, she—like the mother in "Tell Me a Riddle"—must have also found herself constantly "[moving] to the rhythms of others."[17] Yet she has paid a lasting tribute to her own mother (who died before the publication of "Seventeen Syllables") by persevering as a writer:

> I remember that one day long ago my mother found me absorbed in writing a short story on brown wrapping paper. . . . And she said, "When you grow up, you must live in a house on top of a hill, where a cool wind blows, so you can write."
>
> Well, here I am living in a house on top of a hill in Los Angeles, where we are all more or less blissfully smothering to death together in this warm brown cocoon of smog, but sometimes a cool wind does blow. How sweet it is then, especially on an April afternoon when a certain light and a certain breeze combine to make the world so airy and bright and

spacious that one has an illusion of being able to take wing and fly away.

Unlike Tome Hayashi, whose life span as a poet "was very brief, three months at the most," Yamamoto, who received her first rejection slip at fourteen, continues to write in her seventies.[18]

☐ *Notes* ■

1. Susan Koppelman, ed., *Between Mothers and Daughters* (New York: Feminist Press, 1985), 162. Unless otherwise stated, subsequent quotations of Yamamoto's comments are from "Writing" and from my interview with the author, both of which are included in this volume.

2. *Asian-American Authors,* ed. Kai-yu Hsu and Helen Palubinskas (1972; repr. Boston: Houghton Mifflin, 1976), 113.

3. "Life and Death of a Nisei GI: After Johnny Died," *Pacific Citizen,* 1 Dec. 1945: 5; originally published in the column "Small Talk" in the *Los Angeles Tribune,* 26 Nov. 1945: 20–21.

4. Charles L. Crow, "A MELUS Interview: Hisaye Yamamoto," *MELUS* 14:1 (1987): 77.

5. For detailed accounts of Japanese American history, see Roger Daniels, *Concentration Camps, North America: Japanese in the U.S. and Canada during World War II* (Malabar, Fla.: R. E. Krieger, 1981); Ronald Takaki, *Strangers from a Different Shore: A History of Asian Americans* (Boston: Little, Brown, 1989); Yuji Ichioka, *The Issei: The World of the First Generation Japanese Immigrants, 1885–1924* (New York: Free Press, 1988). Elaine H. Kim discusses the relation between Japanese American history and literature in *Asian American Literature: An Introduction to the Writings and Their Social Context* (Philadelphia: Temple University Press, 1982), 122–172. For a description of nisei writers who are Yamamoto's contemporaries, see Yamamoto, "Writing."

6. Stan Yogi, "Legacies Revealed: Uncovering Buried Plots in the Stories of Hisaye Yamamoto," *Studies in American Fiction* 17:2 (1989): 169–181; reprinted in this volume.

7. Valerie Matsumoto, "Desperately Seeking 'Deirdre': Gender Roles, Multicultural Relations, and Nisei Women Writers of the 1930s," *Frontiers* 12:1 (1991): 28.

8. *Aiiieeeee! An Anthology of Asian-American Writers*, ed. Frank Chin, Jeffery Paul Chan, Lawson Fusao Inada, and Shawn Wong (1974; repr. Washington, D.C.: Howard University Press, 1983), xxxiv; *The Big Aiiieeeee! An Anthology of Asian American Writers* (New York: New American Library-Meridian, 1991), 339.

9. Quoted in Dorothy Ritsuko McDonald and Katharine Newman, "Relocation and Dislocation: The Writings of Hisaye Yamamoto and Wakako Yamauchi," *MELUS* 7:3 (1980): 21–38; reprinted in this volume.

10. Crow, "A MELUS Interview: Hisaye Yamamoto," 74.

11. Because of the limited lease imposed by the Alien Land Law, it was also difficult for most rural families to have lasting neighbors. According to Yamamoto, both her family and other farm families she knew "would lease acreage for a couple of years and then move on."

12. Koppelman, *Between Mothers and Daughters*, 162.

13. Cf. Henry James's use of a limited point of view to underscore the social distance between the Old World and the New World in *Daisy Miller*.

14. The two lives have been linked all along through imagery, however. For instance, the phallic "pale green worm" that Jesus places in Rosie's tomato basket echoes the "pale green Parker" with which Tome copies her haiku on good paper. Tome's poetic awakening has been as enthralling as Rosie's sexual awakening.

15. Koppelman describes "Seventeen Syllables" as a "story speaking to the experiences of multiple oppressions—racism and classicism as well as sexism" (*Between Mothers and Daughters*, 162).

16. Tillie Olsen, *Silences* (1965; repr. New York: Dell, 1972), 15.

17. Olsen, *Tell Me a Riddle* (Philadelphia: J. B. Lippincott, 1961), 98.

18. Although some critics think that Yamamoto stopped writing after the publication of "Las Vegas Charley" in 1961, she in fact has been a steadfast contributor of stories, memoirs, and poems to

the Holiday Supplement of *Rafu Shimpo;* she also continues to publish in other journals. Her most recent stories include "Eucalyptus," *Gidra* (1990): 34–36; "Florentine Gardens," *Asian America: Journal of Culture and the Arts* 1 (1992): 10–25; "Reunion," *Rafu Shimpo,* 12 Dec. 1992: A14–15.

❑ Chronology ∎

1885	Japanese government permits the emigration of Japanese nationals.
1907	"Gentlemen's Agreement" established between Japan and the United States whereby the Japanese government agrees to stop issuing passports to laborers who wish to emigrate to America; in return, Japanese immigrants are able to bring in wives and to establish families in America.
1913	Alien Land Law Act passed in California preventing "aliens ineligible for citizenship" from buying land or leasing it for longer than three years.
1921	Hisaye Yamamoto born.
1924	Asian Exclusion Act passed, excluding all "aliens ineligible for citizenship."
1941	United States enters World War II following Japanese attack on Pearl Harbor.
1942	President Franklin D. Roosevelt signs Executive Order 9066; people of Japanese descent residing on the West Coast evacuated to internment camps.
1942–1945	Interned at Poston, Arizona.
1944	Briefly relocated in Massachusetts.
1944	Brother Johnny killed in Grosseto, Italy.
1945–1948	On the staff of the *Los Angeles Tribune,* a black weekly.
1948	"The High-Heeled Shoes" published in *Partisan Review.*
1949	"Seventeen Syllables" published in *Partisan Review.*
1950	"The Legend of Miss Sasagawara" published in *Kenyon Review.*

1950	Receives a John Hay Whitney Foundation Opportunity Fellowship.
1951	"The Brown House" published in *Harper's Bazaar* and "Yoneko's Earthquake" in *Furioso*.
1953–1955	With the Catholic Worker in New York.
1955	Marries Anthony DeSoto and returns to Los Angeles.
1960	"Epithalamium" published in *Carleton Miscellany*.
1961	"Las Vegas Charley" published in *Arizona Quarterly*.
1985	*Seventeen Syllables: 5 Stores of Japanese American Life* published by Kirihara Shoten (Tokyo).
1986	Receives an American Book Award for Lifetime Achievement from the Before Columbus foundation.
1988	*Seventeen Syllables and Other Stories* published by Kitchen Table Press (Latham, N.Y.).
1991	*Hot Summer Winds* shown on PBS's "American Playhouse."

❏ Seventeen
Syllables

☐ Seventeen Syllables

The first Rosie knew that her mother had taken to writing poems was one evening when she finished one and read it aloud for her daughter's approval. It was about cats, and Rosie pretended to understand it thoroughly and appreciate it no end, partly because she hesitated to disillusion her mother about the quantity and quality of Japanese she had learned in all the years now that she had been going to Japanese school every Saturday (and Wednesday, too, in the summer). Even so, her mother must have been skeptical about the depth of Rosie's understanding, because she explained afterwards about the kind of poem she was trying to write.

See, Rosie, she said, it was a *haiku,* a poem in which she must pack all her meaning into seventeen syllables only, which were divided into three lines of five, seven, and five syllables. In the one she had just read, she had tried to capture the charm of a kitten, as well as comment on the superstition that owning a cat of three colors meant good luck.

"Yes, yes, I understand. How utterly lovely,"

From *Seventeen Syllables and Other Stories* (Latham, N.Y.: Kitchen Table: Women of Color Press, 1988), 8–19.

Rosie said, and her mother, either satisfied or seeing through the deception and resigned, went back to composing.

The truth was that Rosie was lazy; English lay ready on the tongue but Japanese had to be searched for and examined, and even then put forth tentatively (probably to meet with laughter). It was so much easier to say yes, yes, even when one meant no, no. Besides, this was what was in her mind to say: I was looking through one of your magazines from Japan last night, Mother, and towards the back I found some *haiku* in English that delighted me. There was one that made me giggle off and on until I fell asleep—

> *It is morning, and lo!*
> *I lie awake, comme il faut,*
> *sighing for some dough.*

Now, how to reach her mother, how to communicate the melancholy song? Rosie knew formal Japanese by fits and starts, her mother had even less English, no French. It was much more possible to say yes, yes.

It developed that her mother was writing the *haiku* for a daily newspaper, the *Mainichi Shimbun,* that was published in San Francisco. Los Angeles, to be sure, was closer to the farming community in which the Hayashi family lived and several Japanese vernaculars were printed there, but Rosie's parents said they preferred the tone of the northern paper. Once a week, the *Mainichi* would have a section devoted to *haiku,* and her mother became an extravagant contributor, taking for herself the blossoming pen name, Ume Hanazono.

So Rosie and her father lived for awhile with two women, her mother and Ume Hanazono. Her mother

(Tome Hayashi by name) kept house, cooked, washed, and, along with her husband and the Carrascos, the Mexican family hired for the harvest, did her ample share of picking tomatoes out in the sweltering fields and boxing them in tidy strata in the cool packing shed. Ume Hanazono, who came to life after the dinner dishes were done, was an earnest, muttering stranger who often neglected speaking when spoken to and stayed busy at the parlor table as late as midnight scribbling with pencil on scratch paper or carefully copying characters on good paper with her fat, pale green Parker.

The new interest had some repercussions on the household routine. Before, Rosie had been accustomed to her parents and herself taking their hot baths early and going to bed almost immediately afterwards, unless her parents challenged each other to a game of flower cards or unless company dropped in. Now if her father wanted to play cards, he had to resort to solitaire (at which he always cheated fearlessly), and if a group of friends came over, it was bound to contain someone who was also writing *haiku*, and the small assemblage would be split in two, her father entertaining the non-literary members and her mother comparing ecstatic notes with the visiting poet.

If they went out, it was more of the same thing. But Ume Hanazono's life span, even for a poet's, was very brief—perhaps three months at most.

One night they went over to see the Hayano family in the neighboring town to the west, an adventure both painful and attractive to Rosie. It was attractive because there were four Hayano girls, all lovely and each one named after a season of the year (Haru, Natsu, Aki,

·Fuyu), painful because something had been wrong with Mrs. Hayano ever since the birth of her first child. Rosie would sometimes watch Mrs. Hayano, reputed to have been the belle of her native village, making her way about a room, stooped, slowly shuffling, violently trembling (*always* trembling), and she would be reminded that this woman, in this same condition, had carried and given issue to three babies. She would look wonderingly at Mr. Hayano, handsome, tall, and strong, and she would look at her four pretty friends. But it was not a matter she could come to any decision about.

On this visit, however, Mrs. Hayano sat all evening in the rocker, as motionless and unobtrusive as it was possible for her to be, and Rosie found the greater part of the evening practically anaesthetic. Too, Rosie spent most of it in the girls' room, because Haru, the garrulous one, said almost as soon as the bows and other greetings were over, "Oh, you must see my new coat!"

It was a pale plaid of grey, sand, and blue, with an enormous collar, and Rosie, seeing nothing special in it, said, "Gee, how nice."

"Nice?" said Haru, indignantly. "Is that all you can say about it? It's gorgeous! And so cheap, too. Only seventeen-ninety eight, because it was a sale. The saleslady said it was twenty-five dollars regular."

"Gee," said Rosie. Natsu, who never said much and when she said anything said it shyly, fingered the coat covetously and Haru pulled it away.

"Mine," she said, putting it on. She minced in the aisle between the two large beds and smiled happily. "Let's see how your mother likes it."

She broke into the front room and the adult conversation and went to stand in front of Rosie's mother, while the rest watched from the door. Rosie's mother was properly envious. "May I inherit it when you're through with it?"

Haru, pleased, giggled and said yes, she could, but Natsu reminded gravely from the door, "You promised me, Haru."

Everyone laughed but Natsu, who shamefacedly retreated into the bedroom. Haru came in laughing, taking off the coat. "We were only kidding, Natsu," she said. "Here, you try it on now."

After Natsu buttoned herself into the coat, inspected herself solemnly in the bureau mirror, and reluctantly shed it, Rosie, Aki, and Fuyu got their turns, and Fuyu, who was eight, drowned in it while her sisters and Rosie doubled up in amusement. They all went into the front room later, because Haru's mother quaveringly called to her to fix the tea and rice cakes and open a can of sliced peaches for everybody. Rosie noticed that her mother and Mr. Hayano were talking together at the little table—they were discussing a *haiku* that Mr. Hayano was planning to send to the *Mainichi*, while her father was sitting at one end of the sofa looking through a copy of *Life*, the new picture magazine. Occasionally, her father would comment on a photograph, holding it toward Mrs. Hayano and speaking to her as he always did—loudly, as though he thought someone such as she must surely be at least a trifle deaf also.

The five girls had their refreshments at the kitchen table, and it was while Rosie was showing the sisters her trick of swallowing peach slices without chewing (she chased each slippery crescent down with a swig of tea) that her father brought his empty teacup and untouched saucer to the sink and said, "Come on, Rosie, we're going home now."

"Already?" asked Rosie.

"Work tomorrow," he said.

He sounded irritated, and Rosie, puzzled, gulped one last yellow slice and stood up to go, while the sisters began protesting, as was their wont.

"We have to get up at five-thirty," he told them, going into the front room quickly, so that they did not have their usual chance to hang onto his hands and plead for an extension of time.

Rosie, following, saw that her mother and Mr. Hayano were sipping tea and still talking together, while Mrs. Hayano concentrated, quivering, on raising the handleless Japanese cup to her lips with both her hands and lowering it back to her lap. Her father, saying nothing, went out the door, onto the bright porch, and down the steps. Her mother looked up and asked, "Where is he going?"

"Where is he going?" Rosie said. "He said we were going home now."

"Going home?" Her mother looked with embarrassment at Mr. Hayano and his absorbed wife and then forced a smile. "He must be tired," she said.

Haru was not giving up yet. "May Rosie stay overnight?" she asked, and Natsu, Aki, and Fuyu came to reinforce their sister's plea by helping her make a circle around Rosie's mother. Rosie, for once having no desire to stay, was relieved when her mother, apologizing to the perturbed Mr. and Mrs. Hayano for her father's abruptness at the same time, managed to shake her head no at the quartet, kindly but adamant, so that they broke their circle and let her go.

Rosie's father looked ahead into the windshield as the two joined him. "I'm sorry," her mother said. "You must be tired." Her father, stepping on the starter, said nothing. "You know how I get when it's *haiku*," she continued, "I forget what time it is." He only grunted.

As they rode homeward silently, Rosie, sitting between, felt a rush of hate for both—for her mother for begging, for her father for denying her mother. I wish this old Ford would crash, right now, she thought, then immediately, no, no, I wish my father would laugh, but it was too late: already the vision had passed through her mind of the green pick-up crumpled in the dark against one of the mighty eucalyptus trees they were just riding past, of the three contorted, bleeding bodies, one of them hers.

Rosie ran between two patches of tomatoes, her heart working more rambunctiously than she had ever known it to. How lucky it was that Aunt Taka and Uncle Gimpachi had come tonight, though, how very lucky. Otherwise she might not have really kept her half-promise to meet Jesus Carrasco. Jesus was going to be a senior in September at the same school she went to, and his parents were the ones helping with the tomatoes this year. She and Jesus, who hardly remembered seeing each other at Cleveland High where there were so many other people and two whole grades between them, had become great friends this summer—he always had a joke for her when he periodically drove the loaded pick-up up from the fields to the shed where she was usually sorting while her mother and father did the packing, and they laughed a great deal together over infinitesimal repartee during the afternoon break

for chilled watermelon or ice cream in the shade of
the shed.

What she enjoyed most was racing him to see who
could finish picking a double row first. He, who could
work faster, would tease her by slowing down until
she thought she would surely pass him this time, then
speeding up furiously to leave her several sprawling
vines behind. Once he had made her screech hideously
by crossing over, while her back was turned, to place
atop the tomatoes in her green-stained bucket a truly
monstrous, pale green worm (it had looked more like an
infant snake). And it was when they had finished a contest this morning, after she had pantingly pointed a
green finger at the immature tomatoes evident in the
lugs at the end of his row and he had returned the accusation (with justice), that he had startlingly brought
up the matter of their possibly meeting outside the
range of both their parents' dubious eyes.
    "What for?" she had asked.
    "I've got a secret I want to tell you," he said.
    "Tell me now," she demanded.
    "It won't be ready till tonight," he said.
    She laughed. "Tell me tomorrow then."
    "It'll be gone tomorrow," he threatened.
    "Well, for seven hakes, what is it?" she had asked,
more than twice, and when he had suggested that the
packing shed would be an appropriate place to find out,
she had cautiously answered maybe. She had not been
certain she was going to keep the appointment until the
arrival of mother's sister and her husband. Their coming seemed a sort of signal of permission, of grace, and
she had definitely made up her mind to lie and leave as
she was bowing them welcome.

So as soon as everyone appeared settled back for
the evening, she announced loudly that she was going
to the privy outside, "I'm going to the *benjo!*" and slipped
out the door. And now that she was actually on her way,
her heart pumped in such an undisciplined way that she
could hear it with her ears. It's because I'm running,
she told herself, slowing to a walk. The shed was up
ahead, one more patch away, in the middle of the fields.
Its bulk, looming in the dimness, took on a sinisterness
that was funny when Rosie reminded herself that it was
only a wooden frame with a canvas roof and three canvas walls that made a slapping noise on breezy days.

Jesus was sitting on the narrow plank that was the sorting platform and she went around to the other side and
jumped backwards to seat herself on the rim of a packing stand. "Well, tell me," she said without greeting,
thinking her voice sounded reassuringly familiar.

"I saw you coming out the door," Jesus said. "I
heard you running part of the way, too."

"Uh-huh," Rosie said. "Now tell me the secret."

"I was afraid you wouldn't come," he said.

Rosie delved around on the chicken-wire bottom
of the stall for number two tomatoes, ripe, which she
was sitting beside, and came up with a left-over that felt
edible. She bit into it and began sucking out the pulp
and seeds. "I'm here," she pointed out.

"Rosie, are you sorry you came?

"Sorry? What for?" she said. "You said you were
going to tell me something."

"I will, I will," Jesus said, but his voice contained
disappointment, and Rosie fleetingly felt the older of
the two, realizing a brand-new power which vanished
without category under her recognition.

"I have to go back in a minute," she said. "My aunt and uncle are here from Wintersburg. I told them I was going to the privy."

Jesus laughed. "You funny thing," he said. "You slay me!"

"Just because you have a bathroom *inside*," Rosie said. "Come on, tell me."

Chuckling, Jesus came around to lean on the stand facing her. They still could not see each other very clearly, but Rosie noticed that Jesus became very sober again as he took the hollow tomato from her hand and dropped it back into the stall. When he took hold of her empty hand, she could find no words to protest; her vocabulary had become distressingly constricted and she thought desperately that all that remained intact now was yes and no and oh, and even these few sounds would not easily out. Thus, kissed by Jesus, Rosie fell for the first time entirely victim to a helplessness delectable beyond speech. But the terrible, beautiful sensation lasted no more than a second, and the reality of Jesus' lips and tongue and teeth and hands made her pull away with such strength that she nearly tumbled.

Rosie stopped running as she approached the lights from the windows of home. How long since she had left? She could not guess, but gasping yet, she went to the privy in back and locked herself in. Her own breathing deafened her in the dark, close space, and she sat and waited until she could hear at last the nightly calling of the frogs and crickets. Even then, all she could think to say was oh, my, and the pressure of Jesus' face against her face would not leave.

No one had missed her in the parlor, however, and Rosie walked in and through quickly, announcing that she was next going to take a bath. "Your father's in the bathhouse," her mother said, and Rosie, in her room, recalled that she had not seen him when she entered. There had been only Aunt Taka and Uncle Gimpachi with her mother at the table, drinking tea. She got her robe and straw sandals and crossed the parlor again to go outside. Her mother was telling them about the *haiku* competition in the *Mainichi* and the poem she had entered.

Rosie met her father coming out of the bath-house. "Are you through, Father?" she asked. "I was going to ask you to scrub my back."

"Scrub your own back," he said shortly, going toward the main house.

"What have I done now?" she yelled after him. She suddenly felt like doing a lot of yelling. But he did not answer, and she went into the bathhouse. Turning on the dangling light, she removed her denims and T-shirt and threw them in the big carton for dirty clothes standing next to the washing machine. Her other things she took with her into the bath compartment to wash after her bath. After she had scooped a basin of hot water from the square wooden tub, she sat on the grey cement of the floor and soaped herself at exaggerated leisure, singing "Red Sails in the Sunset" at the top of her voice and using da-da-da where she suspected her words. Then, standing up, still singing, for she was possessed by the notion that any attempt now to analyze would result in spoilage and she believed that the larger her volume the less she would be able to hear herself think, she obtained more hot water and poured it on until she was free of lather. Only then did she allow herself to step into the steaming vat, one leg first, then the remainder of her body inch by inch until the water no longer stung and she could move around at will.

She took a long time soaking, afterwards remembering to go around outside to stoke the embers of the tin-lined fireplace beneath the tub and to throw on a few more sticks so that the water might keep its heat for her mother, and when she finally returned to the parlor, she found her mother still talking *haiku* with her aunt and uncle, the three of them on another round of tea. Her father was nowhere in sight.

At Japanese school the next day (Wednesday, it was), Rosie was grave and giddy by turns. Preoccupied at her desk in the row for students on Book Eight, she made up for it at recess by performing wild mimicry for the benefit of her friend Chizuko. She held her nose and whined a witticism or two in what she considered was the manner of Fred Allen; she assumed intoxication and a British accent to go over the climax of the Rudy Vallee recording of the pub conversation about William Ewart Gladstone; she was the child Shirley Temple piping, "On the Good Ship Lollipop"; she was the gentleman soprano of the Four Inkspots trilling, "If I Didn't Care." And she felt reasonably satisfied when Chizuko wept and gasped, "Oh, Rosie, you ought to be in the movies!"

Her father came after her at noon, bringing her sandwiches of minced ham and two nectarines to eat while she rode, so that she could pitch right into the sorting when they got home. The lugs were piling up, he said, and the ripe tomatoes in them would probably have to be taken to the cannery tomorrow if they were not ready for the produce haulers tonight. "This heat's not doing them any good. And we've got no time for a break today."

It *was* hot, probably the hottest day of the year, and Rosie's blouse stuck damply to her back even under the protection of the canvas. But she worked as efficiently as a flawless machine and kept the stalls heaped, with one part of her mind listening in to the parental murmuring about the heat and the tomatoes and with another part planning the exact words she would say to Jesus when he drove up with the first load of the afternoon. But when at last she saw that the pick-up was coming, her hands went berserk and the tomatoes started falling in the wrong stalls, and her father said, "Hey, hey! Rosie, watch what you're doing!"

"Well, I have to go to the *benjo,*" she said, hiding panic.

"Go in the weeds over there," he said, only half-joking.

"Oh, Father!" she protested.

"Oh, go on home," her mother said. "We'll make out for awhile."

In the privy Rosie peered through a knothole toward the fields, watching as much as she could of Jesus. Happily she thought she saw him look in the direction of the house from time to time before he finished unloading and went back toward the patch where his mother and father worked. As she was heading for the shed, a very presentable black car purred up the dirt driveway to the house and its driver motioned to her. Was this the Hayashi home, he wanted to know. She nodded. Was she a Hayashi? Yes, she said, thinking that he was a good-looking man. He got out of the car with a huge, flat package and she saw that he warmly wore a business suit. "I have something here for your mother then," he said, in a more elegant Japanese than she was used to.

She told him where her mother was and he came along with her, patting his face with an immaculate white handkerchief and saying something about the coolness of San Francisco. To her surprised mother and father, he bowed and introduced himself as, among other things, the *haiku* editor of the *Mainichi Shimbun,* saying that since he had been coming as far as Los Angeles anyway, he had decided to bring her the first prize she had won in the recent contest.

"First prize?" her mother echoed, believing and not believing, pleased and overwhelmed. Handed the package with a bow, she bobbed her head up and down numerous times to express her utter gratitude.

"It is nothing much," he added, "but I hope it will serve as a token of our great appreciation for your contributions and our great admiration of your considerable talent."

"I am not worthy," she said, falling easily into his style. "It is I who should make some sign of my humble thanks for being permitted to contribute."

'No, no, to the contrary," he said, bowing again.

But Rosie's mother insisted, and then saying that she knew she was being unorthodox, she asked if she might open the package because her curiosity was so great. Certainly she might. In fact, he would like her reaction to it, for personally, it was one of his favorite *Hiroshiges.*

Rosie thought it was a pleasant picture, which looked to have been sketched with delicate quickness. There were pink clouds, containing some graceful calligraphy, and a sea that was a pale blue except at the edges, containing four sampans with indications of people in them. Pines edged the water and on the far-off beach there was a cluster of thatched huts towered over by pine-dotted mountains of grey and blue. The frame was scalloped and gilt.

After Rosie's mother pronounced it without peer and somewhat prodded her father into nodding agreement, she said Mr. Kuroda must at least have a cup of tea after coming all this way, and although Mr. Kuroda did not want to impose, he soon agreed that a cup of tea would be refreshing and went along with her to the house, carrying the picture for her.

"Ha, your mother's crazy!" Rosie's father said, and Rosie laughed uneasily as she resumed judgment on the tomatoes. She had emptied six lugs when he broke into an imaginary conversation with Jesus to tell her to go and remind her mother of the tomatoes, and she went slowly.

Mr. Kuroda was in his shirtsleeves expounding some *haiku* theory as he munched a rice cake, and her mother was rapt. Abashed in the great man's presence, Rosie stood next to her mother's chair until her mother looked up inquiringly, and then she started to whisper the message, but her mother pushed her gently away and reproached, "You are not being very polite to our guest."

"Father says the tomatoes . . ." Rosie said aloud, smiling foolishly.

"Tell him I shall only be a minute," her mother said, speaking the language of Mr. Kuroda.

When Rosie carried the reply to her father, he did not seem to hear and she said again, "Mother says she'll be back in a minute."

"All right, all right," he nodded, and they worked

again in silence. But suddenly, her father uttered an incredible noise, exactly like the cork of a bottle popping, and the next Rosie knew, he was stalking angrily toward the house, almost running in fact, and she chased after him crying, "Father! Father! What are you going to do?"

He stopped long enough to order her back to the shed. "Never mind!" he shouted. "Get on with the sorting!"

And from the place in the fields where she stood, frightened and vacillating, Rosie saw her father enter the house. Soon Mr. Kuroda came out alone, putting on his coat. Mr. Kuroda got into his car and backed out down the driveway onto the highway. Next her father emerged, also alone, something in his arms (it was the picture, she realized), and, going over to the bathhouse woodpile, he threw the picture on the ground and picked up the axe. Smashing the picture, glass and all (she heard the explosion faintly), he reached over for the kerosene that was used to encourage the bath fire and poured it over the wreckage. I am dreaming, Rosie said to herself, I am dreaming, but her father, having made sure that his act of cremation was irrevocable, was even then returning to the fields.

Rosie ran past him and toward the house. What had become of her mother? She burst into the parlor and found her mother at the back window watching the dying fire. They watched together until there remained only a feeble smoke under the blazing sun. Her mother was very calm.

"Do you know why I married your father?" she said without turning.

"No," said Rosie. It was the most frightening question she had ever been called upon to answer. Don't tell me now, she wanted to say, tell me tomorrow, tell me next week, don't tell me today. But she knew she would be told now, that the telling would combine with the other violence of the hot afternoon to level her life, her world to the very ground.

It was like a story out of the magazines illustrated in sepia, which she had consumed so greedily for a period until the information had somehow reached her that those wretchedly unhappy autobiographies, offered to her as the testimonials of living men and women, were largely inventions: Her mother, at nineteen, had come to America and married her father as an alternative to suicide.

At eighteen she had been in love with the first son of one of the well-to-do families in her village. The two had met whenever and wherever they could, secretly, because it would not have done for his family to see him favor her—her father had no money; he was a drunkard and a gambler besides. She had learned she was with child; an excellent match had already been arranged for her lover. Despised by her family, she had given premature birth to a stillborn son, who would be seventeen now. Her family did not turn her out, but she could no longer project herself in any direction without refreshing in them the memory of her indiscretion. She wrote to Aunt Taka, her favorite sister in America, threatening to kill herself if Aunt Taka would not send for her. Aunt Taka hastily arranged a marriage with a young man of whom she knew, but lately arrived from Japan, a young man of simple mind, it was said, but of kindly heart. The young man was never told why his unseen betrothed was so eager to hasten the day of meeting.

The story was told perfectly, with neither groping

for words nor untoward passion. It was as though her
mother had memorized it by heart, reciting it to herself
so many times over that its nagging vileness had long
since gone.

"I had a brother then?" Rosie asked, for this was
what seemed to matter now; she would think about the
other later, she assured herself, pushing back the illu-
mination which threatened all that darkness that had
hitherto been merely mysterious or even glamorous. "A
half-brother?"

"Yes."

"I would have liked a brother," she said.

Suddenly, her mother knelt on the floor and took
her by the wrists. "Rosie," she said urgently, "Promise
me you will never marry!" Shocked more by the request
than the revelation, Rosie stared at her mother's face.
Jesus, Jesus, she called silently, not certain whether she
was invoking the help of the son of the Carrascos or of
God, until there returned sweetly the memory of Jesus'
hand, how it had touched her and where. Still her mother
waited for an answer, holding her wrists so tightly that
her hands were going numb. She tried to pull free. Promise, her mother whispered fiercely, promise. Yes, yes, I
promise, Rosie said. But for an instant she turned away,
and her mother, hearing the familiar glib agreement,
released her. Oh, you, you, you, her eyes and twisted
mouth said, you fool. Rosie, covering her face, began at
last to cry, and the embrace and consoling hand came
much later than she expected.

Yoneko's Earthquake

Yoneko's Earthquake

Yoneko Hosoume became a free-thinker on the night of March 10, 1933, only a few months after her first actual recognition of God. Ten years old at the time, of course she had heard rumors about God all along, long before Marpo came. Her cousins who lived in the city were all Christians, living as they did right next door to a Baptist church exclusively for Japanese people. These city cousins, of whom there were several, had been baptized en masse and were very proud of their condition. Yoneko was impressed when she heard of this and thereafter was given to referring to them as "my cousins, the Christians." She, too, yearned at times after Christianity, but she realized the absurdity of her whim, seeing that there was no Baptist church for Japanese in the rural community she lived in. Such a church would have been impractical, moreover, since Yoneko, her father, her mother, and her little brother Seigo were the only Japanese thereabouts. They were the only ones, too, whose agriculture was so diverse as to include blackberries, cabbages, rhubarb, potatoes,

---

From *Seventeen Syllables and Other Stories* (Latham, N.Y.: Kitchen Table: Women of Color Press, 1988), 46–56.

cucumbers, onions, and canteloupes. The rest of the countryside there was like one vast orange grove.

Yoneko had entered her cousins' church once, but she could not recall the sacred occasion without mortification. It had been one day when the cousins had taken her and Seigo along with them to Sunday school. The church was a narrow wooden building, mysterious-looking because of its unusual bluish-gray paint and its steeple, but the basement schoolroom inside had been disappointingly ordinary, with desks, a blackboard, and erasers. They had all sung "Let Us Gather at the River" in Japanese. This goes:

> *Mamonaku kanata no*
> *Nagare no soba de*
> *Tanoshiku ai-masho*
> *Mata tomodachi to*
>
> *Mamonaku ai-masho*
> *Kirei-na, kirei-na kawa de*
> *Tanoshiku ai-masho*
> *Mata tomodachi to.*

Yoneko had not known the words at all, but always clever in such situations, she had opened her mouth and grimaced nonchalantly to the rhythm. What with everyone else singing at the top of his lungs, no one had noticed that she was not making a peep. Then everyone had sat down again and the man had suggested, "Let us pray." Her cousins and the rest promptly curled their arms on the desks to make nests for their heads, and Yoneko had done the same. But not Seigo. Because when the room had become so still that one was aware of the breathing, the creaking, and the chittering in the trees outside, Seigo, sitting with her, had suddenly flung his arm around her neck and said with concern,

42

"Sis, what are you crying for? Don't cry." Even the man had laughed and Yoneko had been terribly ashamed that Seigo should thus disclose them to be interlopers. She had pinched him fiercely and he had begun to cry, so she had had to drag him outside, which was a fortunate move, because he had immediately wet his pants. But he had been only three then, so it was not very fair to expect dignity of him.

So it remained for Marpo to bring the word of God to Yoneko—Marpo with the face like brown leather, the thin mustache like Edmund Lowe's, and the rare, breathtaking smile like white gold. Marpo, who was twenty-seven years old, was a Filipino and his last name was lovely, something like Humming Wing, but no one ever ascertained the spelling of it. He ate principally rice, just as though he were Japanese, but he never sat down to the Hosoume table, because he lived in the bunkhouse out by the barn and cooked on his own kerosene stove. Once Yoneko read somewhere that Filipinos trapped wild dogs, starved them for a time, then, feeding them mountains of rice, killed them at the peak of their bloatedness, thus insuring themselves meat ready to roast, stuffing and all, without further ado. This, the book said, was considered a delicacy. Unable to hide her disgust and her fascination, Yoneko went straightway to Marpo and asked, "Marpo, is it true that you eat dogs?", and he, flashing that smile, answered, "Don't be funny, honey!" This caused her no end of amusement, because it was a poem, and she completely forgot about the wild dogs.

Well, there seemed to be nothing Marpo could not do. Mr. Hosoume said Marpo was the best hired man he had ever had, and he said this often, because it was an irrefutable fact among Japanese in general that

Filipinos in general were an indolent lot. Mr. Hosoume ascribed Marpo's industry to his having grown up in Hawaii, where there is known to be considerable Japanese influence. Marpo had gone to a missionary school there and he owned a Bible given him by one of his teachers. This had black leather covers that gave as easily as cloth, golden edges, and a slim purple ribbon for a marker. He always kept it on the little table by his bunk, which was not a bed with springs but a low, three-plank shelf with a mattress only. On the first page of the book, which was stiff and black, his teacher had written in large swirls of white ink, "As we draw near to God, He will draw near to us."

What, for instance, could Marpo do? Why, it would take an entire leisurely evening to go into his accomplishments adequately, because there was not only Marpo the Christian and Marpo the best hired man, but Marpo the athlete, Marpo the musician (both instrumental and vocal), Marpo the artist, and Marpo the radio technician.

(1) As an athlete, Marpo owned a special pair of black shoes, equipped with sharp nails on the soles, which he kept in shape with the regular application of neatsfoot oil. Putting these on, he would dash down the dirt road to the highway, a distance of perhaps half a mile, and back again. When he first came to work for the Hosoumes, he undertook this sprint every evening before he went to get his supper, but as time went on he referred to these shoes less and less and in the end, when he left, he had not touched them for months. He also owned a muscle-builder sent him by Charles Atlas which, despite his unassuming size, he could stretch the length of his outspread arms; his teeth gritted then and his whole body became temporarily victim to a

jerky vibration. (2) As an artist, Marpo painted larger-
than-life water colors of his favorite movie stars, all of
whom were women and all of whom were blonde, like
Ann Harding and Jean Harlow, and tacked them up on
his walls. He also made for Yoneko a folding contrap-
tion of wood holding two pencils, one with lead and one
without, with which she, too, could obtain double-sized
likenesses of any picture she wished. It was a fragile in-
strument, however, and Seigo splintered it to pieces one
day when Yoneko was away at school. He claimed he
was only trying to copy Boob McNutt from the funny
paper when it failed. (3) As a musician, Marpo owned a
violin for which he had paid over one hundred dollars.
He kept this in a case whose lining was red velvet, first
wrapping it gently in a brilliant red silk scarf. This
scarf, which weighed nothing, he tucked under his
chin when he played, gathering it up delicately by the
center and flicking it once to unfurl it—a gesture
Yoneko prized. In addition to this, Marpo was a singer,
with a soft tenor which came out in professional quavers and rolled r's when he applied a slight pressure to
his Adam's apple with thumb and forefinger. His violin
and vocal repertoire consisted of the same numbers,
mostly hymns and Irish folk airs. He was especially ad-
dicted to "The Rose of Tralee" and the "Londonderry
Air." (4) Finally, as a radio technician who had spent
two previous winters at a specialists' school in the city,
Marpo had put together a bulky table-size radio which
brought in equal proportions of static and entertainment. He never got around to building a cabinet to
house it and its innards of metal and glass remained
public throughout its lifetime. This was just as well, for
not a week passed without Marpo's deciding to solder
one bit or another. Yoneko and Seigo became a part of

the great listening audience with such fidelity that
Mr. Hosoume began remarking the fact that they dwelt
more with Marpo than with their own parents. He
eventually took a serious view of the matter and bought
the naked radio from Marpo, who thereupon put away
his radio manuals and his soldering iron in the bottom
of his steamer trunk and divided more time among his
other interests.

However, Marpo's versatility was not revealed, as
it is here, in a lump. Yoneko uncovered it fragment by
fragment every day, by dint of unabashed questions, ex-
plorations among his possessions, and even silent ob-
servation, although this last was rare. In fact, she and
Seigo visited with Marpo at least once a day and both of
them regularly came away amazed with their findings.
The most surprising thing was that Marpo was, after
all this, a rather shy young man meek to the point of
speechlessness in the presence of Mr. and Mrs. Hosoume. With Yoneko and Seigo, he was somewhat more
self-confident and at ease.

It is not remembered now just how Yoneko and
Marpo came to open their protracted discussion on religion. It is sufficient here to note that Yoneko was an
ideal apostle, adoring Jesus, desiring Heaven and fearing Hell. Once Marpo had enlightened her on these ba-
sics, Yoneko never questioned their truth. The questions she put up to him, therefore, sought neither proof of
her exegeses nor balm for her doubts, but simply additional color to round out her mental images. For
example, who did Marpo suppose was God's favorite
movie star? Or, what sound did Jesus' laughter have (it
must be like music, she added, nodding sagely, answer-
ing herself to her own satisfaction), and did Marpo suppose that God's sense of humor would have appreciated

the delicious chant she had learned from friends at
school today:

> *There ain't no bugs on us,*
> *There ain't no bugs on us,*
> *There may be bugs on the rest of you mugs,*
> *But there ain't no bugs on us?*

Or did Marpo believe Jesus to have been exempt from
stinging eyes when he shampooed that long, naturally
wavy hair of his?

To shake such faith, there would have been required a most monstrous upheaval of some sort, and it
might be said that this is just what happened. For early
on the evening of March 10, 1933, a little after five
o'clock this was, as Mrs. Hosoume was getting supper,
as Marpo was finishing up in the fields alone because
Mr. Hosoume had gone to order some chicken fertilizer,
and as Yoneko and Seigo were listening to Skippy, a tremendous roar came out of nowhere and the Hosoume
house began shuddering violently as though some giant
had seized it in his two hands and was giving it a good
shaking. Mrs. Hosoume, who remembered similar, although milder experiences from her childhood in Japan, screamed, "*Jishin, jishin!*" before she ran and
grabbed Yoneko and Seigo each by a hand and dragged
them outside with her. She took them as far as the
middle of the rhubarb patch near the house, and there
they all crouched, pressed together, watching the world
about them rock and sway. In a few minutes, Marpo,
stumbling in from the fields, joined them, saying,
"Earthquake, earthquake!" and he gathered them all in
his arms, as much to protect them as to support
himself.

Mr. Hosoume came home later that evening in a

stranger's car, with another stranger driving the family Reo. Pallid, trembling, his eyes wildly staring, he could have been mistaken for a drunkard, except that he was famous as a teetotaler. It seemed that he had been on the way home when the first jolt came, that the old green Reo had been kissed by a broken live wire dangling from a suddenly leaning pole. Mr. Hosoume, knowing that the end had come by electrocution, had begun to writhe and kick and this had been his salvation. His hands had flown from the wheel, the car had swerved into a ditch, freeing itself from the sputtering wire. Later it was found that he was left permanently inhibited about driving automobiles and permanently incapable of considering electricity with calmness. He spent the larger part of his later life weakly, wandering about the house or fields and lying down frequently to rest because of splitting headaches and sudden dizzy spells.

So it was Marpo who went back into the house as Yoneko screamed, "No, Marpo, no!" and brought out the Hosoumes' kerosene stove, the food, the blankets, while Mr. Hosoume huddled on the ground near his family.

The earth trembled for days afterwards. The Hosoumes and Marpo Humming Wing lived during that time on a natural patch of Bermuda grass between the house and the rhubarb patch, remembering to take three meals a day and retire at night. Marpo ventured inside the house many times despite Yoneko's protests and reported the damage slight: a few dishes had been broken; a gallon jug of mayonnaise had fallen from the top pantry shelf and splattered the kitchen floor with yellow blobs and pieces of glass.

Yoneko was in constant terror during this experience. Immediately on learning what all the commotion was about, she began praying to God to end this violence. She entreated God, flattered Him, wheedled Him, commanded Him, but He did not listen to her at all—inexorably, the earth went on rumbling. After three solid hours of silent, desperate prayer, without any results whatsoever, Yoneko began to suspect that God was either powerless, callous, downright cruel, or nonexistent. In the murky night, under a strange moon wearing a pale ring of light, she decided upon the last as the most plausible theory. "Ha," was one of the things she said tremulously to Marpo, when she was not begging him to stay out of the house, "you and your God!"

The others soon oriented themselves to the catastrophe with philosophy, saying how fortunate they were to live in the country where the peril was less than in the city and going so far as to regard the period as a sort of vacation from work, with their enforced alfresco existence a sort of camping trip. They tried to bring Yoneko to partake of this pleasant outlook, but she, shivering with each new quiver, looked on them as dreamers who refused to see things as they really were. Indeed, Yoneko's reaction was so notable that the Hosoume household thereafter spoke of the event as "Yoneko's earthquake."

After the earth subsided and the mayonnaise was mopped off the kitchen floor, life returned to normal, except that Mr. Hosoume stayed at home most of the time. Sometimes if he had a relatively painless day, he would have supper on the stove when Mrs. Hosoume came in from the fields. Mrs. Hosoume and Marpo did all the field labor now, except on certain overwhelming days when several Mexicans were hired to assist them.

Marpo did most of the driving, too, and it was now he
and Mrs. Hosoume who went into town on the weekly
trip for groceries. In fact Marpo became indispensable
and both Mr. and Mrs. Hosoume often told each other
how grateful they were for Marpo.

When summer vacation began and Yoneko stayed
at home, too, she found the new arrangement rather in-
convenient. Her father's presence cramped her style:
for instance, once when her friends came over and it
was decided to make fudge, he would not permit them,
saying fudge used too much sugar and that sugar was
not a plaything; once when they were playing paper
dolls, he came along and stuck his finger up his nose
and pretended he was going to rub some snot off onto
the dolls. Things like that. So on some days, she was
very much annoyed with her father.

Therefore when her mother came home breathless from the fields one day and pushed a ring at her, a
gold-colored ring with a tiny glasslike stone in it, saying, "Look, Yoneko, I'm going to give you this ring. If
your father asks where you got it, say you found it on
the street." Yoneko was perplexed but delighted both by
the unexpected gift and the chance to have some secret revenge on her father, and she said, certainly, she
was willing to comply with her mother's request. Her
mother went back to the fields then and Yoneko put the
pretty ring on her middle finger, taking up the loose
space with a bit of newspaper. It was similar to the
rings found occasionally in boxes of Crackerjacks, except that it appeared a bit more substantial.

Mr. Hosoume never asked about the ring; in fact,
he never noticed she was wearing one. Yoneko thought
he was about to, once, but he only reproved her for the
flamingo nail polish she was wearing, which she had

applied from a vial brought over by Yvonne Fournier, the French girl two orange groves away. "You look like a Filipino," Mr. Hosoume said sternly, for it was another irrefutable fact among Japanese in general that Filipinos in general were a gaudy lot. Mrs. Hosoume immediately came to her defense, saying that in Japan, if she remembered correctly, young girls did the same thing. In fact she remembered having gone to elaborate lengths to tint her fingernails: she used to gather, she said, the petals of the red *tsubobana* or the purple *kogane* (which grows on the underside of stones), grind them well, mix them with some alum powder, then cook the mixture and leave it to stand overnight in an envelope of either persimmon or taro leaves (both very strong leaves). The second night, just before going to bed, she used to obtain threads by ripping a palm leaf (because real thread was dear) and tightly bind the paste to her fingernails under shields of persimmon or taro leaves. She would be helpless for the night, the fingertips bound so well that they were alternately numb or aching; but she would grit her teeth and tell herself that the discomfort indicated the success of the operation. In the morning, finally releasing her fingers, she would find the nails shining with a translucent red-orange color.

Yoneko was fascinated, because she usually thought of her parents as having been adults all their lives. She thought that her mother must have been a beautiful child, with or without bright fingernails, because, though surely past thirty, she was even yet a beautiful person. When she herself was younger, she remembered she had at times been so struck with her mother's appearance that she had dropped to her knees and mutely clasped her mother's legs in her arms. She

51

had left off this habit as she learned to control her emotions, because at such times her mother had usually
walked away, saying, "My, what a clinging child you
are. You've got to learn to be a little more independent."
She also remembered she had once heard someone
comparing her mother to "a dewy, half-opened
rosebud."

Mr. Hosoume, however, was irritated. "That's no
excuse for Yoneko to begin using paint on her fingernails," he said. "She's only ten."

"Her Japanese age is eleven, and we weren't
much older," Mrs. Hosoume said.

"Look," Mr. Hosoume said, "if you're going to
contradict every piece of advice I give the children,
they'll end up disobeying us both and doing what they
very well please. Just because I'm ill just now is no reason for them to start being disrespectful."

"When have I ever contradicted you before?"
Mrs. Hosoume said.

"Countless times," Mr. Hosoume said.

"Name one instance," Mrs. Hosoume said.

Certainly there had been times, but Mr. Hosoume
could not happen to mention the one requested instance on the spot and he became quite angry. "That's
quite enough of your insolence," he said. Since he was
speaking in Japanese, his exact accusation was that she
was *nama-iki,* which is a shade more revolting than being merely insolent.

"*Nama-iki, nama-iki?*" said Mrs. Hosoume. "How
dare you? I'll not have anyone calling me *nama-iki!*"

At that, Mr. Hosoume went up to where his wife
was ironing and slapped her smartly on the face. It was
the first time he had ever laid hands on her. Mrs. Hosoume was immobile for an instant, but she resumed

her ironing as though nothing had happened, although she glanced over at Marpo, who happened to be in the room reading a newspaper. Yoneko and Seigo forgot they were listening to the radio and stared at their parents, thunderstruck.

"Hit me again," said Mrs. Hosoume quietly, as she ironed. "Hit me all you wish."

Mr. Hosoume was apparently about to, but Marpo stepped up and put his hand on Mr. Hosoume's shoulder. "The children are here," said Marpo, "the children."

"Mind your own business," said Mr. Hosoume in broken English. "Get out of here!"

Marpo left, and that was about all. Mrs. Hosoume went on ironing, Yoneko and Seigo turned back to the radio, and Mr. Hosoume muttered that Marpo was beginning to forget his place. Now that he thought of it, he said, Marpo had been increasingly impudent towards him since his illness. He said just because he was temporarily an invalid was no reason for Marpo to start being disrespectful. He added that Marpo had better watch his step or that he might find himself jobless one of these fine days.

And something of the sort must have happened. Marpo was here one day and gone the next, without even saying good-bye to Yoneko and Seigo. That was also the day that the Hosoume family went to the city on a weekday afternoon, which was most unusual. Mr. Hosoume, who now avoided driving as much as possible, handled the cumbersome Reo as though it were a nervous stallion, sitting on the edge of the seat and hugging the steering wheel. He drove very fast and about halfway to the city struck a beautiful collie which had dashed out barking from someone's yard. The car jerked with the impact, but Mr. Hosoume drove right on and Yoneko, wanting suddenly to vomit, looked back and saw the collie lying very still at the side of the road.

When they arrived at the Japanese hospital, which was their destination, Mr. Hosoume cautioned Yoneko and Seigo to be exemplary children and wait patiently in the car. It seemed hours before he and Mrs. Hosoume returned, she walking with very small, slow steps and he assisting her. When Mrs. Hosoume got in the car, she leaned back and closed her eyes. Yoneko inquired as to the source of her distress, for she was obviously in pain, but she only answered that she was feeling a little under the weather and that the doctor had administered some necessarily astringent treatment. At that Mr. Hosoume turned around and advised Yoneko and Seigo that they must tell no one of coming to the city on a weekday afternoon, absolutely no one, and Yoneko and Seigo readily assented. On the way home they passed the place of the encounter with the collie, and Yoneko looked up and down the stretch of road but the dog was nowhere to be seen.

Not long after that the Hosoumes got a new hired hand, an old Japanese man who wore his gray hair in a military cut and who, unlike Marpo, had no particular interests outside working, eating, sleeping, and playing an occasional game of *goh* with Mr. Hosoume. Before he came Yoneko and Seigo played sometimes in the empty bunkhouse and recalled Marpo's various charms together. Privately, Yoneko was wounded more than she would admit even to herself that Marpo should have subjected her to such an abrupt desertion. Whenever her indignation became too great to endure gracefully, she would console herself by telling Seigo that, after all, Marpo was a mere Filipino, an eater of wild dogs.

Seigo never knew about the disappointing new

hired man, because he suddenly died in the night. He and Yoneko had spent the hot morning in the nearest orange grove, she driving him to distraction by repeating certain words he could not bear to hear: she had called him Serge, a name she had read somewhere, instead of Seigo; and she had chanted off the name of the tires they were rolling around like hoops as Goodrich Silver-TO-town, Goodrich Silver-TO-town, instead of Goodrich Silvertown. This had enraged him, and he had chased her around the trees most of the morning. Finally she had taunted him from several trees away by singing "You're a Yellow-streaked Coward," which was one of several small songs she had composed. Seigo had suddenly grinned and shouted, "Sure!" and walked off leaving her, as he intended, with a sense of emptiness. In the afternoon they had perspired and followed the potato-digging machine and the Mexican workers— both hired for the day—around the field, delighting in unearthing marble-sized, smooth-skinned potatoes that both the machine and the men had missed. Then in the middle of the night Seigo began crying, complaining of a stomach ache. Mrs. Hosoume felt his head and sent her husband for the doctor, who smiled and said Seigo would be fine in the morning. He said it was doubtless the combination of green oranges, raw potatoes, and the July heat. But as soon as the doctor left, Seigo fell into a coma and a drop of red blood stood out on his underlip, where he had evidently bit it. Mr. Hosoume again fetched the doctor, who was this time very grave and wagged his head, saying several times, "It looks very bad." So Seigo died at the age of five.

Mrs. Hosoume was inconsolable and had swollen eyes in the morning for weeks afterwards. She now insisted on visiting the city relatives each Sunday, so that she could attend church services with them. One Sunday she stood up and accepted Christ. It was through accompanying her mother to many of these services that Yoneko finally learned the Japanese words to "Let Us Gather at the River." Mrs. Hosoume also did not seem interested in discussing anything but God and Seigo. She was especially fond of reminding visitors how adorable Seigo had been as an infant, how she had been unable to refrain from dressing him as a little girl and fixing his hair in bangs until he was two. Mr. Hosoume was very gentle with her and when Yoneko accidentally caused her to giggle once, he nodded and said, "Yes, that's right, Yoneko, we must make your mother laugh and forget about Seigo." Yoneko herself did not think about Seigo at all. Whenever the thought of Seigo crossed her mind, she instantly began composing a new song, and this worked very well.

One evening, when the new hired man had been with them awhile, Yoneko was helping her mother with the dishes when she found herself being examined with such peculiarly intent eyes that, with a start of guilt, she began searching in her mind for a possible crime she had lately committed. But Mrs. Hosoume only said, "Never kill a person, Yoneko, because if you do, God will take from you someone you love."

"Oh, that," said Yoneko quickly, "I don't believe in that, I don't believe in God." And her words tumbling pell-mell over one another, she went on eagerly to explain a few of her reasons why. If she neglected to mention the test she had given God during the earthquake, it was probably because she was a little upset. She had believed for a moment that her mother was going to ask about the ring (which, alas, she had lost already, somewhere in the flumes along the canteloupe patch).

56

Background
to the Stories

Writing

This is the sum total of my published work: two pieces in *Partisan Review,* one each in *Kenyon Review, Harper's Bazaar, Furioso, Frontier, The Carleton Miscellany,* and *Arizona Quarterly.* There have also been contributions over the years to *Pacific Citizen, Crossroads, Rafu Shimpo, Kashu Mainishi, Sangyo Nippo,* and *The Catholic Worker.* I also put in a couple of years with the *Los Angeles Tribune,* which Fred Fertig, erstwhile pastor to the Nisei, once described as the "most creatively-edited Negro newspaper" in the country. The stories in *Partisan Review, Harper's Bazaar, Furioso* and its successor *The Carleton Miscellany* made Martha Foley's list of "distinctive" short stories for their particular years, with the one in *Furioso* reprinted in her anthology as one of the *Best American Short Stories of 1952.* But, alas, when I have occasion to fill out a questionnaire, I must in all honesty list my occupation as housewife. And I don't know of any Nisei dedicated to serious writing as a life work: neither do I know of any Nisei gathering together these days to discuss literature. (I understand there is a Mitsu Yamamoto, no relation, whether male or female, Nisei or what, I do not know, who had stories in the *New Yorker* and *Redbook* in the latter 1950s.)

This could hardly be ascribed to any flaw in the Japanese character, since there is testimony to the contrary all the way from Lady Murasaki to Yasunari Kawabata. But there is something in the nature of the Nisei, in his wholeminded acceptance of the American criterion of success—and I suppose

From *Rafu Shimpo,* 20 December 1968. Reprinted in *Amerasia Journal* 3:2 (1976): 126–133.

this is connected with the alacrity with which Japan accepted westernization (as she had previously absorbed all the conveniences of Chinese civilization)—which would preclude literature for the time being. For a writer proceeds from a compulsion to communicate a vision and he cannot afford to bother with what people in general think of him. We Nisei, discreet, circumspect, care very much what others think of us, and there has been more than one who has fallen by the wayside in the effort to reconcile his inner vision with outer appearances.

Too, there is the matter of language. English is to us, after all, the second tongue, and while we retain even less of the original language, we do not find ourselves as proficient in English as she is writ as a practitioner in it must necessarily be. Even those of us who would use the language as a means of livelihood generally lack the ability to sling it around, stretch it, knead it, pull it apart—much less pull rabbits out of it.

However, there was a gaggle of Nisei who in their youth found outlet in the pre-war pages of this newspaper [*Rafu Shimpo*] and other vernaculars, and they had a community of sorts. Some passed on early: George Watanabe, sensitive, poetic; Sam Hohri, our own Orwell in more ways than one—but he was technically an Issei; Chico Sakaguchi, who also danced the can-can at a UCLA dance festival (her brothers all seem to have become doctors); Tomomasa Yamazaki, who once in awhile amused himself by writing under the byline Les Harakiri; Carl Kondo, specialist in the ironic vignette. There were real poets, Helen Aoki and Toyo Suyemoto, and a variegated assortment of columnists—Joe and Mary Oyama, Henry Mori, Kay Tateishi, Ayako Noguchi, Kenny Murase, Lily Yanai, Harry Honda, Yas Nakanishi; and there was Roy Kawamoto (called Bull) who doubled in sports and linoleum blocks which brightened up the pages of the *Kashu Mainichi*. There were also Larry Tajiri, Togo Tanaka, and Roy Takeno, but these were all journalists already, working seriously at their craft. Toshio Mori had already had work published in *The Clipper*.

More glamorously, to the east, there was Mae Ninomiya Clarke, editor of movie magazines, and Japanese college students on the Eastern seaboard banded together under theology student Masatane Mitani and were loosely held together by "visitations" made and reported on by Toru Matsumoto. Among those he visited were Yoko Matsuoka, perennial delegate to youth conferences, and Tom Komuro, who later came west.

I have no doubt omitted names because, as the years rush pell-mell by, details of every kind have begun to elude me, but many of those named can be encountered still as by-lines in the English sections of the Japanese press. Others have gone on to be included in the success stories of other fields of endeavor. I am 47, which is the median age of the Nisei, which is to say that most are either younger or older. So I guess we have all arrived at the middle of the journey or thereabouts, and if there had been a true writer amongst us, he would certainly have reared his head or at least shown his hand by now.

But the way I fell into writing for awhile was that I had early contracted the disease of compulsive reading. I read anything I could get my hands on, all kinds of junk, especially in the summertime when I had no access to the school library, and I found myself beginning to look forward to the English sections of the Japanese-language newspapers with a feeling of having found my element. One day I remember taking pen in hand to write to Kay Tateishi, who wrote a column called "Tish for Tash," to chide him about borrowing an item from a columnist named E. V. Durling who used to write in the daily papers. Kay printed the note in its entirety, and I must say, to see my very own words in print, it was like some heady wine. I was hooked for life. It didn't help any when my English teacher at Excelsior, Elizabeth Chapin (afterwards Luttrell), gave me an A for one of my compositions and put it in a school anthology.

So I became a contributor, at first hiding under the pseudonym Napoleon—as an apology for my little madness—and then growing bolder and signing my very own name. For a writer must possess an enormous ego, absolutely certain that he is the greatest writer of the century and absolutely certain that the most important thing in life is to communicate his vision. Of course, there will be moments of doubt, but these convictions must be strong enough to override the precarious periods. We imitate God when we create, the God who created us and all the things about us out of His overflowing love. We have to retain a sense of uniqueness (I am the only one who has lived this particular life in this particular way and no one can duplicate it) and when we give in to this suspicion that we are, if not superfluous, at best expendable—why, if we are not able to accept this knowledge and go on from there, we at least will "not go gentle into that good night."

This was also the beginning of one of the most extensive collections of rejection slips extant. The first one came from the old *Pictorial Review*, I think it was. Or maybe the *Delineator*. Anyway, my first rejection slip at fourteen so depressed me that I tore up the returned story in little bits and pieces and scattered them along the orange and walnut groves there on Studebaker Road, all the way home from the country mailbox.

When Kay Tateishi left on a Japanese government scholarship (my cousin Isamu Masuda was also a recipient the same year), he asked me to replace him as a columnist. However, Ruth Kurata had already asked Kenny Murase, so there we were, writing insults at each other, and nobody really asked me to stop writing, so I kept writing. I remember Editor Roy Takeno, whose mother had tried to teach me the rudiments of Japanese at language school, cautioning me to go easy on the "ubiquitous characteristics of the Nisei." This was my introduction to the word "ubiquitous" and to the awareness that there was a definite Nisei personality which was definitely not to be made fun of.

Simultaneously, there were stints on yearbooks in high school and junior college, and there was encouragement from Lela May Garver, teacher of English, who passed on two Memorial Days ago at the retired teachers' community in Santa Barbara. At Compton, I met Emily Higuchi Munoz and Mary Kitano Diltz. Emily also wrote for the Japanese newspapers and Mary became editor of the junior college newspaper. Mary also later wrote her *Snafu* for the *Rafu Shimpo,* subsequently going to work for the old *Daily News* and CBS Television. There was also Mary Nakahara Kochiyama who was later to become known as a one-woman USO for the 442nd and who now publishes a yearly family bulletin called *Christmas Cheer* from New York's Harlem where she is an ardent worker for black rights.

Then came World War II and the *Poston Chronicle,* which might be looked back upon as a fun newspaper. Topaz Relocation Center's *Trek* magazine published the best creative writing and Jimmy Yamada, who later came to our camp, was the brightest star (particularly in a short story called "Gaudeamus Igitur"). In Poston I met Henry Mori, also Cherry Obayashi Tom who had occasionally contributed poetry to the Japanese newspapers and who later, as a student at Wells College, won a literary prize from *Tomorrow* magazine. My good friend was Wakako Nakamura Yamauchi, who not only paints but who has written several short stories in recent years which, while they are not as technically adept as they might be (for that matter, mine ain't either), are nevertheless very moving. But, of course, I am prejudiced. Pauline Bates Brown, our second Reports Officer—of the first, the less said the better—thought I should write the Great Nisei Novel. And I was delighted to find out that there lived in our very own block a pioneer Nisei newspaperman, the late Franklin Sugiyama.

Oh, the unlooked-for flotsam and jetsam that floats to the surface when one plunges headlong into memory—did you know that I once wrote a mystery serial? I had completely forgotten it till now, and the title of the story escapes me, but it seems to me there was a murder on the train en route to the relocation center. Although I don't remember who dunnit, I remember Editor Sus Matsumoto worming the story out of me, installment by installment.

Both Bean Takeda, who had published his own *Japanese American Mirror* in pre-war years, and I applied for the job on the *Los Angeles Tribune* after seeing the ad in the *Pacific Citizen.* The whole purpose of adding a Japanese to the staff of a Negro newspaper had been not only to welcome the returning Japanese (this was 1945, and Li'l Tokio, which had become Bronzeville during the war, was in the process of reconversion), but to make the newspaper more solvent by inviting Japanese advertising. The ad had specified a man, but I was hired. I doubt if my presence on the staff attracted even one line of Japanese advertising or even one Japanese subscriber. Later on, I came to see why I had been hired instead of Bean. He was too normal. My perceptive employers, heir to all the ambiguities of the Negro intellectual in a white society, had sensed in me kinship. For a writer must be a neurotic, treasuring his neurosis as the well-spring of his creativity at the same time keeping it enough in hand so that he doesn't go off half-cocked on some tangent. If you think this is easy . . .

But I learned a great deal from the *Tribune*'s publisher and its editor. In fact, the whole apprenticeship has profoundly, if you will pardon the expression, colored the rest of my life.

One day, proofreading, I was sullenly returning some corrected galleys to the linotypist, when the publisher went by.

"Your elbow's black," he said, meaning that I was quite grimy with printer's ink.

"Oh, so's your old man!" I retorted.

When I realized what it was I had said and after I got over my laughing fit (naturally this put me in high good humor for the rest of the day), the publisher merely remarked, "I'll bet you stayed awake all night thinking that one up."

Meanwhile, a young girl reporter from the *Christian Science Monitor* came to interview me as a specimen of returning Japanese, also the actress Ruby Berkeley Goodwin who was doing free-lance writing at the time. And I made Walter Winchell's column as an oddment: "An LA Negro newspaper's movie critic is named Husaye (sic) Yamamoto . . . a poultry journal's editor is named Russell Duck . . ." On Helen Sawa's recommendation, the Women's International League for Peace and Freedom, Pasadena branch, sponsored me at one of the International Institutes at Whittier College, and there I met Aldous Huxley, but I was so unnerved by the unexpected encounter that I couldn't think of a thing to say. All I remember is that he was wearing white socks.

One of the exchange newspapers that used to come into the *Tribune* was Dorothy Day's *Catholic Worker* and I was instantly drawn to it. I saved all the copies and took them home and accumulated an eight-year file before I finally did something about it.

It was my first acceptance by a literary magazine that detoured me. I had originally sent the story to the *New Yorker*, only this time, instead of putting the homeless story in the round file, as was my wont, I sent it off in another envelope to the *Partisan Review.* This was my undoing. The incredible letter from Mr. Rahv came and I was at long last a writer, at age 26.

"How long did it take you to write the story?" Albert Saijo asked.

"All my life," I answered.

What he wanted, of course, was the answer in days and hours and minutes. I think I dashed it off in a couple of hours, compared to the days and days I have been wallowing in this true confession. But all my life before had been laying the groundwork for that first published short story.

It was my brother Jemo who had made the writing possible by agreeing to help support me for a few months after I decided to leave the *Tribune.* I also had the posthumous help of another brother, Johnny, who died at 19 in Italy. Suddenly, however, a child came to live with me and this made a great deal of difference in my mode of existence. But Jemo gamely agreed to help and I continued to write. For a writer must have someone willing to finance creativity or have something else to fall back on. I understand only a handful of writers in the whole country, perhaps ten, making a living at it, serious writers that is. The rest have to do hack writing on the side or teach or do gardening in order not to die. That was the elegant poet Rainer Maria Rilke of whom it was written, ". . . The Duinese elegist, divinest sponger of all . . ."

This arrangement worked out until my brother decided to get married. The John Hay Whitney Foundation came to the rescue after Beatrice Griffith Thompson, author of *American Me,* urged me to apply for one of the first Opportunity Fellowships. For a whole year, I was really a writer, sending the child off next door to be baby-sat, bringing him home for lunch and a nap, and sending him back next door for a couple more hours. But I remember he used to pound on the door, demanding to be let in, or he would wedge himself between the typewriter and me and, spreading out his arms, say, "Don't type!"

Yet I managed to translate the whole of Rene Boylesve's "L'Enfant à la Balustrade" from French into English and to sell a couple of stories. Also to collect another batch of rejection slips. During this time I met Ward Moore, author of several novels who came to interview me for the *San Francisco Chronicle* as part of a double interview with Carlos Bulosan, the Filipino writer. Ward also did an article on the returning Japanese for *Fortnight*. It was while he was in charge of book reviews for *Frontier* that Nisei names like Gompers Saijo and George Yamada were signed to an occasional review.

I had excellent long-distance criticism from a brilliant Hawaiian Nisei, Daniel Kanemitsu, who later went on to study at Columbia University, and local criticism from Albert Saijo. The former, reading between the lines of my short stories, begged me to go easier on the father figure in them as well as on myself, and the latter wryly advised me to keep my output down to one story every five years. I also heard from Yvor Winters, poet and professor at Stanford, who suggested applying for a fellowship there; the poet Elizabeth Bishop; and there accumulated a small sheaf of inquiries from literary agents and publishers (some of them had been put up to it by the Foundation) who invited me to submit work. There was that wire from a magazine in New York asking if three hundred dollars was acceptable payment for a slight story which I had originally written for the *Pacific Citizen* and which I decided to send somewhere else first. All this was highly gratifying, except that throughout that year of subsidized writing, I was gradually coming to the conclusion that I didn't contain enough information to be a writer. For, looking back, it seems that I slept unconscionably long, that it was the sheer gall of ignorance that propelled me towards writing, that I came tardy to this most awkward groping towards light.

So when I had to check in with Dr. Robert C. Weaver, now Secretary of Housing and Urban Development (HUD), who was then director of the Opportunity Fellowships, I guess I was apologetic.

"Why," said Dr. Weaver, "we're expecting you to win the Pulitzer Prize in five years."

"Or the Nobel Prize in ten?" I said.

But we knew we were just joshing. A couple of others on fellowships that same year did just fine: one of them was the singer Leontyne Price and another was Julian C. Nava, professor of history at San Fernando Valley State and Board of Education member.

It was the *Catholic Worker* that had stuck in my craw for so many years, with its non-violence, voluntary poverty, love for the land, and attempt to put into practice the precepts of the Sermon on the Mount, which beckoned me now like a letter from home. So, after the fellowship had run out and my brother and his wife Yuri had moved in with us to make the living easier, the child and I headed for Peter Maurin Farm on Staten Island. The farm, with its daily Mass, cockroaches, weaving, bedbugs, homemade whole wheat bread, poison ivy, was home for us for a couple of years, except for brief forays into New Jersey, Maryland and Massachusetts, and even now, when we have been back in California for over a dozen years, we feel like an extension of the *Catholic Worker* family. Among the members of the family was Peggy Baird Conklin, who numbered among her former husbands Malcolm Cowley and who had been Hart Crane's companion on his last voyage.

Then I settled down to becoming a housewife and mother to five kids, except that unsettling events like death and illness fell thick and heavy there for awhile and I faltered, yearning, I guess, for a little more peace and order than it was at that time possible to have. Nervous breakdown is the popular term for it, anxiety the clinical name. The psychiatrist at Resthaven, and it was well named, said my illness stemmed from fear of responsibility. But he eased me out after a month, although I was allowed to be back and tell him all my troubles from time to time. I never go past the place, nestled on a knoll above Chinatown amidst a stand of eucalyptus, without a sense of deep gratitude.

After that, while expecting another child and therefore having to take it easy, I took to writing again as a form of therapy. In that period, around 1960, I wrote three stories and sent them off one by one. They all came back one by one, and I sent them off again, this time to be accepted by *Carleton Miscellany, Arizona Quarterly,* and the *Rafu Shimpo.* It must have been about this time, too, that there found its way to me by a most circuitous route an airmail letter from a young Englishman teaching in the Sudan. He was writing a book on Gladstone and wanted further elaboration on a fleeting reference to Gladstone which he had come across in a short story of mine in an old *Partisan Review* of ten years previous! It was like hearing from someone halfway across the world years and years after one has forgotten throwing into the sea a bottle containing a trivial message.

I remember that one day long ago my mother found me absorbed in writing a short story on brown wrapping paper. My mother was of a literary bent herself, and her father before her. And she said, "When you grow up, you must live in a house on top of a hill, where a cool wind blows, so you can write."

Well, here I am living in a house on top of a hill in Los Angeles, where we are all more or less blissfully smothering to death together in this warm brown cocoon of smog, but sometimes a cool wind does blow. How sweet it is then, especially on an April afternoon when a certain light and a certain breeze combine to make the world so airy and bright and spacious that one has an illusion of being able to take wing and fly away. It is on such days that the chores go easy, lightened by the remarkable cadence of such as "Though worlds of wanwood leafmeal lie . . ."

As for writing, this is about it.

"... I Still Carry It Around"

In this inescapably Bicentennial Year, we are here to look back upon an experience which is part of the darker side of American tradition. It is a tradition we share with the so-called Native American, with his background of being herded into reservations, and the Black, whose forebears were kept as chattel on Southern plantations.

Perhaps, hearing names like Dachau, Buchenwald, Auschwitz or Maidenek, we know that our concentration camp experience was comparatively benevolent. However, we also know that it, too, should never have happened.

Any extensive literary treatment of the Japanese in this country would be incomplete without some acknowledgment of the camp experience. It was a trauma which many Japanese who were incarcerated choose to ignore today, on the grounds that it is past history, over and done with, or that it is simply not a very interesting topic to bring up. It is some of our more sensitive children who have uncovered this uncomfortable period in our history and who, aghast, have insisted on looking at it in the full light of day, in order to try and comprehend how such a thing could have ever happened in a country where one million speeches have been delivered on the delights of freedom.

It is an episode in our collective life which wounded us more painfully than we realize. I didn't know myself what a lump it was in my subconscious until a few years ago when I

Excerpt from a paper presented at "A View from the Inside" symposium, Oakland Museum, October 15, 1976; published in *Rikka* 3:4 (1976): 11–19.

watched one of the earlier television documentaries on the subject, narrated by the mellow voice of Walter Cronkite. To my surprise, I found the tears trickling down my cheeks and my voice squeaking out of control, as I tried to explain to my amazed husband and children why I was weeping.

James and Jeanne Wakatsuki Houston report a similar response when they undertook research for their book, *Farewell to Manzanar,* among Mrs. Houston's relatives. Under probing, the memories of camp, long locked up, came tumbling out, accompanied by tears.

I think, looking over the whole of Japanese American creative literature, which does not yet span three complete generations, that we will find the Nisei writer choosing not to dwell on his camp experience. Perhaps this was all to the good, for his own health and well being. Perhaps this was because, as Albert Saijo pointed out ("The Nisei as an American," *Pacific Citizen,* Jan. 7, 1959), it was a complex event whose ambiguities further muddled our identities. Perhaps it was because the Nisei, in the years after the war, was preoccupied with survival. Whatever, it is more often the Sansei writer who goes back to the subject of evacuation again and again, sometimes to the point of obsession. Well, it is fashionable now to dig down to one's roots, and the younger writer has come to maturity in an atmosphere of ethnic consciousness and militancy. Also, the younger writer is generally more educated and therefore more articulate, as well as more self-probing, in this age of self-examination. We Nisei went to Japanese school because it was expected of us; the Sansei elects to learn Japanese in high school and college because he urgently wants to. We Nisei tend to be unobtrusive; the Sansei goes around nonchalantly wearing a *hi-no-maru* [rising sun] T-shirt. Sometimes all this has had the effect of arousing the older writer to go back to that neglected territory, with the feeling that he may have a few things to say on the subject.

Interview with Hisaye Yamamoto

This interview was conducted by correspondence, most of it during November 1992. I wished to elicit written responses from Hisaye Yamamoto for various reasons. For a start, given my two auto accidents earlier that year, I dreaded the prospect of negotiating the steep hill to her house. Secondly, some of my questions seemed so personal that I would have hesitated to ask them face to face. Furthermore, I was aware it might not be easy to make Ms. Yamamoto—known for her modesty—talk about herself. Most significantly, I had discovered through our informal exchanges that her letters can be as evocative and riveting, and as full of humorous sketches and pointed reflections, as is her published work. I am glad she agreed to a written interview.

KC: Were you exposed to literature at a very early age?

HY: No deliberate exposure to literature, except that my brothers and I, as children of Japanese immigrants, got by osmosis the myths and fairy tales (and ghost stories!) of Japan. Our first language was Japanese. Later, we read these stories in our Japanese school textbooks, but by then we had been exposed to similar reading in western literature. My favorites at first were *The Red Fairy Book, The Blue Fairy Book*—where I probably first encountered "Snow White," "Hansel and Gretel," "The Mermaid"; and at Japanese school, "Urashima Taro" and "The Peach Boy" were among the first folk tales read. By now, it's all a jumble with the Brothers Grimm, Hans Christian Andersen. I do remember that my favorite time in the classroom was when the teacher read aloud to us, although I now can recall only *Dr. Dolittle* as one of the treats.

KC: At the beginning did you feel self-conscious being an Asian American writer? Did you feel a sense of constraint?

HY: In the act of writing I can't remember self-consciousness. It seemed a perfectly natural thing to do. But yes, when my words actually appeared in print, there was definitely some constraint. I used the pseudonym "Napoleon" for awhile, but then I became accustomed to publishing and began to sign my real name.

KC: Were there fellow nisei writers?

HY: I came across Japanese American writing very early, in the bundles of Japanese American newspapers bought by my folks in order to make hot caps, shaped much like the soldiers' caps, to protect young seedlings planted in cold weather. This wasn't long after I learned how to read English—maybe when I was eight or nine?—and I still remember glamorous nisei poets' names like Sophronia Aoki and one twelve-year-old poet whose first name was Sierra, which I thought was lovely. And, if I remember correctly, there was an Aunt Polly who answered questions from nisei readers much like Dear Abby and Ann Landers do now. Except, knowing nisei, I rather suspect the questions were made up by Aunt Polly. This was in the late 1920s. So I might have realized about that time that it was possible for nisei to write for publication.

But I didn't really begin writing myself till several years later, about age fourteen. I began contributing oddments to the English section of the *Kashu Mainichi* (the *Japan California Daily News* which, alas, seems to be breathing its last after recently being purchased by a Japanese corporation which moved operations from Little Tokyo to Glendale). In the years before the war, the *Kashu* had a very hospitable, undiscriminating feature page every weekend, edited by Ruth Kurata. Later, I wrote a regular column called variously "Napoleon's Last Stand," "Don't Think It Ain't Been Charmin'" and "Small Talk," which last I retained for the column I did in the camp newspaper and subsequently every week for the *Los Angeles Tribune* (and later on a few times for the *Kashu* in the fifties).

So it seems I was trying things on for size under a very permissive feature page policy. By the late thirties and early forties, I believe Ruth's husband Tomomasa Yamazaki was the feature editor. (He died in the South Pacific in World War II, and, after the war, she was on the staff of *Motor Trend,* one of the Patterson magazines, as R. K. Yamazaki.).

KC: Do you feel that the position of Asian American writers has changed since you started?

HY: Considerably. It's a lot more "honorific," to use a friend's adjective. We had very limited response when we first were being published, but now, with ethnic literature courses available on the university level and ethnic literature "politically correct" or even mandatory in textbooks, we're being read as examples of Asian American writing. Just among Japanese American writers is some marvelous and variegated talent— R. A. Sasaki, Cynthia Kadohata, Holly Uyemoto, David Mura, Karen Tei Yamashita, Lonny Kaneko, James Masao Mitsui, Garrett Hongo, Sylvia Watanabe, others. Other Asian Americans like Maxine Hong Kingston and Amy Tan have been on best-seller lists. Then there's Jessica Hagedorn, David Wong Louie, Gish Jen. I haven't read Gus Lee's book yet, but have come across an excerpt which is intriguing. So now, some of the earlier writers, Wakako Yamauchi, Lawson Inada, and Frank Chin are coming out with new books. And Jeff Chan, too, I hope, and Shawn Wong.

KC: Rosie in "Seventeen Syllables" is a little bored with her friends' much ado over the new coat. What was your chief obsession at her age?

HY: I think my own interests were pretty much run-of-the-mill. Comic books (Superman, Batman, Flash Gordon) and radio (Jack Benny, Fred Allen, Vic and Sadie) and swing music (Glenn Miller, Tommy Dorsey, the Inkspots, Herb Jeffries). Radio was the common medium then; there was no TV. I guess my favorite thing was reading, indiscriminate reading, anything I could get my hands on. In school, the required reading was more structured: Shakespeare, Beowulf, Longfellow, stuff like that.

Oh, I forgot the movies. We were crazy about the movies and went every chance we got. It was only a dime for kids (25¢ for adults, 35¢ for loges), and we liked everything—

westerns, gangster films, musicals, comedies. I remember my folks liked Johnny Weismuller in the Tarzan movie so much that they sat through it twice. But all that combat with lions and tigers scared me and I went out in the lobby to wait for them. My mother admired Robert Taylor's widow's peak and Myrna Loy's mouth when she sang [in *The Prizefighter and the Lady*], as I remember. I liked fluff—Jeannette MacDonald and Nelson Eddy, Dick Powell and Ruby Keeler in all those musicals, and I remember the English teacher liking *It Happened One Night* so much that she arranged for the theater in Bellflower to show it especially for our school.

My mother was so taken by one Tanaka Kinuyo* movie, way back in the thirties, that she bought all the records from that film. So, from hearing her play the songs I learned them and can remember most of the words today. Very melancholy songs, for the most part, on the sentimental side. We saw quite a few Japanese films, silent, usually narrated by the *benshi*, the man who stood to one side of the platform and did all the speaking parts, including women and children. After a while, absorbed in following the story, one forgot he was there. When Japan invaded Manchuria, that was when the spate of war-oriented movies were brought over, and I'm sure any nisei who attended those films remembers the militaristic music from them, a very contagious kind of music—not that we really understood the words. I recall seeing Kabuki at Moneta Japanese school, but vaguely—too young to appreciate it. I believe it was a travelling troupe from Japan, with all the elaborate costumes. It must have lasted hours—there were mattresses in the front, so children could be put there when they fell asleep. It's coming back to me—there were quite a few programs of this type that we attended, not all Kabuki, but selections from Kabuki, with other dances interspersed.

KC: Were you at all drawn to Japanese art or literature when you were growing up?

---

*A famous Japanese film actress who starred in countless movies, starting in the thirties as an ingenue.

HY: Although the influence of Japanese art and literature came with our Japanese school studies, most of public schooling emphasized English and American literature and history. The Japanese influences we took for granted, not as any specialized field of study, just as Italians no doubt enjoy opera in their everyday life without categorizing it as classical music.

I don't remember reading Japanese as literature, only as school lessons. But the Japanese American writers in the newspapers, even though the outside world didn't recognize them as such, were faithfully followed: the Oyamas, Molly [Mary] Oyama Mittwer and Joe Oyama; Kenny Murase, Toyo Suyemoto, Dr. Yasuo Sasaki, Helen Aoki Kaneko, Carl Kondo, Ellen Noguchi Nakamura, Sam Hohri, many more.

KC: Rosie seems to have a pretty good time in school. Can you tell us something about your own experience in Japanese language school and public school? Were most of your teachers and fellow students in public schools Caucasians?

HY: School was fun; I looked forward to it. In Japanese school we were expected to use Japanese, but we jabbered away in English. For lunch, though, we looked forward to being able to take *onigiri* (rice triangles) and *umeboshi* (pickled plums) instead of baloney sandwiches.

In public school there were contacts of many extractions—Italian, Armenian, Mexican, French, Dutch, Basque, Jewish, Portuguese, whites that were called Okies as differentiated from whites that were called Americans. There were always some Japanese Americans around, but in high school I recall only one Korean and one African American. My brothers had Chinese classmates, but I can't recall a single one at the schools I went to. As far as I can recall, all the teachers were Caucasian. It was only after the war, I believe, that Japanese Americans were hired as teachers here in California. It was a big deal when one nisei fellow was hired locally by the post office before the war.

KC: What about your friends?

HY: I guess my friends in school were both Japanese and Caucasian. When I attended a mini-reunion of women from my high school not long ago, only the Japanese alumnae remembered me.

KC: Were you a star pupil?

HY: I wasn't very consistent in my schoolwork. I remember flunking typing and gym, or pretty nearly. But somehow I was named valedictorian when I graduated from grammar school, and although I didn't attend my high school graduation, someone who saw a program said my name was on it as a lifetime California Scholarship Federation member. I missed about a month of my junior college classes but was named salutatorian. I really didn't learn much in school, as I look back. I was unconscious most of the time, unaware.

KC: Thinking back to Rosie again, how good was/is your Japanese?

HY: My spoken and written Japanese is practically nonexistent. While my aunt was alive, there was somebody to converse with in Japanese. But you have to use a language to keep it from getting rusty. About the only time I use it nowadays is to answer queries from Tony [HY's husband], who is studying *katakana* [a phonetic Japanese syllabary] and *hiragana* [a cursive Japanese syllabary] on his own, so I guess I still retain some rudimentary knowledge from the twelve years of Japanese school once or twice a week.

KC: When you were Rosie's age, did you also help out on the farm?

HY: No, I didn't help out in the fields, although most of my friends did. I remember one classmate who was commended for being able to heft crates of cabbage just like a man. But I was excused, possibly because I was the only girl in the family, or maybe because I always had my nose in a book. But just before evacuation, I picked strawberries along with almost everybody else in our farm colony there in Oceanside, because the fellow who bought up the crops was paying wages we could save toward our unknown future.

I see all the advantages of that farm life now and am wistful about it. The fresh air and fresh vegetables—it was a pretty healthy life. So I putter around in my backyard now, trying to recapture some of that old agrarian feeling. My childhood dream was to have a little house all to myself, painted green, with a white picket fence around the flowers in the yard, and, inside, books, books, books, with maybe a narrow cot (one has to sleep sometime).

KC: Tell us something about your neighborhood when you were growing up. In the story the Hayashis visit the Hayanos. Did you live close to other Japanese American families and relatives?

HY: Our family and other farm families we knew moved quite frequently. The Alien Land Law prohibited Japanese from owning land, so most of the families would lease acreage for a couple of years and then move on. We moved at least four times in the Redondo Beach area, then inland to Downey, Artesia, Norwalk, Hynes (the Greatest Hay and Dairy Center in the world), which is now known as Paramount, and finally down to Oceanside. The availability of land to lease came down in a kind of pipeline from other Japanese, usually friends of the family who had come from the same area in Japan. So there was this kind of floating community that we belonged to, with village and prefectural picnics every year, the annual *mochi-tsuki** around Christmas time, the Japanese school events. Even leasing became illegal, according to Yuji Ichioka's *Issei*, but, as he notes, there were ways of getting around the law.

There wasn't much mingling with the white community, although there were probably some lasting contacts formed with some landlords, business people, neighbors.

KC: The multi-racial cast in your stories is remarkable, especially since most of them were written long before this country embraces multiculturism. In "A Fire in Fontana," your memoir about working for the *Los Angeles Tribune*, you identified viscerally with the black victims of racism. When did you become aware of racial prejudice?

---

* A new year ritual in which mochi (a special glutinous rice) was pounded, shaped, sold, and eaten. Yamamoto describes this custom in detail in "Las Vegas Charley."

HY: Southern California has always been a melting pot, at least in my experience. I gradually became aware of discrimination and when we Japanese were singled out for mass detention during the war, that really opened my eyes to what prejudice can lead to. And my education on this subject was furthered when I went to work for the *Los Angeles Tribune*.

KC: You said in "Writing" that Little Tokyo "had become Bronzeville" during the war. How did African Americans and Japanese Americans get along in the community after the war?

HY: Little Tokyo was gradually reclaimed by the Japanese after the war (it's being taken over by Japan now). The *Tribune*, in hiring a Japanese, had in mind a collaboration between the returning Japanese and the African American community. Almena (Davis) Lomax in her vision was far ahead of her time. However, I wasn't the activist type that could have established connections between the two communities, which generally went on their separate ways.

KY: In "Seventeen Syllables" there is this dizzying encounter between Rosie and Jesus Carrasco. How were interracial relationships looked upon in those days? Did your own parents give you a hard time when you dated non-Japanese Americans?

HY: Interracial relationships were on the whole frowned upon, but here and there such linkage did occur. The only cautionary note about intermarriage from my father was once when he warned me about marrying a white man. But otherwise neither my parents nor I devoted much thought to such possibilities, probably because I didn't really "date" till junior college, and by then I was pretty much on my own. (I was sixteen when I enrolled at Compton Junior College.)

KC: Dorothy Ritsuko McDonald said of John Okada's *No-No Boy* that while the "good" characters—Ichiro, Kenji, Emi— have Caucasian features, the more problematic characters, such as Ichiro's parents, have stereotypical Asian features— short, flat-chested, etc. Both Rosie in "Seventeen Syllables" and Yoneko (as well as her mother Mrs. Hosoume) are drawn to non-Japanese men, such as Jesus Carrasco and Marpo. To what extent were nisei influenced by dominant (Euro-American) standards of beauty?

HY: I am sure we were brainwashed by the movies we saw, to wish for blond hair, tall stature, etc. Wasn't there something in Monica Sone's autobiography about this? But I'm sure most nisei accepted their looks sooner or later. I remember one young columnist in the *Poston Chronicle* expressing her preference for her own skin color over white skin. Perhaps, unconsciously, we still compare ourselves to the white stereotypes of beauty, the movie stars.

KC: What about Japanese influence? Were you brought up according to any rigid gender stereotypes that your parents might have carried to America?

HY: No recollection of my parents being that rigid about anything. They were Americanized as a result of being here. There *were* parents of friends who insisted on their children conforming to Japanese ideals. Some were sent to Japan for their education—these children came back to be categorized as kibei (like Wakako's Kiyoko character in *And the Soul Shall Dance*). They usually knew Japanese better than English and were probably more comfortable in the company of issei than with their nisei peers.

But even in our case the Japanese ideals (of the Meiji era) were held up to us children. Reprimands usually included mention of the exemplary behavior of Japanese children, how quiet they were and obedient, how demure the girls were and how brave the boys.

KC: You turned twenty-one in camp. What were you doing before the evacuation? Had you not been interned, what do you think you would have done during those three years?

HY: Pre-war, I was keeping house for my father and three brothers in Oceanside, also trying to write (and getting rejection slips). I was doing a weekly column for the *Kashu Mainichi*. Probably my reading was also at its peak then. And just before evacuation we were harvesting strawberries for the man who bought up the crops and hired us to pick them.

I can't imagine what I would have done if we hadn't

been sent to camp. I loved that place (it became Camp Pendleton after we left), the view of the ocean, the near-perfect climate—probably I would have stayed there and continued sending manuscripts to possible publishers.

KC: Your graphic description of the burning of the Hiroshige in "Seventeen Syllables" reminds me of other literary descriptions about issei burning art objects and heirlooms in the wake of Pearl Harbor. Did that connection ever cross your mind? Did your family have to burn Japanese keepsakes before going to the camps?

HY: No, I didn't connect the destruction of family treasures after Pearl Harbor with the burning of the Hiroshige, which was purely imaginary. Down in Oceanside, we did bury Japanese textbooks and magazines and such, and I remember my youngest brother throwing his *kendo* uniform into the same hole. One neighbor offered his Japanese sword to a Caucasian man who used to check the water gauges on the mesa, and this man informed the FBI, so our neighbor was taken away to detention. Probably the government confiscated the sword as contraband.

KC: Unlike most critics of your work, I do have sympathy for the issei father figures in your stories. Do you think that the criteria for manhood are similar in Japan and in America? Are there distinctive Japanese American criteria?

HY: Japan and the U.S., as I understand it, have differing codes of conduct for men, but maybe they both boil down to glorifying the "macho" image—men as the stronger physically, as the heads of the household, harking back to the samurai for Japanese men and to knights for Western men? Not sure, since there was in the past this exaggerated martial code about *bushido* for Japanese men which probably accounted for the *kamikaze* pilots and such. With women's lib, though, there is this new move for men here to "reclaim their manhood," etc. I don't know where all this is leading. There's bound to be a reaction against it.

KC: I understand that your own father, when he was interned by the American government, lost a son—your brother—who was killed when fighting for America. How did that family tragedy mark him?

HY: When my brother died in Italy, my other two brothers and I had been in Massachusetts for about a month. Griefstricken, our father begged us to come back to camp. So we did, even though the WRA [War Relocation Authority] tried its best to talk us out of returning.

KC: In the mid-1950s you volunteered some time at the Catholic Worker farm in Staten Island. What precipitated your decision? How did Paul, your adopted son, find it?

HY: The *Catholic Worker* newspaper was one of the *Tribune* exchanges, and it was my job to cull items from the exchanges. The *Worker* fascinated me, so I began taking the copies home and re-reading them. After I left the *Tribune,* I subscribed (a penny a copy, or 25¢ a year), and the more I read it, the more I wanted to be part of the movement. So I finally was able to go and see for myself what living in community was like, although I guess camp was a type of living in community, enforced and on a massive scale. I've come across one analysis that my choice was a natural outcome of the internment. I thought it was because Paul was a cradle Catholic, and I intended to respect that but I also wanted him to become the best type of Catholic there was—a Catholic Worker. As he told people, "I'm the Catholic and she's the Worker." I fed the chickens and rabbits usually, sometimes cooked if there was no one else around to do it, cleaned cupboards, sorted clothing that came in, and wrote for the paper. Paul had several of Dorothy Day's grandchildren to play with, as well as neighbor children, and he was fond of the community's "hermit," Leonard, who had built a cabin for himself down in the woods and who was the community's Jack-of-all-trades. So when Paul and I would go for a walk and he saw a fender, for instance, he would hide it in the woods and we would pick it up on the way back "for Leonard" (guess who had to carry it?). He later went to school at St. Louis Academy for girls, a boarding school which had a day school for locals. After all that, he married a Lutheran girl and became a Lutheran. (I'm not a Catholic.)

KC: Do you remember your reaction when your first story—
"The High-Heeled Shoes"—was accepted for publication?

HY: Yes, because in the same mail I got some family news that
was of some concern, so my joy at having the story accepted
was tempered by this news.

KC: Can you say something about the publishing history of
"Seventeen Syllables"? Did you spend a long time writing that
story? What was your reaction when it was accepted for publication? What was your parents' reaction?

HY: "Seventeen Syllables" was the second story I submitted
to *Partisan Review*. I understand Philip Rahv, a co-editor, was
a man of multifarious interests who was fascinated with little-
known aspects of life in America, so maybe that was why he
published my stuff. I was in my later twenties. In those days—
unlike now—I wrote very easily, little re-writing if at all, so I
don't remember any particular difficulties with it. It kind of
wrote itself. When it was accepted, I guess I was happy, but
by then I had had other acceptances so I may have taken it in
stride.

 My mother died September 1, 1939, the day Hitler
marched into Poland. So she didn't live to see "Seventeen Syllables." Neither she nor my father read English very well, so I
doubt that they would have been interested. My aunt later
read Kats Kunitsugu's translation in a local Japanese women's
literary magazine and she commented, "Ah, so you remember
some of your mother's stories?" And I had to say, "No, but I
remember yours."

KC: "Seventeen Syllables" suggests a certain conflict between
female creativity and domestic responsibility. Do you experience any such conflict in your own life?

HY: Oh, sure. When I want to write it's very difficult to get to
writing (like I should be vacuuming right now, instead of an-
swering these questions; and I'll have to stop soon in order to
prepare supper). Writing now is something I do in my spare
time, except that I don't have any spare time.

KC: What is your impression of *Hot Summer Winds*, the

American Playhouse adaptation of "Seventeen Syllables" and "Yoneko's Earthquake"?

HY: I like the film very much. That's a Japanese American first, I believe—Emiko both writing the script and directing the film. She had been saving anecdotes about Japanese Americans for years, so she incorporated quite a bit of her data into the film, using my stories as a very loose frame.

KC: What about the happy ending? Isn't it quite different from the way you end your two stories?

HY: Yes, but Emiko is more sanguine than I am.

KC: Who are some of your favorite writers?

HY: Eclectic taste, but I've been reading a lot of Asian American writing in recent years. There's so much now. Recently, everything from Eleanor Clark, to Thomas Mann, to Karen Tei Yamashita, Cynthia Kadohata, Anne Tyler. The most perfect short story I've read is Tillie Olsen's "Tell Me a Riddle." But someone who knows her said she was still working on it. My favorite "novel" is Vikram Seth's *The Golden Gate,* in sonnet form. It has a very appealing sansei heroine. I guess if I had endless time I'd read more slowly, savoring—the King James Bible, Shakespeare, Yeats—and get into some of this pile of books I bought intending to read.

KC: Why did you translate René Boylesve's *L'Enfant á la Balustrade* during the year you were on a John Hay Whitney Foundation Opportunity Fellowship? Was the translation published?

HY: I was charmed by it in school and thought it should be available in English. Never published, but it's still around here somewhere. I also expected I wouldn't be very prolific, so the translation was to fill in the down time, so I wouldn't feel guilty.

KC: Have you ever taken any formal courses in creative writing?

HY: No, I haven't taken any formal writing courses, which I could probably benefit from. I'm very arrogant about what I

write. That is to say, I don't show my work in progress to anyone usually. If it gets accepted and published, it's there for
anyone to see, bloopers and all, but then it's too late.

KC: How comfortable are you with the label Asian American
writer or woman writer or feminist writer?

HY: Any label is okay, or no label.

KC: Have there been any surprising responses to your stories?

HY: Robert Rolf sent me some student papers from Tokyo
which were approving of the wife giving up her haiku in order
to be obedient to her husband; these were from women students, so I see women's lib hasn't made much of an inroad into
everyday Japanese life.

KC: Some Asian American writers have said how the Asian
and the non-Asian communities often react differently to their
writings. Do you also feel confronted by a double audience?

HY: Generally, more interest from Asians than from non-
Asians, more interest from women than from men, that I can
see. But it was a WASP male, Robert Payne, who made the
KPFK tape by Jeanne Sakata of "Seventeen Syllables." And
ditto, Professor Robert Rolf, also white, who edited *Seventeen
Syllables* for Kirihara Shoten; and Professor Charles Crow,
who has examined my stories very carefully in a couple of his
critical essays. And it was Professor Susan Koppelman, white,
who encouraged me to send my stories to Kitchen Table. So
I've been surprised at the interest in my stories from both
Asian and non-Asian, I guess. And in five stories ["Seventeen
Syllables," "Yoneko's Earthquake," "The Legend of Miss Sasagawara," "The Brown House," "Las Vegas Charley"] especially, that I wrote so long ago, never dreaming that they would
be reprinted and read so many years later, by those with
different emphases—ethnic, feminist, regional—a matter of
great astonishment.

KC: Speaking of these different emphases, any thoughts on
the relationship between politics and aesthetics? Do you feel
that a writer should have a political agenda or should their
politics emerge spontaneously?

HY: I call myself a Christian anarchist, but I'm not sure my beliefs come through in the stories. If they're part of me, however, some sense of it must be evident, but I leave that for you to judge.

A fiction writer who has a political agenda will probably consciously or unconsciously incorporate it into his work, don't you think? Either way is acceptable to me, just so the writing is good.

KC: What do you mean by "Christian anarchist"?

HY: I'm a Christian because I believe that Jesus Christ is the Son of God. And an anarchist because I agree that "the government is best which governs least," the government by mutual consent in small groups—communities—is the ideal form of democracy. This includes pacifism. Peter Maurin, the French peasant who was a co-founder of the Catholic Worker movement, wrote "Easy Essays" which explained his views. Sometimes the essays were rephrasings of theologians like Emmanuel Mounier, Jacques Maritain, etc. I don't vote.

KC: In "Writing" you describe something of the influence your mother had on you as a writer. How would you compare your relationship with your mother and your relationship with your own children? What do they think of your writing?

HY: I never tried to steer my children in any particular direction, except to make sure they would take advantage of the music training in the schools (I'm a frustrated musician). My mother was the one who encouraged me to seek higher education, my father not so much. Of course, there's a generation gap between us and our kids—they came of age after the sixties so we had to adjust ourselves, as best we could, to rock and roll, to marijuana, to people living with each other without being married, etc. As one friend shrugged, "After the first one . . ." I took the remark and the shrug to mean that there was no longer shock and protest after the first child lived with a partner without marriage. She had several children (all very accomplished and in the public eye, by the way), as we did, so, we got used to this even though we didn't really approve of it. As one older friend commented, "They (the younger genera-

85

tion) enter into these relationships so naturally and simply," that we can't help but accept the arrangements.

I doubt that the children read my stories as literature. But they have sat up and taken notice on occasion, as when one daughter, who is a Quality Paperback Club member, was quite impressed when *Seventeen Syllables* was listed as an alternate QPB offering.

KC: In what sense is "Seventeen Syllables" the story of your mother, as you told Koppelman?

HY: The reason I call it my mother's story is that, like most women, she didn't fulfill her potential. She had us kids to look after, on top of all the housework and working alongside my father in the fields. I remember when she was president of the Japanese school mothers' club, the group was very active, with such projects as Chinese cooking lessons and tie-dye sessions. She had a variety of interests and also tried out all kinds of dishes on us (recipes from the Japanese newspapers and the women's magazines from Japan, I suppose), which other nisei don't seem to know about, like ice-cold gelatinous noodles in summer with an ice-cold sauce that (as I remember) tasted like part soy sauce, part vinegar—I've never had any since.

Anyway, this short story has been reprinted in so many textbooks and anthologies that I've lost count. It's amazing. So I have this theory that my mother is behind the scenes there somewhere, making sure her story reaches the widest possible audience.

❏ Critical Essays

ROBERT T. ROLF ■

The Short Stories of Hisaye Yamamoto, Japanese American Writer

Hisaye Yamamoto was born in Redondo Beach, California, in 1921; her parents hail from Kumamoto Prefecture.[1] She apparently began writing at an early age, for she "received her first rejection slip at the age of fourteen."[2] As a young woman, she published where she could, in school magazines, for example, and finally began to appear in nationwide journals in 1948. Her short stories, poems, and other writings have appeared in many Japanese American and regional publications, as well as in such nationally-known ones as *Arizona Quarterly, Carleton Miscellany* (formerly *Furioso*), *Harper's Bazaar, Kenyon Review,* and *Partisan Review.* Still, her total literary output is relatively small; she seems to have put aside her writing to a large extent after marrying in her thirties. She is now often listed as Hisaye Yamamoto DeSoto; she has five children and has gone on to grandmotherhood.

Yamamoto's short stories have been anthologized regularly (no fewer than twenty times); this and the surge of interest and activity in ethnic studies the past decade or so have helped to keep her name prominent. My discussion will be confined to seven short stories of the years 1948 to 1961, all of which appeared in the above well-known, and thus accessible, journals. A truly thorough study of her career would involve ferreting out all of her various writings tucked away

From *Bulletin of Fukuoka University of Education* 31 : 1 (1982): 71–86.

in a variety of sources, some rather esoteric, the *Kashu Maini-chi, Rafu Shimpo,* and *Sangyo Nippo,* to name a few.

Although I will limit myself to her more widely known stories, I will still have plenty to talk of. Indeed, her star as a short story writer was rising in the early 1950s; from 1949 to 1952 five of her stories received some form of national recognition, "with 'Yoneko's Earthquake' reprinted as one of the *Best American Short Stories of 1952.*"

Hisaye Yamamoto's early life looks extremely diverse. The above period of her most conspicuous literary success was preceded by three years writing for the *Los Angeles Tribune,* a black newspaper, 1945–1948, and followed by two years of volunteer work on Staten Island at a rehabilitation farm affiliated with the *Catholic Worker* (1953–1955). Miss Yamamoto had been drawn there by the nonviolence and selfless idealism of the Catholic Worker Movement.[3] Her experiences in New York City provide material for the story "Epithalamium," or "wedding poem"; it seems that with her marriage she left the Catholic community to return to California.

Hovering over all the events of her life, however, is a central fact of existence for almost any prewar West Coast Japanese American, that of the war. What the Japanese attack on Pearl Harbor brought their American cousins on the West Coast is well known and well documented. Some 110,000 Japanese Americans, both non-citizen Issei and citizen Nisei alike, were deprived of their liberty solely on account of their ancestry, and forced to live for most of the war in one of ten so-called "relocation camps," nearly all hastily constructed in desolate, barely habitable locations. Miss Yamamoto must have turned twenty-one in or on her way to her wartime home, the Poston Relocation Camp, out in the Arizona desert near the California border.

The rationale for the relocation was that the Japanese Americans were potential spies or agents of the Japanese government, and as such had to be removed from the West Coast which was felt to be in imminent danger of invasion. The fact that more than half of the West Coast Japanese were native-born Americans and their parents were peaceful and productive long-term residents was buried under an avalanche of hostility toward Japan, indigenous white racism, and early

90

1942 "bad-war-news" hysteria. The Issei had been prohibited by law from obtaining citizenship and there were special statutes proscribing their purchase of land.

The lives of Hisaye Yamamoto and the other Japanese Americans of her time were shaped by a combination of factors: the cultural attitudes the Issei brought from Japan; the open and institutionalized racism of pre–Civil-Rights-Movement America; the unique experience of the relocation camps; the strong Americanizing influences of compulsory education in English and the pervasive popular culture (radio, movies, music, and so on), and, finally, life as a small minority whose values were threatened by the sheer volume of those of the majority culture on all sides.

Hisaye Yamamoto's stories, of course, spring from that experience. Of the seven stories to which I will refer, three involve sketches of prewar rural California Japanese American life: "Seventeen Syllables," "Yoneko's Earthquake," and "The Brown House." One story, "The Legend of Miss Sasagawara," is set in a wartime relocation camp; another is a brief vignette of postwar Japanese American life in Los Angeles, "The High-Heeled Shoes." "Epithalamium," as noted, draws upon Yamamoto's Staten Island period, and "Las Vegas Charley" attempts to convey the whole sweep of the Japanese American experience through the portrayal of the life of one Issei man, Charley.

Yamamoto's Style

To begin with a few comments on style, Yamamoto's method of narrative exposition is generally inductive. Her perception is microcosmic; she begins with a particular incident in the lives of her characters and goes on to suggest its wider significance. In "The High-Heeled Shoes," for example, she begins with a specific incident, an obscene phone call. She employs the first person, and even uses the present tense, maintaining it successfully for better than two pages, to create a sense of immediacy and urgency.

> In the middle of the morning, the telephone rings. I am the only one at home. I answer it. A man's voice says softly, "This is Tony."[4]

She returns to the present tense in the story's last few paragraphs, but the middle and largest section consists of reminiscences, philosophizing, and other ruminations that use the phone call as a point of departure and range even to a critique of the usefulness of Gandhian nonviolence for a young woman in pervert-infested Los Angeles. The story is successful; she has much to say, and quickly and intelligently imparts a sense of the fears of the young working woman.

The one story where she abandons this tight focus is "Las Vegas Charley," her attempt at a mini-epic of Japanese American life. "Las Vegas Charley" is, in my view, the least successful of the stories under discussion. There are several reasons, one being the basic unsuitability of the short story form for a Rootsian narrative. (Unfortunately, Yamamoto has never published a novel.) Another is her tendency in "Charley" to romanticize Japanese American life. And, there is more narrative distance toward Charley than other Yamamoto protagonists, no doubt to impart a certain universality to his experiences, but with the unfortunate result that he elicits less concern.

Significantly, only in "Charley" does Yamamoto begin with generalizations, including rather unremarkable comments on the phenomenon of Las Vegas, that oasis of decadence and entertainment in the Great Desert of American Puritanism. Still, "Charley" does have its merits; it ends strongly as the tale stops being that of an Issei Everyman and zooms in on just plain Charley, the slot machine-addict Japanese dishwasher, who once had a wife, farm, and family. And, of course, it is of considerable importance as a sympathetic portrayal of an Issei man, a "redressing" of Yamamoto's frequently unsympathetic characterizations of Issei fathers in her stories of a decade or so before.

The social context of Yamamoto's stories is significant, but her sensibility seems more that of an artist than historian. In her better stories, the world of the Issei and Nisei takes shape naturally as she works her way out from some illuminating moment in the lives of her characters. Both the individuals and their environments come into focus; we see the forest *and* the trees. Only in "Las Vegas Charley" does she often seem to be chronicling an age, a cultural experience, rather than trying to suggest the texture of individual lives.

It was Yamamoto's language that first attracted me to her writing; it is quintessentially American, marked by precision, playfulness, and irony. To illustrate what I mean, let me stop picking on "Charley" and refer to "Yoneko's Earthquake," my personal favorite, along with "The Brown House."

Yoneko is ten years old, a farmer's daughter, fascinated by Marpo, their twenty-seven-year-old Filipino Catholic farmhand. One day there is an earthquake and days of aftershocks, which refuse to stop despite Yoneko's prayers to Marpo's God. During the quake an electric power line falls on her father's car; he lives but receives such a shock that he can no longer do a proper day's work. Yoneko's mother and Marpo must do most of the labor. She apparently becomes pregnant, for she seems to undergo an abortion; at about the same time, Marpo makes an abrupt departure. When Yoneko's younger brother dies soon after, her mother feels it is retribution for the abortion and turns to Christianity to expiate her guilt.

Yamamoto's irony is evident as she has the adult events of the story seen through the little girl's perception of Yoneko. She does not understand the real nature and significance of all that has happened among her parents and Marpo.

Using a child as protagonist also affords Yamamoto a convenient means of understating events. She never actually says that Marpo and Yoneko's mother have an affair or that there is an abortion, but things are so obvious that only a child would not know what is going on. This light touch is characteristic of Yamamoto.

Both the precision and playfulness of Yamamoto's language can be appreciated from the following:

> Once Yoneko read somewhere that Filipinos trapped wild dogs, starved them for a time, then, feeding them mountains of rice, killed them at the peak of their bloatedness, thus insuring themselves meat ready to roast, stuffing and all, without further ado. This, the book said, was considered a delicacy. Unable to hide her disgust and her fascination, Yoneko went straightway to Marpo and asked, "Marpo, is it

true you eat dogs?", and he, flashing that smile, answered, "Don't be funny, honey!" This caused her no end of amusement, because it was a poem, and she completely forgot about the wild dogs.

The bulk of the first sentence describing the cooking of dogs is a masterfully concise description, worthy of a Hemingway, but then Yamamoto's playful spirit enters the picture, her imagery adjusted to the child's perception, and it is "stuffing and all, without further ado." Yamamoto's feel for the charm and humor of American speech is revealed in Marpo's disarming retort, "'Don't be funny, honey.'"

There are many examples of Yamamoto's ear for the color and humor of American speech. "The Brown House" is a treasure-trove of such little gems. The house of the title is a gambling establishment run by Chinese. The struggling Issei farmer Mr. Hattori leaves his wife and five preschool boys out in the car while he goes in to reconnoiter. Later, the impatient Mrs. Hattori begins sending her oldest to fetch papa, and the child returns accompanied by a portly Chinese woman bearing a plate of Chinese cookies.

> Although the woman was about Mrs. Hattori's age, she immediately called the latter "mama," assuring her that Mr. Hattori would be coming soon, very soon. Mrs. Hattori, mortified, gave excessive thanks for the cookies which she would just as soon have thrown in the woman's face. Mrs. Wu, for so she had introduced herself, left them after wagging her head in amazement that Mrs. Hattori, so young, should have so many children and telling her frankly, "No wonder you so skinny, mama."[5]

The line "'No wonder you so skinny, mama'" represents a real coup, a deft stroke of characterization, and funny, besides.

On another visit, the house is raided and "all kinds of people—white, yellow, brown, and black" make a run for it. A black man piles into the back of the Hattori car and Mrs. Hattori generously grants him sanctuary. Later, Mr. Hattori appears and drives his brood away, unaware of the man hiding on the floor in back.

> They were almost a mile from the brown house before the man in back said, "Thanks a million. You can let me off here."
>
> Mr. Hattori was so surprised that the car screeched when it stopped. Mrs. Hattori hastily explained, and the man, pausing on his way out, searched for words to emphasize his gratitude. He had always been, he said, a friend of the Japanese people; he knew no race so cleanly, so well-mannered, so downright nice. As he slammed the door shut, he put his hand on the arm of Mr. Hattori, who was still dumbfounded, and promised never to forget this act of kindness.
>
> "What we got to remember," the man said, "is that we all got to die sometime. You might be a king in silk shirts or riding a white horse, but we all got to die sometime."(118)

Again, the black man's dialogue is a brilliant mini-character sketch, as well as being a humorous example of one minority stereotyping another, and from a 1951 story at that. Clearly, the young Yamamoto had already developed a sophisticated understanding of the irrationality and ubiquity of racial stereotyping. This is also apparent from Mr. Hosoume's attitude toward Filipinos in "Yoneko's Earthquake."

Mr. Hattori is incensed that his wife has allowed a black into their car; she defends her actions, points out the inconsistencies in her husband's attitudes, and is severely beaten by him for her efforts. In time she finally leaves him, unable to bear his compulsive gambling. Later, a teenage nephew is sent as an emissary, and a confrontation ensues between the Japanese-speaking Issei and English-speaking Nisei, a bit overdrawn, but humorous, nonetheless.

> This nephew . . . about seventeen . . . a coiffure . . . like . . . a painted wig. . . . kept his hands in his pockets, straddled the ground, and let his cigarette dangle to one side of his mouth as he said to Mr. Hattori, "Your wife's taken a powder."
>
> The world actually turned black for an instant for Mr. Hattori as he searched giddily in his mind for another possible

interpretation of this ghastly announcement. "Poison?" he queried, a tremor in his knees.

The nephew cackled with restraint. "Nope, you dope," he said. "That means she's leaving your bed and board."

"Talk in Japanese," Mr. Hattori ordered, "and quit trying to be so smart."(120)

The nephew is sketched with an uncharacteristically heavy hand, but the central incident of the scene, the Issei unable to understand the slang expression "to take a powder," seems to be a favorite of Japanese American commentators illustrating their generation and culture gaps. It must have a ring of truth for them, and, every American is familiar with the spirit of this passage, an intelligent attempt to disarm an explosive confrontation through the humorous revelation of its essential absurdity.

Most of Yamamoto's characters are Japanese Americans, Issei and Nisei. Their values, especially those of the former, often appear quite Japanese. For example, the family is a central concern; it must be made financially secure and its fortunes promoted. There is a preference for male children ("Seventeen Syllables"), the wife is expected to sacrifice herself for the family (Mrs. Hattori), and filial piety exerts a strong psychological pull ("Las Vegas Charley").

There is also concern for what might be termed racial purity. One feature of Yamamoto's style is the inclusion, for emphasis or effect, of Japanese words (sometimes with an English translation). The heroine of "Epithalamium" marries an alcoholic and wonders how to break it to her mother, in whose eyes the man would have another strike against him in addition to his illness. That is, "Sooner or later, her mother would have to learn that her daughter married an alcoholic, and a *hakujin* (white) at that."[6]

Blacks, also, can be viewed adversely, as seen earlier in "The Brown House," where the issue is not marriage but merely a ride in the Hattori car. Mr. Hattori's aversion to blacks seems physical. "'A *kurombo!*' he said. And again, 'A *kurombo!*' He pretended to be victim to a shudder" (118).

All in all, the black man in "The Brown House" is portrayed with sympathy; it is Mr. Hattori who comes off the worse in this confrontation. Many other non-Japanese characters appear in Yamamoto's stories, including another black, a seaman friend of the white alcoholic in "Epithalamium." He is mentioned but briefly and portrayed rather neutrally.

As for Chinese, in addition to the delightful Mrs. Wu in "The Brown House," there is Dick Chew, the Las Vegas restaurateur who employs old Charley. The description of Mr. Chew is of interest:

> [He] owned several cafes in the city, staffed by white waitresses and by relatives he had somehow arranged—his money was a sharp pair of scissors that snipped rapidly through tangles of red tape—to bring over from China. Mr. Chew dwelt, with his wife and children, in a fabulous stucco house which was a showplace (even the mayor had come to the housewarming). He left most of the business in the hands of relatives and went on many vacations . . . one year . . . even . . . as far as England. . . .[7]

This passage is followed by a contrasting description of the destitution and drudgery of Charley's life, although, later, Chew is revealed to be capable of at least a small act of charity.

The image of Chinese in Yamamoto's stories is perhaps less than flattering, but, in the final analysis, they seem basically kind-hearted and philosophical. During their second encounter, Mrs. Wu adds a sack of Chinese firecrackers to her customary gift of Chinese cookies, and says to the exasperated Mrs. Hattori, "'This is America' . . . 'China and Japan have war, all right, but (she shrugged) it's not our fault. You understand?'" (117).

Other ethnic Americans are described positively. There are the Filipino farmhand Marpo in "Yoneko's Earthquake," the flower-loving little girl Margarita in "The High-Heeled Shoes," and the amiable teenager Jesus, who gives the innocent Nisei heroine of "Seventeen Syllables" her first kiss. Even the drunken sailor of "Epithalamium" comes off well, all in all, because he is so manly and attractive that Yuki Tsumagari marries him in spite of herself.

It is non-ethnic whites that seldom seem to come alive. There are nebulous, neutral figures such as the white waitresses in "Las Vegas Charley" and the camp nurses in "The Legend of Miss Sasagawara," and there is a passing reference to a common stereotypical image, that of the "golden-haired goddess," in "Epithalamium" (64). But other than Marco, the Italian-American seaman, the only major white character is Mother Marie, the head of the Staten Island community in the same story. She functions as an authority figure of sorts for the heroine Yuki, whose reading of Western literature had led her to New York. "Epithalamium" contains references to Gerard Manley Hopkins, Flaubert, and Roman Catholic liturgy.

Of the seven stories, only "Epithalamium" does not deal directly with life in Japanese American communities and is set in the East rather than Far West. And, interestingly, the only two well-rounded white characters appear in this story, where finally Yuki, too, must return to California and the psychological shelter of the Japanese American community.

Whites have little place in the four California stories or in the almost entirely Japanese world of the relocation camp in "The Legend of Miss Sasagawara." In "Las Vegas Charley" the tragedy of the elderly protagonist is his isolation. He leaves California and the Japanese American community, and winds up in Las Vegas, which, Yamamoto stresses, is no place for a Japanese. He was Kazuyuki Matsumoto as a young man in Japan and Mr. Matsumoto when a family man and farmer among the Japanese in California. Now, alone in Nevada, he is reduced to a stereotypical nickname, in short, he has lost his dignity and meaning, having been wrenched from the Japanese community by the dislocation of the war.

Removed from the sheltering womb, Charley does have encounters with whites, for example a drunken soldier, described as the man who dropped the bomb on Hiroshima and as frantic with guilt. However, Charley is unable to give his own reactions to the man, because, despite a lifetime spent in America, he still cannot speak English very well (305).

Charley's other encounters include two incidents in which his life is threatened just after the war by hostile anti-Japanese drunks. One is a "white" and the other a "Mexican"; Yamamoto's depiction of them affords a revealing juxtaposition. The "white" puts Charley at knife point and, with no prior explanation, delivers a right/wrong, with me or against me question, "'Are you Japanese or Chinese?'" Only Charley's confused silence saves him. The "Mexican," on the other hand, merely grabs Charley by the arm and says that he has to "keel" him because the Japanese killed his son in the war. Charley is able to reason with the "Mexican" easily; "somehow a Mexican had not been as intimidating as a white man." "'Mexicans, Japanese, long time good friends,' Charley had answered. 'My boy die in the war, too. In Italy. I no hate Germans. No use'" (306). Charley feels a familiarity with the "Mexican" inasmuch as he had hired many Mexican farm workers before the war. He "had been their boss" (306). With white Americans the relationship must have been different, as they were his bosses in the relocation camp.

The Theme of Sex

Having examined the language and characters of Yamamoto's stories, let us take a look at two of their prominent themes: first of all, sex, and, later, Japanese and American cultural tensions. Sexuality is approached entirely from the point of view of the female characters, nearly all of whom—Issei, Nisei, and the white Mother Marie—struggle with their sexual instincts.

Sex is characterized by its unsavoriness or even perversion, whether real or imagined. The high heels of the story "The High-Heeled Shoes" are worn by an otherwise naked man, lounging in a car parked along a Los Angeles street, door open to expose himself as he leers at the incredulous heroine walking by one morning on her way to work. As we saw, the story begins with an obscene phone call, which triggers memories of other brushes with perverts in Los Angeles. The extreme of degeneracy represented by a naked man in high-heeled shoes is contrasted with the flowers and innocence of the little neighborhood girl Margarita. Such a juxtaposition is common in these stories. The female characters fight to repress a part of their true natures; they do not seem to trust their inner feelings, at least not when sexual.

Yamamoto's stories can be seen as forming, in part, a fictional chronology of the sexual progress of one such Japanese American woman, from the innocence of a ten year old to an eventual, much delayed capitulation to male sexuality in her thirties. The uncomprehending innocence of Yoneko is set against the deterioration of her parents' relation: apparent adultery, abortion, and remorse. "'Never kill a person, Yoneko,'" her mother says to her in the end, "'because if you do, God will take from you someone you love'" (282).

In "Seventeen Syllables," tenth-grader "Rosie fell, for the first time, entirely victim to a helplessness delectable beyond speech," when given her first kiss by twelfth-grader Jesus. But the "beautiful sensation" is quickly overshadowed by "the reality of Jesus' lips and tongue and teeth and hands" and Rosie frees herself forcibly and returns on the run to the refuge of a Japanese American family gathering. Finally, later, Rosie's mother tells her of her own youthful indiscretion in Japan, of a still-born, illegitimate half-brother, of how she had forsworn suicide in the incident only for escape to America and a hastily-arranged marriage with a young man "of simple mind . . . but . . . kindly heart." Then, her desperately unhappy mother implores her earnestly, frantically, "'Rosie . . . Promise me you will never marry!'"

Rosie is forced to agree, because it is her mother, but in truth she wants the symbolically-named Jesus Carrasco: "Jesus, Jesus, she called silently, not certain whether she was invoking the help of the son of the Carrascos or of God, until there returned sweetly the memory of Jesus' hand, how it had touched her and where." Rosie's acquiescence is described as her "familiar glib agreement," and thus appears perfunctory. As the story ends, the mood between mother and daughter is one of mutual disenchantment: Rosie with her mother for projecting her dilemma onto her, and the mother with Rosie for her unconcern. Her mother looks dissatisfied, perhaps with Rosie's weakness, having given in to parental authority with an evident lack of spirit, although she herself had followed her emotions as a girl in Japan: "Oh, you, you, you, her (mother's) eyes and twisted mouth said, you fool."

It is difficult, and perhaps unwise, to try to pinpoint the exact nature of the emotions of the two women, but it does seem safe to say that they find themselves unable to communicate unreservedly, especially Rosie, who does not tell her mother of her own unhappiness. Rosie internalizes the concomitant frustration, locking it within where it can eat away at her, undermining the natural development of her personality. Whoever may be to blame, she has been hurt and something lost in her relationship with her mother.

The sexual awareness of Yamamoto's heroine continues to expand in "The Legend of Miss Sasagawara," where she is a young camp inmate, a first-person narrator of the story of the camp's star attraction, the lovely but withdrawn Miss Sasagawara, a professional ballet dancer, nearing forty, who deteriorates from eccentricity to psychosis when forced by camp life to live with her father. A Buddhist priest, he virtually beams with self-satisfaction over his satori and nirvana, recently achieved after the death of his wife and through the freedom from social responsibilities of the simple life of an elderly detainee.

That much of Miss S's problem is sexual is clear from descriptions of her innocent but abnormal voyeurism and interest in much younger men. Sympathy entirely belongs to her, however, and blame is clearly placed on her father, who neglects her human needs to attain his own selfish salvation. Still, it may be inferred that Miss S serves as a negative cautionary model for the narrator. Miss S is desirable (her naked body is described as trim and youthful) and she herself desires, but the only man in her life is her father, who has devoted himself to the systematic negation of natural desires and instincts. Thus isolated, her thwarted drives and repressed emotions work within to destroy her mental equilibrium.

In "The High-Heeled Shoes," the Yamamoto heroine seems to be in her mid or late twenties working in Los Angeles after the war, with other women for companions, reading copiously but finding no way in books to cope with the impersonality and abnormality of sexual expression in the big city. Finally, in "Epithalamium," the Yamamoto heroine, in her thirties now, has found romance and begun a sex life at last. In the environment of the New York religious community, however, the heroine's love becomes a matter of defilement. Of Marco and Yuki, we are told:

> There was scarcely a nook or cranny of the Community that
> they had not defiled. . . . she had urgently sensed that it was

against God's will . . . each moment stolen for love had been unmistakably tainted. (57)

Juxtapositions of the sacred and the profane, the divine and the carnal, that had been tentatively put forward in "Seventeen Syllables" are developed more complexly in "Epithalamium." The Yamamoto heroine, Yuki, finally opts for life—she will be no second Miss Sasagawara—but she feels she is betraying not only her mother by marrying a white alcoholic, but even God by having sex with the man.

Such a repressed attitude toward sex is believable, in the light of the descriptions of the Yamamoto heroine's parents in the earlier stories. The fathers are gruff and distant (although the only mention of Yuki's father in "Epithalamium" is positive), lost in work or gambling. They take out their frustrations on their wives, whose subsequent misogamy colors their education of their daughters.

Cultural Conflict and the Search for Values

Another important element of Yamamoto's stories is their insight into Japanese American family life and the clash of Japanese and American values. The Issei immigrants faced not only white racism, but also a vastly different culture. Often it was their own children, the Nisei, who unwittingly confronted the Issei with the alien values in their own homes, so that it becomes difficult to distinguish clearly between inter- and intra-cultural confrontations, since the two are closely intertwined. The nature and extent of the cultural difference is evoked brilliantly, when Yamamoto renders the formal, often formulaic Japanese speech of the Issei directly into English. The result is not simply unidiomatic; at best it has a quaint charm, and at worst sounds absurdly indirect or self-effacing.

One of several such passages is in "Seventeen Syllables," where Mrs. Hayashi, the frustrated wife of a farmer, has regularly contributed haiku to a Japanese newspaper in San Francisco, much to her uncomprehending husband's dismay. One day there is a surprise visitor to the Hayashi farm, a dignified, well-dressed Japanese man who has come to inform her she has won a haiku competition and to deliver her prize, a Hiroshige print.

> Handed the package with a bow, she bobbed her head up and down numerous times to express her utter gratitude.
>
> "It is nothing much," he added, "but I hope it will serve as a token of our great appreciation for your contributions and our great admiration of your considerable talent."
>
> "I am not worthy," she said, falling easily into his style. "It is I who should make some sign of my humble thanks for being permitted to contribute."
>
> "No, no, to the contrary," he said, bowing again.

Providing the title of "Seventeen Syllables," the haiku poetic form functions as a symbol of the incomplete communication between the Issei parent and Nisei child. The story opens with daughter Rosie (soon to receive her first kiss from Jesus, as we recall) being shown a haiku by her mother. Rosie had not even known of this important area of her mother's inner life, so this revelation represents an important opportunity to establish complete communication between mother and daughter. But, we are told of Rosie and the haiku, "Rosie pretended to understand it no end, partly because she hesitated to disillusion her mother about the quantity and quality of Japanese she had learned in all the years she had been going to Japanese school every Saturday (and Wednesday, too, in the summer)."

Her mother does her best to explain the poem, but finally gives up the attempt as hopeless. "Resigned," mother returns to haiku writing—in Japanese; and, Rosie is left to her solitary thoughts—in English.

> The truth was that Rosie was lazy; English lay ready on the tongue but Japanese had to be searched for and examined, and even then put forth tentatively (probably to meet with laughter). It was so much easier to say yes, yes, even when one meant no, no. Besides, this was what was in her mind to say: I was looking through one of your magazines from Japan last night, Mother, and towards the back I found some *haiku*

in English that delighted me. There was one that made me
giggle off and on until I fell asleep—

> It is morning, and lo!
> I lie awake, comme il faut,
> Sighing for some dough.

Now, how to reach her mother, how to communicate the melancholy song? Rosie knew formal Japanese by fits and starts,
her mother had even less English, no French. It was much
more possible to say yes, yes.

At the conclusion, Rosie promises her mother never to
marry—with "her mother . . . holding her wrists so tightly that
her hands were going numb." At the end of the emotional Issei
mother/Nisei daughter confrontation, and the story, "Rosie,
covering her face, began at last to cry, and the embrace and
consoling hand came much later than she expected." Need-
less to say, being forced by a language gap to say yes, yes,
when in one's heart it is no, no, places a heavy strain on
parent/child relations. Parental expectations arrived at in a
foreign, Japanese context might seem unrealistic or unreason-
able in an American one. Nevertheless, parents are parents,
regardless of how well they speak English, and the inability to
conform honestly with their wishes could create psychological
pressure and guilt feelings. In "Epithalamium," the heroine
Yuki at first uses humor to neutralize her guilt feelings toward
her mother for being unmarried at thirty. But this typically
American ploy does not always overcome the pressure of her
Issei mother's expectations, and Yuki at times feels inadequate, calling herself "a *katawa*. . . . a freak" (65).
  Much of the dilemma of the Yamamoto heroine results
from a confusion of values. There is a searching for moral authority, a strong need for a father figure. The Issei fathers
in her stories have difficulty adjusting their role concepts
to the needs of American life. They are often stern and
uncommunicative.
  In "Epithalamium," the father is described as sympathetic, but in "Seventeen Syllables," after fleeing the trauma
of her first kiss, Rosie hurries to join her father in the sanctu-

ary of their Japanese bathhouse, only to meet with infuriating rejection rather than understanding.

> "Are you through, Father?" she asked. "I was going to ask you to scrub my back."
>
> "Scrub your own back," he said shortly, going toward the main house.
>
> "What have I done now?" she yelled after him. She suddenly felt like doing a lot of yelling. But he did not answer.

In "Yoneko's Earthquake," the image of the father is also generally unpleasant. Still, on balance, the Issei fathers in Yamamoto's stories do not appear especially unkind to their children; it is their wives who suffer most at their hands.

We have seen the put-upon or frustrated wives of "The Brown House" and "Yoneko's Earthquake." In "Seventeen Syllables," the difficulty and refinement of Mrs. Hayashi's haiku create a barrier not only between her and Rosie, but between her and Mr. Hayashi as well. In a possessive rage nearly worthy of Jake LaMotta in the film *Raging Bull*, Mr. Hayashi routs the innocent newspaperman from his house, and wantonly, systematically, destroys the Hiroshige print his wife has just won. First, he smashes it viciously with an axe, and, then, douses it with kerosene and burns it.

"Seventeen Syllables" also contains a vivid sketch of a neighbor woman, Mrs. Hayano, who was once "the belle of her native village" in Japan, but is now "stooped, slowly shuffling, violently trembling (*always* trembling)." We are told explicitly that her affliction began with the birth of her first child, a girl. Because of the old country need for a son, and despite Mrs. Hayano's ill health, she is destroyed by the births of four children, ironically all girls. Rosie is delighted by the company of her four pretty friends but it is "painful" for her to watch the hobbled, inarticulate Mrs. Hayano. Rosie senses something is wrong, but apparently the Issei adults do not. Amid such a muddle of values and conscience, Rosie is forced to conclude that "it was not a matter she could come to any decision about."

The Yamamoto heroine seeks beyond the Japanese American world for a viable system of values, for moral authority. However, Gandhian nonviolence ("The High-Heeled Shoes") proves inadequate and Catholic self-denial ("Epithalamium") unrealistic, in providing a model for moral female behavior. Likewise, Buddhist ritual had seemed somehow empty, to judge from the characterization of Reverend Sasagawara; his nirvana becomes unfeeling egoism in the contexts of both family and camp life.

The slight, sensitive Yamamoto heroine needs physical protection and emotional shelter to survive in America. On the one hand is the strong, manly (albeit generally sodden) presence of the Italian-American sailor with the perhaps symbolic East/West name Marco, and, on the other, is the familiar intimacy and gentility of Japanese-style daily life, the sushi, sashimi, and kindly "aunty" of the ending of "The High-Heeled Shoes."

The Yamamoto heroine does feel the need for Japanese cultural continuity. The Issei parents may provide a somewhat bewildering example at times, but their dedication and single-mindedness inspire loyalty. A Nisei's loyalty to his parents may represent not only the familiar virtue of "filial piety," but also a way of maintaining identity as a member of a small minority in America. In "Epithalamium," the heroine spends two years in the black and white world of the Catholic community. Standing in the way of her acceptance of Catholicism is its failure to recognize the efficacy of Buddhist salvation, for accepting a faith that could not admit her parents to its Heaven "would be equivalent to rejecting her mother and father, and Yuki could not bring herself to cause this irreparable cleavage" (66).

The short stories of Hisaye Yamamoto are skillfully written and hold the reader's interest through their gentle wit and deft characterization. In the course of depicting the progress from girlhood innocence to womanhood of one Japanese American girl, much of the experience of the American Nisei is revealed: the distinctive problems of their bicultural family life; the extent of their ties to the culture of the old world, Japan; and, the relationship of the Japanese Americans to other Americans.

The predicament of the Yamamoto heroine, faced with many systems of values, none quite right for her, suggests the contemporary and ongoing problem of how we should live our lives. Yuki, in "Epithalamium," comes out of hiding and, in her own way, plunges once again into life, armed with only her sense of life's essential absurdity (for example, her awareness of what an incongruous pair she and Marco make) and the reassuring possibility that life does go on, as Hopkins said, "Because the Holy Ghost over the bent/World broods with warm breast and with ah! bright wings" (67). There is room for hope in Yamamoto's world, though her mention of the martyrs St. John the Baptist and St. Sabina warns that life is also marked by suffering and uncertainty.

In the last of these seven stories, "Las Vegas Charley" (1961), Yamamoto lays aside the chronicle of her heroine and moves to male characters and an assessment of the Japanese American experience, focusing on the Issei. And, she concludes that although old Charley appeared amiable and carefree, his life may have been a quiet tragedy, unlike that of his pessimistic, sobersided young Nisei doctor, who works too much and so envies Charley's smoking, drinking, and gambling.

The Nisei go on living knowing at least that however difficult things become, life was probably harder for their Issei parents. The reaffirmation of life in Yamamoto's stories is neither obvious nor facile; her attitude is highly ambivalent, which seems appropriate to the complexity of the issue. Still, her intelligent reticence may make the little hope she does extend all the more of a comfort.

☐ *Notes* ■

1. This study was presented at the 27th Annual Kyushu Seminar in American Literature, hosted jointly by the Fukuoka American Center and Kyushu University, May 9 and 10, 1981. The contents are entirely my responsibility, but I would like to acknowledge gratefully the invaluable aid in gathering materials of the following people: Dr. Frederick Richter; Dr. Thomas E. Swann; Dr. Thomas Cogan; Mr. Russell Leong; Prof. Kazuhiro Ebuchi; Mrs. Margaret H. Rolf; and, especially, Mrs. Hisaye Yamamoto DeSoto.

2. "Relocation and Dislocation: The Writings of Hisaye Yamamoto and Wakako Yamauchi," by Dorothy Ritsuko McDonald and

Katharine Newman, *MELUS: Ethnic Women Writers I,* Vol. 7, No. 3, Fall, 1980, p. 23.

3. *Encyclopedia Brittanica* describes the Catholic Worker Movement as a "Roman Catholic lay movement in the U.S. and Canada, emphasizing personal reform, radical agrarianism, absolute pacificism, and the personal practice of the principles in Jesus' Sermon on the Mount. The *Catholic Worker,* a monthly tabloid publication, was founded in 1933 by Dorothy Day. . . . A group gathered in New York City under Miss Day's leadership. . . . Their example was followed in the U.S. and Canada by local groups. . . . Before World War II there were 35 of these groups, maintaining a strict pacifist position, but many young persons associated with the movement entered the armed services, and houses of hospitality went out of existence. The movement never regained its prewar influence . . ." In fact, however, the Catholic Worker Movement appears to be alive and well. Materials sent by Mrs. DeSoto include copies of the *Catholic Worker* (published nine times a year in New York), the *Catholic Agitator* (published 10 times yearly in Los Angeles), and many recent clippings from the *Los Angeles Times* reporting on such CWM volunteer activities as caring for impoverished immigrant Latino families and the homeless elderly on Los Angeles' Skid Row and providing supervised playground facilities for poor children. Each *Catholic Agitator* lists ten regular CW activities in the Los Angeles area, including hospitality houses, hospitality kitchens, free medical and legal clinics, an "at-cost food store," the "Justice Bakery," and the playground.

4. "The High-Heeled Shoes," *Partisan Review* 15 (Oct., 1948), p. 1079. Subsequent references by page number only.

5. "The Brown House," *Asian-American Authors,* ed. by Kai-yu Hsu & Helen Palubinskas. (Boston: Houghton Mifflin, 1972), p. 116. Subsequent references by page number.

6. "Epithalamium," *Carleton Miscellany,* Fall, 1960, p. 66. Subsequent references by page number.

7. "Las Vegas Charley," *Arizona Quarterly,* Winter, 1961, pp. 303–304. Subsequent references by page number.

Hisaye Yamamoto:
A Woman's View

Hisaye Yamamoto has chronicled Japanese American social history in her short stories. In "The Brown House" (1951), "Seventeen Syllables" (1949), and "Yoneko's Earthquake" (1951), we are introduced to Japanese American rural life, *issei-nisei* relationships, Japanese American attitudes towards Filipinos, Chinese, Mexicans, and Blacks, and the position of *issei* women in the community. "Las Vegas Charley" (1961) traces the life of an *issei* widower from Japan to the California farms to the internment camps to Las Vegas, where he works as a dishwasher and gambles his wages away until he dies. In "The Legend of Miss Sasagawara" (1950), Yamamoto records part of the Japanese American internment experience. The story is set in a desert camp. We catch glimpses of how families lived and interacted as well as of how internment affected their behavior. The bizarre actions and appearance of Miss Sasagawara, a social deviant in the Japanese American community, is seized upon by her fellow inmates, who use her to help relieve their tension, boredom, and sense of insecurity.

When asked about her motivation to write, Yamamoto has said:

> I guess I write (aside from compulsion) to reaffirm certain basic truths which seem to get lost in the shuffle from generation to generation, so that we seem destined to go on

From *Asian American Literature: An Introduction to the Writings and Their Social Context* (Philadelphia: Temple University Press, 1982), 157–163, 304–305.

109

making the same mistakes over and over again. If the reader is entertained, wonderful. If he learns something, that's a bonus.[1]

Most of Yamamoto's stories have something to say about the relationship between the *issei* and *nisei* generations, who are brought together in stories essentially addressed to fellow *nisei* almost as a warning to them not to lose the experiences of their parents, which they (and she) can only partially understand. This warning is never made at the expense of the *issei*. Neither are the *nisei* blamed for failing to understand completely. Generally, the stories are told from the viewpoint of a *nisei* narrator who sees the *issei* as through a glass darkly, without ever fully comprehending the feelings and actions of the older persons. The understanding is incomplete partly because of communication difficulties, but also because of the self-absorption of the *nisei,* who are intent upon conquering other worlds. Yamamoto demonstrates the impossibility of anyone's ever fully understanding the motivations and experiences of others, but she is not pessimistic. What the *issei* have lived through is in danger of being lost to their children, but if the *nisei* make a conscious effort to learn from what the *issei* have experienced, the *nisei* may also learn to understand themselves.

In "The Brown House," the imperfect communication and cultural differences between *issei* and *nisei* is seen in the interchange between the immigrant and his American-bred teenage nephew:

This nephew, who was about seventeen at the time, had started smoking cigars when he was thirteen. He liked to wear his amorphous hat on the back of his head, exposing a coiffure neatly parted in the middle which looked less like hair than like a painted wig, so unstintingly applied was the pomade which held it together. He kept his hands in his pockets, straddled the ground, and let his cigarette dangle to one side of his mouth as he said to Mr. Hattori, "Your wife's taken a powder."

The world actually turned black for an instant for Mr. Hattori as he searched giddily in his mind for another possible interpretation of this announcement. "Poison?" he queried, a tremor in his knees.

The nephew cackled with restraint, "Nope, you dope," he said. "That means she's leaving your bed and board."

"Talk Japanese," Mr. Hattori ordered, "and quit trying to be so smart!"

Abashed, the nephew took his hands out of his pockets and assisted his meager Japanese with nervous gestures. . . .

"Tell her to go jump in the lake," Mr. Hattori said in English, and in Japanese, "Tell her if she wants the boys, to come back and make a home for them."[2]

The humor in the passage is not derived from Hattori's inability to speak colloquial English but from the role reversal later in the passage. The *nisei* who cackled "Nope, you dope," is transformed into a bumbling fool whose broken Japanese needs to be assisted by "nervous gestures." Hattori gives a final flourish to the conversation with a quip of his own in American slang. But the *nisei* and the *issei* know what it is to have two different identities based on two different language abilities.

The language gap between first- and second-generation Japanese Americans is only one sign of the differences in cultural orientation, whether slight or vast, that impede mutual understanding. Yamamoto portrays the situation with succinct humor in "Seventeen Syllables," when Rosie's mother tries to read her *haiku:*

"Yes, yes, I understand. How utterly lovely," Rosie said, and her mother, either satisfied or seeing through the deception and resigned, went back to composing.

The truth was that Rosie was lazy; English lay ready on the tongue but Japanese had to be searched for and examined and even then put forth tentatively (probably to meet with laughter). It was so much easier to say yes, yes, even when one meant no, no. Besides, this was what was in her mind to say: I was looking through one of your magazines from Japan last night, Mother, and towards the back I found some *haiku* in English that delighted me. There was one that made me giggle off and on until I fell asleep:

—It is morning, and lo
I lie awake, comme il faut
sighing for some dough.

Now, how to reach her mother, how to communicate the melancholy song? Rosie knew formal Japanese by fits and starts, her mother had even less English, no French. It was much more possible to say yes, yes.

The juxtaposition of *issei* and *nisei* provides the basis for much of the subtle humor in Yamamoto's stories, a gentle humor that is never derived at the expense of either generation. In "Las Vegas Charley," Noriyuki and Alice telephone their old *issei* father long distance every month to find out whether he is "still alive and kicking." The five *nisei* girls in "Seventeen Syllables" are busy swallowing peach slices without chewing them while their parents are visiting politely in the living room. And, in the same story, Rosie decides to sneak off to the fields to meet Jesus, the Chicano farmhand, while she is bowing her aunt and uncle welcome. In "The Legend of Miss Sasagawara," the internment camp Christmas party is a "gay, if odd celebration." The first performance is by an old *issei,* who delivers a speech in an exaggerated Hiroshima dialect. In the next, a young *nisei* imitates Frank Sinatra while the girls in the audience scream and pretend to faint. Then the *issei* sing old Japanese songs and perform the *dojo-suki,* a Japanese comic folk dance, while the *nisei* sing quartets or do hula dances, wearing grass skirts and brassieres. Besides humorous contrast, the juxtaposition of the *nisei* narrator's observations of the *issei* performances gives poignance to the imperfectness of her perceptions: she knows less than the readers about what is really going on in the lives of the elders.[3]
Superficially, everything seems as "normal" and wholesome as it seems to the innocent narrator. But beneath the surface are violent undercurrents, situations fraught with dangers and potential sorrows of which the narrator is only vaguely aware. The reader has premonitions that eventually the callow *nisei* will come to know those sorrows first-hand.

Yamamoto's stories are consummately women's stories. What accomplished Asian American male writers like Louis Chu, John Okada, and Carlos Bulosan could only imagine, Yamamoto presents fully. "Yoneko's Earthquake" and "Seventeen Syllables" are stories of *issei* mothers told through the oblique visions of their *nisei* daughters. In the former, the violence and tragedy of the mother's experience and the daughter's ingenuousness and self-absorption are sharply contrasted. In the course of the story, the mother falls in love with the hired man, conceives a child by him, gets an abortion, and loses the lover. Her youngest child dies suddenly, and she is condemned to a life of toil beside a husband rendered impotent during an earthquake. We know, as Yoneko does not, that her mother's life is scarred by heartaches and toil. Yoneko does not understand, as the reader does, the significance of the ring, the earthquake, or the sudden departure of Marpo, the Filipino farmhand. Yoneko understands these events only in relation to her own superstition and decision to become a "freethinker."

Yoneko has a little girl's "crush" on Marpo, whose colorful presence on the farm brings excitement to farm life for her. From Marpo, Yoneko learns about Jesus, Heaven, and Hell. She adorns her beliefs with "additional color to round out her mental images" in the way childish imaginations comfortably integrate the literal with the abstract. She wants to know:

> [Who] was God's favorite movie star? . . . and did Marpo suppose that God's sense of humor would have appreciated the delicious chant she had learned from friends at school today:
>
> > There ain't no bugs on us,
> > There ain't no bugs on us,
> > There may be bugs on the rest of you mugs,
> > But there ain't no bugs on us?

When God does not answer her call during the earthquake and Marpo leaves the farm unexpectedly, Yoneko stops "believing."

The merging of wish and reality in the child's mind, as well as the child's confusion of anger and guilt, are depicted in "Seventeen Syllables":

> Rosie . . . felt a rush of hate for both—for her mother for begging, for her father for denying her mother. I wish this old Ford would crash, right now, she thought, then immediately, no, no, I wish my father would laugh, but it was too late; already the vision had passed through her mind of the green pick-up crumpled in the dark against one of the mighty eucalyptus trees they were just riding past, of the three contorted, bleeding bodies, one of them hers.

The same skill used in portraying a little girl's psychology is brought to the depiction of female adolescence. Rosie notes without much thought that her mother cooks, washes, cleans house, and does the farmwork in the fields by day and then becomes a poetess by night. Her more prosaic father dislikes his wife's hobby and loses his temper when she wins a prize for her *haiku*. She never completely understands why her mother writes poetry or why the father stops her, although we are made to feel that someday she might. Rosie's candid adolescent charm and wholesomeness, especially in her world "so various, so beautiful, so new"* with the attentions of an adolescent farmhand, Jesus, are starkly contrasted with the sordid secret her mother burdens her with at the end of the story.

Rosie is half-child, half-woman. She jokes and plays with her friends, but she is confused by the strange emotions awakened when Jesus kisses her. She is both elated and perturbed. In her excitement, she holds imaginary conversations with him in the fields, but she hides from his sight when he actually appears, peering at him from between cracks in the privy walls. Rosie is brought to the threshold of adulthood, frightened and apprehensive, when her mother talks to her as woman to woman. She weeps like the child she is, after recalling how Jesus had touched her like the woman she will become. Her life and her mother's life cross at the moment when the mother makes Rosie promise she will never marry at the very moment she is attracted to a man for the first time.

---

*This phrase was eliminated from the definitive version of "Seventeen Syllables."—Ed.

In both "Yoneko's Earthquake" and "Seventeen Syllables," there is a foreboding sense that the cheerful narrators' worlds will be transformed, eventually, into something not quite "so various, so beautiful, so new." There is a warning that they might inherit the worlds of their mothers, stifled and circumscribed, condemned to lives of drudgery devoid of romance or beauty with only their strength and quiet endurance to keep their spirits alive.

In "The Legend of Miss Sasagawara," the "normal," psychologically healthy young narrator and her friend are in the internment camps, dreaming of finishing college, finding "good jobs," and marrying "two nice, clean young men, preferably handsome, preferably rich, who would cherish us forever and a day." Like Rosie and Yoneko, however, these two girls will eventually face the same realities that confront Mari Sasagawara, who responds to her loveless life by going insane. How the younger girls will respond has something to do with the extent to which they can derive lessons from Mari Sasagawara's experience.

In Yamamoto's stories, men and women both seek ways to transcend their frustration and difficulties. Hattori in "The Brown House" and Matsumoto in "Las Vegas Charley" turn to gambling. In "The Legend of Miss Sasagawara," Reverend Sasagawara seeks escape through spiritual transcendence. The men are afflicted either by weakness or by callousness. In "Yoneko's Earthquake" and "Seventeen Syllables," the husbands are hard-working and serious but unable to tolerate their wives' efforts to create beauty and poetry. They ultimately crush their wives and shackle them to a life of endless toil beside them, not necessarily because they are evil, but because they cannot tolerate independence of any kind in their wives. Yamamoto's women, on the other hand, possess strength that arises from a combination of madness and a thirst for beauty and meaning in their lives. Most of them are unable to resist oppression without losing their spirit and their sanity. In this lies the kernel of the mothers' warning to their daughters.

Something of Yamamoto's attitudes towards women can be seen in a comment she made in a 1953 book review:

> It has been said that women are organically incapable of genius, and with this I agree, since I am unable to think of a single name to squelch the rhetorical question, "Has there ever been a woman philosopher?" (At the same time, I am rather puzzled as to what has been added to the world by all these male geniuses with their intricate and conflicting systems of thought.)[4]

In "Seventeen Syllables," the *nisei* narrator is warned by her mother not to let herself be dominated when she grows up. As the woman watches her husband burn the poetry prize she has won, she turns to her daughter:

> Suddenly, her mother knelt on the floor and took her by the wrists. "Rosie," she said urgently, "Promise me you will never marry!" Shocked more by the request than by the revelation [that her mother had married her father not out of love but out of desperation], Rosie stared at her mother's face. . . . She tried to pull free. Promise, her mother whispered fiercely, promise. Yes, yes, I promise, Rosie said. But for an instant she turned away, and her mother, hearing the familiar glib agreement, released her. Oh, you, you, you, her eyes and twisted mouth said, you fool. Rosie, covering her face, began at last to cry, and the embrace and consoling hand came much later than she expected.

There is here a warning to *nisei* to catch the "basic truths" without being trapped by the particulars, which differ from person to person and generation to generation. The mother has been subdued, and the legacy of the mother will be passed on to the daughter. But there is still the chance that the daughter might come to comprehend the meaning of her mother's experience in time to benefit from it.

☐ *Notes* ■

1. Kai-yu Hsu and Helen Palubinskas, eds., *Asian-American Authors* (Boston: Houghton Mifflin Co., 1972), p. 113.

2. Hisaye Yamamoto, "The Brown House," in Hsu and Palubinskas, eds., *Asian-American Authors,* pp. 119–120.

3. Hisaye Yamamoto, "Las Vegas Charley," *Arizona Quarterly 17,* no. 4 (winter 1961): 303–322; Hisaye Yamamoto, "The Legend of Miss Sasagawara," *Kenyon Review* 12, no. 1 (winter 1950): 99–115.

4. Hisaye Yamamoto, "The Shakers," *Frontier* 14, no. 12 (Oct. 1953): 22.

CHARLES L. CROW ■

The *Issei* Father in the Fiction of Hisaye Yamamoto

Hisaye Yamamoto's five superbly crafted stories of the Japanese American experience, published between 1949 and 1961, are a saga in miniature. They are vignettes from the struggle of the first generation of immigrants to California (the *Issei*), the life they built on the farmlands there, and the disruption of that life by the Second World War. The stories also portray the emergence of their children (the *Nisei*), who were born in America and grew to maturity in the nineteen thirties and forties, and ultimately achieved the assimilation into the middle-class American mainstream denied their parents. Like most Japanese American authors, Yamamoto explores the frustrated relationship between these two generations—a relationship which changed abruptly and forever in the relocation centers during the war.[1]

For Yamamoto, two themes emerge from this generational conflict. The first, present in every one of the stories, is the failure of the fathers of the first generation. Sometimes withdrawn and indifferent, sometimes violent, the father figure is presented with images of sterility, death, and disintegration. The five stories can be seen as an extended quarrel with or perhaps rite of exorcism against this generalized *Issei* male, and their fine technical experiments in narration as ways to channel the powerful emotions he evokes. Only in the last story, which describes his death, is her old antagonist forgiven.

From *Für eine offene Literaturwissenschaft: Erkundungen und Erprobungen am Beispiel US-amerikanischer Texte*, ed. Leo Truchlar (Salzburg, Austria: Wolfgang Neugebauer Verlag GmbH, 1986), 34–40.

The second theme is the struggle of the Japanese American woman to express herself. Against the spirit-destroying male, Yamamoto sets a series of sensitive women, wives who are broken and daughters who sometimes escape. In several *Nisei* children and adolescents, we may suspect a covert portrait of the artist as a young woman, and witness the growth of her consciousness and her art, both of which have painful birth in the cruelty of the *Issei* father.

The issues are drawn in their full complexity in "Seventeen Syllables" (1949), her first published story, and in "Yoneko's Earthquake" (1951)—two stories of the death of the heart set in the pre-war countryside.

The victim in "Seventeen Syllables" is Ume Hanazono, whose death we can speak of as a murder, even though she was not a 'real' person; yet in a sense she was real, the pen name and alter ego of a farm wife, created to voice, in classical Japanese *haiku,* the feelings she could not reveal to her husband or her daughter. Yet Ume Hanazono's "life span, even for a poet, was very brief—perhaps three months at most." She wins a *haiku* contest in a San Francisco Japanese-language periodical. The editor arrives to offer congratulations and award the prize, a woodblock print by Hiroshige, when the poet's husband decides that enough is, after all, enough. He is outraged by his wife's artiness and the disruption of the tomato harvest, so he drives the editor from the house, smashes the framed print with an axe, and burns the fragments with kerosene. Ume Hanazono will never write, or live, again; she is survived by the ordinary farm woman, Mrs. Hayashi, who is found by her daughter, "watching the dying fire."

Images of death and sterility are piled up as Mrs. Hayashi, in a last bid for self-expression, tries to tell her daughter, in English, the secrets of her life. She came to America and married "as an alternative to suicide" after a love affair in Japan with "the first son of one of the well-to-do families of the village." Mrs. Hayashi tells how "the two had met whenever and wherever they could, secretly, because it would not have done for his family to see him favor her—her father had no money; he was a drunkard and a gambler besides. She had learned she was with child; an excellent match had already been arranged for her lover. Despised by her family, she had given birth to a stillborn son, who would be seventeen now." The number seventeen, the years since the birth of the lost son, and the syllables of the *haiku,* link the two failures of love in her life.

Considering the ineptitude and brutality of the men she has known, it is not surprising that Mrs. Hayashi turns to her daughter with the plea that she never marry. It is equally predictable that the *Nisei* daughter, Rosie, who is entering her teens and has just had her own first romantic episode, cannot respond to her mother's wishes. She has heard these revelations with reluctance, revelations which would, she knew, "level her life, her world to the very ground." Thus the story ends with apparent frustration, the mother unable to pass the accumulation of her experience across the barriers of culture, language, and generation to Rosie.

A similar broken connection marks the conclusion of "Yoneko's Earthquake," a story closely linked in theme and setting, and my favorite among Yamamoto's works. Since Yoneko is a younger child than Rosie, she can see but understand little of the events of the story. The narrator follows her thoughts, using her as a 'reflector' in the manner of Henry James's *What Maisie Knew.* Events are set in motion by the Long Beach earthquake of 1933, which causes Yoneko's father to have a nervous collapse, rendering him incapable of managing the farm. (His invalidism may be considered an emblem of the withdrawal and ineffectiveness with which Yamamoto generally accuses the *Issei* male.) The reader understands, as Yoneko cannot, the implications of the events which follow: the unexplained silver ring, actually a gift from Marpo, the hired man, to Yoneko's mother, symbol of the love blossoming between the pair, who are thrown together in running the farm during Mr. Hosoume's incapacity; the argument culminating in Mr. Hosoume striking his wife; the disappearance of the hired man; the trip to the Japanese hospital for what can only be an abortion. The central, unnamed event of the story thus parallels the birth of the stillborn son in "Seventeen Syllables." The result is to leave Mrs. Hosoume, Yoneko's mother, no longer the "half-opened rosebud" someone once called her,

121

but broken as effectively as the beautiful collie Mr. Hosoume runs down on the trip to the hospital. (He does not look back.) When, later, Yoneko's little brother dies of appendicitis, Mrs. Hosoume takes refuge from her guilt in religious fanaticism. "Never kill a person, Yoneko," Mrs. Hosoume blurts out one evening, "because if you do, God will take from you someone you love." Without pausing to consider the ambiguities in this appeal, Yoneko instantly rejects it: "I don't believe in that, I don't believe in God."

The two girls have had their lives 'leveled' by the complex legacies forced upon them, their homes wrecked by events for which the earthquake may stand as symbol. Both stories end in the apparent refusal or inability of the daughters to comprehend their mothers' message. Yet Elaine Kim, the most distinguished critic of Asian American literature, feels, speaking of "Seventeen Syllables," that "there is still the chance that the daughter might come to comprehend the meaning of her mother's experience in time to benefit from it."[2] I agree, and suggest that the note of hope is augmented by the specific qualities of Rosie and Yoneko, not noted by Professor Kim. It is no incidental quirk of characterization, I suggest, that Rosie is a natural clown and mimic, able to conjure up an entire variety show for a friend at school recess: "She held her nose and whined a witticism or two in what she considered was the manner of Fred Allen; she assumed intoxication and a British accent to go over the climax of the Rudy Vallee recording of the pub conversation about William Ewart Gladstone; she was the child Shirley Temple piping, 'On the Good Ship Lollipop'; she was the gentleman soprano of the Four Inkspots trilling, 'If I Didn't Care.'" In other words, Rosie has inherited her mother's skill with language, though these whimsies are so far from the formal poetry in another tongue that neither mother nor daughter could recognize in them the evidence of this gift, this point of contact. Similarly, Yoneko's word games and rhymes mark her as an incipient artist. At the story's end, "whenever the thought of Seigo [her dead brother] crossed her mind, she began composing a new song, and this worked very well." We can imagine Rosie and Yoneko not only understanding and benefiting from their mothers' defeat by the *Issei* father, as Kim suggests, but someday making it the subject of their art.

Just such a transformation into art, and the transmission of experience between women, are explored in "The Legend of Miss Sasagawara" (1950), the first of Yamamoto's stories to describe life in the relocation centers. The "legend" is recorded and told by a first-person narrator, a young woman whose passage into adulthood is touched by the title character.

Miss Sasagawara is a former ballet dancer, interned in Arizona with her father, a dignified and respected widower who is a Buddhist priest. She is an object of fascination to the camp because of her beauty and her strangely youthful appearance (despite her thirty-nine years), her dramatic mannerisms, and eccentric behavior. Gradually the stories, the legends, which gather around her reveal that she is mad. Yet in intervals of lucidity, between treatment, Miss Sasagawara organizes a dance class for children, and, on one occasion, speaks to the narrator with memorable kindness during a chance meeting at the camp's shower facility. At the end, however, the two women have gone in separate directions: Miss Sasagawara to a California state mental institution, the narrator to a college in the east.

Yet the madwoman has made her mark on the narrator. When the narrator returns to the camp on a visit from college, she learns that Miss Sasagawara has been committed after being discovered one morning in the bedroom of a neighbor boy, staring at his sleeping form. The narrator tries to apply the imperfect wisdom she has gained from her college psychology courses, and "sagely explained that Miss Sasagawara had no doubt looked upon Joe Yoshinaga as the image of either the lost lover or the lost son. But my words made me uneasy by their glibness, and I began to wonder seriously about Miss Sasagawara for the first time."[3] In spite of the self-directed irony, the narrator's probably half-right attempt to understand Miss Sasagawara is an important step in her own education, and leads her to the discovery, back in college, of a poem the older woman has published. The poem is about a man "whose lifelong aim had been to achieve Nirvana, that saintly state of moral purity and universal wisdom." After the death of his wife, as the narrator paraphrases the poem, he is able to concentrate his efforts on this goal:

> This man was certainly noble. . . . But say that someone else, someone sensitive, someone admiring, someone who had not achieved this sublime condition and who did not wish to, were somehow called to companion such a man. Was it not likely that the saint . . . would be deaf and blind to the human passions rising, subsiding, and again rising, perhaps in anguished silence, perhaps within the same room? The poet could not speak for others, of course, she could only speak for herself. But she would describe this man's devotion as a sort of madness, the monstrous sort which, pure of itself and so with immunity, might possibly bring troublous, scented scenes to recur in the other's sleep. (115)

The *Issei* father can blight as effectively through withdrawal as violence. Miss Sasagawara's identity has remained somehow unfocussed, as her ambiguous age and mother/lover roles indicate (as the narrator surmised); finally her father's madness has become her own, and she is bound forever in anguished silence.

More than any of her other stories, however, this one makes explicit the redemptive power of art. The narrator, as she writes, is no longer the callow bobby-soxer who once fantasized with her friend Elsie about "two nice, clean young men, preferably handsome, preferably rich, who would cherish us forever and a day" (101). The ironic tone of this memory is the voice of a mature speaker, to whom Miss Sasagawara has spoken, nakedly, as she once did in the shower, and who has understood. "The Legend of Miss Sasagawara," given to us by this artist, is proof that speech shaped into art, even in English, can transmit the experience of Japanese American women, and leap the barriers which defeated the *haiku* poet Ume Hanazono.

The three stories considered thus far dramatize the struggle of the emerging female artist with the *Issei* father. In "The Brown House" (1951) and in "Las Vegas Charley" (1961), this issue seems to vanish; yet it is still present, I would argue, imbedded in the relationship of the narrator, and, at a deeper rhetorical level, the implied author, with the father figure.

"The Brown House" is a domestic tragedy set in the same pre-war countryside as "Yoneko's Earthquake" and "Seventeen Syllables." The flaw of Mr. Hattori, the father, is gambling—the disease to which "Las Vegas Charley" also succumbs—a form of dissipation, a way of making nothing out of something, which destroys the family's discipline and way of life. The setting is familiar; what is new for Yamamoto is her refusal to use a sensitive girl as a first-person narrator or a Jamesean reflector. In fact the Hattori children are all boys. Thus depriving herself of an obvious point of sympathetic contact, Yamamoto constructs a narrative voice which is detached, clinical, even cruel: "The quarrel continued through supper at home, touching on a large variety of subjects. It ended, in the presence of the children, with Mr. Hattori beating his wife so severely that he had to take her to the doctor to have a few ribs taped. Both in their depths were dazed and shaken that things should have come to such a pass."[4]

Held at a distance, viewing the Hattoris through the narrator's cold eyes, we see no 'depths.' They are flattened to characters in a Punch-and-Judy show, and we say, in effect, what fools these mortals be. We may regard "The Brown House" as discipline the author has imposed on herself in preparation for her final step. She has separated herself from the female victim described in her earlier stories; now she will defeat her adversary by comprehending him, by assuming his identity. In "Las Vegas Charley" Yamamoto, for the first time, enters the thoughts of the *Issei* father.

"Las Vegas Charley" summarizes the entire span of *Issei* and *Nisei* history into the 1950s; its title character is a reprise of most of the destructive features the author has seen in her male characters. Kazuyuki Matsumoto, known as Charley, is a neglectful son and a severe parent, *tsumara-nai* (a worthless fellow) like his own father. He drinks too much, begins to gamble with the seductive flower cards, loses his farm, and slides eventually into the role of dishwasher in a Las Vegas restaurant, an embarrassment to his son and daughter-in-law. Yet our understanding of Charley is shaped by the feel-

125

ings which the inarticulate man could not voice for himself, but which the sympathetic third-person narrator can express for him. Thus we learn of his love for his young wife, who died in bearing their second son, of his memories of Japan, and his affection for his sometimes cruel mother, whose letters he never manages to answer.

The decline in Charley's life may be traced through the story's many descriptions of food and eating. Yamamoto gives three pages to a loving catalogue of the dishes which Charley's farming community used to prepare for New Year's day. This was the high point of Charley's life, when his farm prospered and "he had a young wife to share his bed."[5] Likewise it was the highpoint of the *Issei* community in California. Though they had failed to gain equal participation in American society, in the twenties and thirties the *Issei* had created a stable way of life: the old ways and values still held, and hard work was rewarded with some material prosperity.[6] The troubles of Charley's middle years, though begun by the death of his wife, are followed by other hardships which are shared by the community: the Great Depression and the farm quotas of the Roosevelt administration. Charley must send his sons away to their grandmother in Japan. When they return to him a few years later, they are like strangers. Charley can afford to feed them only a poor fare of soup and vegetables. The good times never return.

Instead, there comes the great turning point of *Issei* history, the war and the relocation camps, from which Charley's son Isamu leaves for the army and is killed in Italy. Charley himself "settled for a job as a cook in one of the mess halls" (314), a *Nisei* spinster rejects his gift of a bag of apples, and he sinks deeper into the pattern of gambling with the flower cards. After the war Charley is no longer a producer of food, or even a cook, but a washer of other people's dirty plates in a restaurant by night, a gambler by day. Charley himself can hardly eat at all, as his teeth begin to rot and fall out. Visiting his surviving son Noriyuki in Los Angeles to be fitted with dentures, he discovers that his daughter-in-law resents having to prepare separate meals for her children, her husband and herself, and "a bland, soft diet for toothless Charley"

(319), and so he returns early to Las Vegas with poorly adjusted false teeth, still unable to chew anything solid.

When Charley dies, his Americanized, middle-class son has "lived through a succession of conflicting emotions about his father—hate for rejecting him as a child; disgust and exasperation over that weak moral fiber; embarrassment when people asked what his father did for a living; and finally, something akin to compassion, when he came to understand that his father was not an evil man, but only an inadequate one with the most shining intentions, only one man among so many who lived from day to day as best they could, limited, restricted, by the meager gifts Fate or God had doled out to them . . ."

The son's emotions are those Yamamoto has dramatized in her cycle of stories about the *Issei* father, with whom she has finally achieved peace. The struggling, growing female artist shown in the early stories, who distanced her emotion with cold irony in "The Brown House," has reached a nearly serene understanding with Charley, and can see her longtime tormentor with "something akin to compassion." The circle is closed, and Yamamoto is like Prospero saying of Caliban, "This thing of darkness I acknowledge mine." Yet Yamamoto could forgive the *Issei* father only after imagining his toothless, helpless humiliation, then his death. Since then her art has been locked in silence.

☐ *Notes* ∎

1. The best of the small amount of criticism on Yamamoto is by Elaine H. Kim. See *Asian American Literature: An Introduction to the Writings and Their Social Context* (Philadelphia: Temple University Press, 1982), pp. 157–163; "Asian American Writers: A Bibliographical Review," *American Studies International* 22 (Oct. 1984), 55–56. See also Charles L. Crow, "Home and Transcendence in Los Angeles Fiction," in *Los Angeles in Fiction,* ed. David Fine (Albuquerque: University of New Mexico Press, 1984), pp. 189–203, for a discussion of "Yoneko's Earthquake" in the context of Southern California regionalism.

2. Kim, *Asian American Literature*, p. 163.

3. "The Legend of Miss Sasagawara," *Kenyon Review* 12 (Winter 1950), 114. Subsequent references in text.

4. "The Brown House," in *Asian-American Authors,* ed. Kai-yu Hsu and Helen Palubinskas (Boston: Houghton Mifflin Co., 1972), p. 119. The story was originally published in *Harper's Bazaar* (Oct. 1951).

5. "Las Vegas Charley," *Arizona Quarterly* 17 (Winter 1961), 305. Subsequent references in text.

6. See Elaine H. Kim's chapter "Japanese American Family and Community Portraits," *Asian American Literature*, pp. 122–172, for historical background.

☐ DOROTHY RITSUKO McDONALD
and KATHARINE NEWMAN ■

Relocation and Dislocation: The Writings of Hisaye Yamamoto and Wakako Yamauchi

I. Survivors

Two young women, their lives frozen by Executive Order 9066 (Japanese Relocation Act of 1942), became close friends during the long boring months of their confinement in the camp at Poston, Arizona. Fortunately there was a "library" of a few old books and some magazines which, somehow, had traveled to the camp by various routes. Hisaye Yamamoto who "had early contracted the disease of compulsive reading" introduced her younger friend, Wakako [Nakamura] Yamauchi, to Thomas Wolfe, James T. Farrell, Marcel Proust, and the *New Yorker*.[1] When they sat on the barrack steps, day after day, they discussed writing, although at that time, Wakako thought of herself as a painter and thought of Hisaye as someone beyond her powers of emulation. Then there was the *Poston Chronicle* and Hisaye wrote for that, and for a Buddhist magazine and for a mimeographed camp magazine, and sent out material to the *New Canadian*.

But beyond literature, deeper than any boredom, was the unremitting tragedy of this confinement. They watched and saw what internment was doing to families whose sons

---

From MELUS 7:3 (Fall 1980): 21–38. The section on Wakako Yamauchi's work has been omitted for the purposes of this edition.

129

had to decide between fighting for America or being moved to Tule Lake Camp preparatory to shipment to Japan.[2] People who had never been allowed to become American citizens, who had just lost the homes and savings of years, now had to face estrangement from their own children. The younger generation, American-born, had to face the betrayal of democracy that had allowed American citizens to be incarcerated without cause. Although not as devastating as the Holocaust or Hiroshima, the "Camp Experience" left a deep wound in the lives of Japanese Americans. It was a psychological trauma for all of the 110,000 people who were incarcerated, but there were added tragedies for Hisaye and for Wakako: Hisaye's nineteen-year-old brother, having joined the American Army, was killed at Grosseto, Italy; Wakako's father died in the very last days of confinement, a victim of the stress of the years at Poston and the shock of the atom bomb and the defeat of Japan. Years later, when her husband and children asked her about her stay in Poston, Hisaye Yamamoto found tears flowing down as the memories came back.[3] And when Wakako was asked to read some poetry written during the Relocation, she prefaced her reading with some explanations:

> The Sansei accused us of not wanting to talk about the evacuation experience. And it's true. I speak for hundreds of Nisei like myself, or perhaps just people like myself, who are sometimes overwhelmed by a current of events we can neither understand nor stem. . . .
>
> And when we do see those old photographs of the mass evacuation . . . we can see the mirror of our tragedy. Few of us can hold back the tears that most often smack of self-pity, but maybe somewhere behind those tears we know that this is the event that changed the course of our lives, and though there were those among us who had more insight, more courage, whatever path we chose, we have survived—whole. Maybe that's why so many of us remain silent about our camp experience. Maybe in our silence we ask you to honor us for that—survival. We ask that you not indulge us with pity, neither then nor now. The fact of our survival is proof of our valor. And that is enough.[4]

The friendship between the two women has remained sturdy over the years. Now they are both well established writers, with certain similarities in their work. Both show the deterioration of the family, the changing role of women, the bleakness of farm life, the transformation of Japanese traditions into Japanese American culture. They make us aware of Japanese American history, of the thousands of Japanese men who arrived in America to make their fortunes in its "gold-paved streets" and then (they dreamed) to return in triumph to their homeland, there to live in their traditional family structure. But making that fortune was not easy. Some men with families—the families that Yamamoto and Yamauchi usually write about—farmed in the desert valleys of the American West, barely wresting a living during the depression years. The bachelors were migrant farm workers, harvesting fields and orchards, and, in their boredom, gambling and drinking away their wages. Their difficulties in surviving in an entirely alien civilization weakened them, and there are only a few strong male figures in the authors' works.

This is not to say that their women are pure and heroic. But there is the pathos in the stories of arranged marriages that are unsatisfactory, forcing the romantic women into adultery and into longing to return to a beautiful illusory Japan. There is also the pathos of the women born in America and the conflicts they feel as they try to blend the traditions of their parents with those of their own country. There is the pathos of the resultant stress on the traditional family structure, weakened even more by the Relocation. These writers have reproduced a sorrowful society—and their key word is survival.

Their differences are at once apparent in their responses to a formal question: how have Japanese traditions affected their writings? Wakako Yamauchi wrote, stressing her personal involvement with her characters and their stories:

> If I tried to tell you in a scholarly way how my Japanese background has affected my writing, it would be a long time before you heard from me. I can only say that in my writing I reach inside and plunder—I use every experience, everything I know as a person, as a woman, as a divorcee, as a mother, and

yes, as a child of Japanese parents. My childhood and being Japanese American is an integral part of the person I am today. I write from these experiences and I consider myself an American writer.

Hisaye Yamamoto, on the other hand, moves outward, with a blend of irony, forbearance, and connectedness:

> I'm sure the Japanese tradition has had a great influence on my writing since my parents brought it with them from Japan and how could they not help but transmit it to us? I even wonder if I would have been a writer at all without this tradition to go by, since most of the stories seem to deal with this interaction of the Japanese tradition with the American experience. And even while I have come to look upon the American experience with a jaundiced (yellow) eye, I appreciate being able to communicate in the English language and just plain being alive at this time and in this place.[5]

Yamauchi writes totally within the Japanese American community; Yamamoto sees a world in interaction (though seldom with Anglos in it). They pace off at different distances from their subjects and see them from different perspectives. In short, two women, two friends, two people with similar experiences, are still very different as writers.

II. Hisaye Yamamoto

Yamamoto received her first rejection slip at the age of fourteen and persisted in her aspiration to be a writer until she received her first acceptance from a major periodical when she was twenty-six. In the years between, she completed the program at Compton Junior College, contributed to school, college, and small magazines, and wrote even while she was at Poston. After her release from camp she went to Los Angeles and obtained a reporter's job on the only newspaper that would hire a Japanese: the Negro *Los Angeles Tribune*. She worked there from 1945 to 1948. Her first story, "The High-

Heeled Shoes" appeared in 1948. [. . .] More essay than story, unlike those that followed, it has the Yamamoto hallmarks:

1. References to literary materials outside the Japanese American tradition. This shows her wide reading. In this story, Freud, Ellis, Stekel, Krafft-Ebbing, and Robert Browning are mentioned. In "Epithalamium," she quotes extensively from Gerard Manley Hopkins as well as echoing Spenser's poem. This strategy lifts her stories into the wider world of European-American culture and adds surprise and new angles of perspective.
2. References to actual events, place, or people. In this story she names Wakako Yamauchi as the friend who has given her the plants from which the narrator is picking pansies in the story.
3. Lists, particularly of foods, flowers, and oddments that give sensory appeal as well as substantiating the reality of the story. In "The High-Heeled Shoes," she is irritated when the phone rings because she fantasizes that it is a salesman and she does not have money to buy from him. She lists what she would have bought by week's end if she only had money.
4. Soliloquies and imaginary dialogues. Here she has a talk with Gandhi about non-violent responses versus the suffering of women attacked by rapists. Gandhi does not come off well.

The keynote in all of Yamamoto's work is her use of her own mind: she is analytic, meditative, honest, compassionate, and ironic. Whether she uses the first person or a narrator, the final word is usually hers—and it is frequently so open-ended that the reader feels there are stories and meanings as yet unguessed implicit in each tale.

Yamamoto's pervasive love for humanity is found in "The High-Heeled Shoes." The protagonist ("I") is confronted with sexual perversions: she receives an obscene telephone call at the story's beginning and this propels her mind into "unlovely, furtive things" about other encounters with men that she and her friends have had. The most startling was the time she caught sight of a pair of legs in black high-heeled shoes sticking out from the open door of a "dusty-blue, middle-aged sedan." As she approached and glanced in, she discovered that the shoes were worn by a naked man reclining on the front seat . . . and she was, "with frantic gestures, being enjoined to linger awhile."

The narrator calls on her reading for some understanding of this frightening experience but concludes: "Reading is reading, talking is talking, thinking is thinking, and living is different." However, she regards both incidents as caused by society and does not blame the men, believing that they were part of "a great dark sickness on the earth that no amount of pansies, pinks, or amaryllis, thriving joyously in what garden, however well-ordered and pointed to with pride, could ever begin to assuage."

There is a final paragraph: her aunt calls, thus purifying the telephone from the contamination of the obscene caller, and she offers to come over for dinner, bringing food with her. This is the only "Japanese" touch in a story all too universal: "ricecakes with Indian bean frosting, as well as pickled fish on vinegared rice. She has also been able to get some yellow-tail, to slice and eat raw." Yamamoto, as narrator, comments, "It is possible she wonders at my enthusiastic appreciation, which is all right, but all out of proportion."

What remains with the narrator is: "Whatever, whatever—I knew I had discovered yet another circle to put away with my collection of circles." A similar personal revelation of the sickness of humankind was revealed in "Wilshire Bus," a 1950 story, which deals with a Japanese American woman's fear of being identified as Chinese by a drunken bigot. Shocked at finding this weakness in herself, she lost "her saving detachment . . . and she was filled once again in her life with the infuriatingly helpless, insidiously sickening sensation of there being in the world nothing solid she could put her finger on, nothing solid she could come to grips with, nothing solid she could sink her teeth into, nothing solid."[6]

She has written two stories about gamblers: "The Brown House" (1951), and "Las Vegas Charley" (1961). The former has a jocose tone: Mr. Hattori, weary of trying to make a living growing strawberries, seeks out a Chinese house where he can try his luck at gambling. The appearance of the house is whimsical: "recently painted brown and relieved with white window frames. . . . To the rear of the house was a ramshackle barn whose spacious blue roof advertised in great yellow letters a ubiquitous brand of physic."

During the travail, as the Hattoris come to argue and their marriage nearly expires, there are humorous incidents, such as a police raid and the semi-friendship between Mrs. Wu, wife of the manager of the brown house and Mrs. Hattori, who must wait, hour upon hour, in the car with the [five] little children. The children come to acquire a taste for the Chinese cookies that Mrs. Wu brings to the car and Mrs. Hattori becomes quite attached to the Chinese woman. But Mrs. Wu, looking at them, concludes "she had never before encountered a woman with such bleak eyes."[7] As the story ends, the reader goes back over it and sees that it never was humorous, that human interaction is "a collection of circles."

Las Vegas Charley began life as Kazuyuki Matsumoto, a prosperous young immigrant farmer until the death of his beloved wife in childbirth broke his spirit. Ultimately he has become a dishwasher in a restaurant in Las Vegas, spending his free time gambling. As he grows old, he becomes closer to his son and daughter-in-law in Los Angeles. Finally Charley dies, and the doctor who has attended him, complaining of his own frustration at seeing his patients die, comments:

> "Well, at least your father had a good time—he drank, he gambled, he smoked; I don't do any of these things. All I do is work, work, work. At least he enjoyed himself while he was alive."

> And Noriyuki—who, without one sour word, had lived through a series of conflicting emotions about his father . . . finally, [reaching] something akin to compassion, when he came to understand that his father was not an evil man, but only an inadequate one with the most shining intentions, only one man among so many who lived from day to day as best they could, limited, restricted by the meager gifts Fate or God had doled out to them—could not quite agree.

Yamamoto's honesty also shows through in this story, because she sums up Kazuyuki Matsumoto's reaction, after one son is killed and the other leaves for Tule Lake:

> As for himself, he would be quite content to remain in the camp the rest of his life—free food, free housing, friends, flower cards; what more could life offer. It was true that he had partially lost his hearing in one ear, from standing by those hot stoves on days of unbearable heat, but that was a small complaint. The camp hospital had provided free treatment, free medicines, free cottonballs to stuff in his bad ear.[8]

Obviously the future "Las Vegas Charley" was not of heroic mould, even so his adjustment to camp is, by contrarieties, an indictment of it. A story like this in 1961, too, would have sufficient distance in time to arouse little disapproval. This was not the case in 1950 when Yamamoto's story, "The Legend of Miss Sasagawara" was accepted by the *Kenyon Review*.[9] This is probably her finest piece of writing and it is still one of the most evocative of all stories of the camp experience (as Wakako Yamauchi says, people did not want to talk about that experience). It is possible that the success of the story results from the way she controlled her own emotions as she wrote, for this time she used a filtered intelligence of a girl obviously herself to give the story through random glimpses of Miss Sasagawara. The rest of the other witnesses are unreliable: an ambulance driver, a teenaged boy, a hysterical woman, and people who love gossip for its own sake, not realizing the human anguish behind bizarre actions.

Miss Sasagawara, aged thirty-nine, has had no regrets that she has never married because she has traveled "all over the country a couple times, dancing in the ballet. . . . she's had her fun." But now, her mother having died, she is confined in a portion of a barracks with her father, a Buddhist priest. Yamamoto explains how adversely the pursuit of the Buddhist-Nirvana—"that saintly state of moral purity and universal wisdom"—can affect those close to the would-be saint. The daughter is the victim of a man who wished to "extinguish within himself all unworthy desire and consequently all evil, to concentrate on that serene, eight-fold path."

136

The relocation camp experience ironically freed the Reverend Sasagawara from worldly responsibilities, including those to his daughter. She, however, is filled with admiration of his superior being. But a full explanation comes to the narrator in later years when, in a college library, she finds an old poetry magazine which includes "the first published poem of a Japanese-American woman who is, at present, an evacuee from the West Coast making her home in a War Relocation Center in Arizona."

In other words, this is a poem which Miss Sasagawara wrote in the middle of the war, at the time of this story, before she was permanently committed to a mental institution. In an "erratically brilliant" poem, she questions: would not such a saint be "deaf and blind to the human passions" of another who does not wish to attain this sublime condition and wishes instead to respond to the "passions rising in anguished silence in the selfsame room?" The poet (who is Miss Sasagawara) regards the saint's intense idealism as madness, not seeing that she herself will only find freedom from this Buddhist idealism through her own madness.

The story operates on two levels. The news of the unhappy dancer comes to the reader in sporadic items, but the picture of life in the camp is sustained and highly informative. The young narrator sits on the front stoop with her best friend, using such phrases as "Oooh" and "Wow!" while watching the other people and slapping mosquitoes. We learn that two Army cots pushed together make a double bed for a husband and wife, that an apple crate makes a night table, that people eat in the mess hall by age classification. We have the complete program of the block Christmas entertainment. We can almost taste the boredom. But when the story ends, it is with Miss Sasagawara's own poem, her voice really heard at last, and the details fall into the background of this tragic story of a woman beset jointly by the frustrations of her own culture and by the imprisonment imposed on her by her fellow Americans.

In a pair of stories, "Seventeen Syllables" and "Yoneko's Earthquake," Yamamoto depicts life on the little tenant farms before the War. So specific is she that the reader even learns about the two days' work and one night's discomfort that girls in Japan were glad to endure in order to have their fingernails "shining with a translucent red-orange color." Both of these stories are examinations of unhappy marriages; in one the wife seeks release through the writing of haiku, in the other, through intimacy with the Filipino farmhand after her husband is invalided in an earthquake. In the first, the wife begs the teenaged, blossoming daughter to promise never to marry. Yamamoto's realism hits its own low in the second story when the child, Yoneko, is annoyed by the invalid's threatening to pick his nose and wipe the snot on her and her friends' paper dolls.

Yamamoto selects as her main characters those who are hurt, who have deviated from the norm, who are grasping for some bits of beauty in their desperation: gamblers dreaming of the gifts they will heap on their loved ones when they make the big payoff, a ballet dancer being driven insane by confinement with a religious fanatic, a farmer's wife who writes haiku in the evenings, women who take lovers in order to find the love of which they have been cheated—all those who seek but lose are of interest to Yamamoto, and somehow she wins our understanding, largely through the accepting interpretations of the narrator.

In one late story, however, she goes even further; she makes the female narrator herself neurotic. In "Epithalamium," the woman, Yuki Tsumagari, shows no apparent guilt in her tumultuous love affair with an Italian-American alcoholic seaman at a Catholic community for social rejects on Staten Island. Yuki herself is not a reject; up until now she has been supporting herself and now, at thirty-one, remains unmarried by choice. Though her mother, back in her earlier years, had urged marriage on her, her father had said, untraditionally, to leave her alone. Now an inexplicable love has come. As lovers, the Italian Marco and Japanese Yuki use all the secluded spots near the community, which neighbors a seminary. She even suffers a secret miscarriage; but though the narrator uses such words as "defile," "terrible," and "sordid" to describe their lovemaking, a love for all humanity hovers over the entire story, making it right for Yuki to marry the seaman while he is drunk. In "Epithalamium," Yamamoto is not only forgiving sin; she has her persona, Yuki, embracing it. And in so doing, Yuki is acknowledging the inevitability of

138

suffering and accepting the fact that this marriage will be as much a burden as a glory. On the way back to the Community after they are married, "with Marco slumped heavily against her," Yuki keeps remembering Hopkins: "The world is charged with the grandeur of God. . . ."[10] She hopes that this is a sign from God that she has chosen the right way. But her thoughts then ramble on to the missal of the day which had told the story of St. Sabina, a Roman widow who, having become a Christian, was beheaded under the Emperor Hadrian, and secretly buried. "However," the missal had added, "it was not certain whether such a woman had existed at all." Yamamoto thus enigmatically turns the story of a strong love and a sad wedding into a legend for the bride to ponder—what is God's reality after all?

Yamamoto's most recent publication, "what might be the second chapter of an autobiography," is "Life among the Oilfields."[11] Here are the familiar Yamamoto hallmarks: the contacts with non-Japanese children, the delights of the American candy store, the smells of her mother's kitchen, all the details that bring into near-camera realism the seasons of farming, the frequent moves, the constrictions of poverty— the life of the Nisei a generation ago. There is the self-deprecation (the teacher wonders what to do with "this deluded Oriental shrimp with second-grade pretensions").

But the realism of the story is set off by the epigraph from Fitzgerald and the conclusion. A speeding sports car, coming up the asphalt road in the oilfields, strikes her little brother, tosses him to the side of the road, and keeps on going. The child has not been killed, only badly bruised, to the relief of the sister, the child Hisaye. But the mature woman, keeping her detachment, muses:

> When I look back on that episode, the helpless anger of my father and my mother is my inheritance. But my anger is more intricate than theirs, warped by all that has transpired in between. For instance, I sometimes see the arrogant couple from down the road as young and beautiful, their speeding open roadster as definitely and stunningly red. They roar by; their tinkling laughter, like a long silken scarf, is borne back by the wind. I gaze after them from the side of the road,

where I have darted to dodge the swirling dust and spitting
gravel. And I know that their names are Scott and Zelda.

Another recent piece reinforces the continuing strand, from
oilfields to the present, the determination to appreciate "just
plain being alive at this time and in this place":

Survival

The freeway yonder, deferred
for a time, has at last come
through. At first the razed lots
reminded of war's aftermath but
gradually they merged under tree
and flower and weed to make an
impromptu park where children
stalked one another in hiding
games, where humming bird hovered
over nicotiana, where bumblebee
buzzed the wisteria and hollyhock,
where there was room for gopher,
field mouse, skunk, opossum,
golden garden spider, fat snail,
mating lizards, king snake skating
through the grass, and raccoon
sneaking over here to up-end the trash
in the dark of night.

They must have all gone
somewhere. The neighborhood
owl, giant and white, has eaten
three kittens of our Manx,
leaving only bloody traces
of intestine smeared on the driveway
where he swooped to dine. Only
the runt of the litter, whom one
would have thought the easiest
prey, remains. It grows
by leaps and bounds, having
now all the milk
to itself.[12]

☐ *Notes* ∎

1. Hisaye Yamamoto, "Writing," *Amerasia Journal*, Vol. 3, No. 2 (1976), 126–133, rpt. from *Rafu Shimpo*.

2. Yamauchi treats this boredom and tragedy in "The Sensei," *Yardbird Reader*, No. 3 (1974), indirectly in "Shirley Temple Hotcha-cha," *Rafu Shimpo*, Holiday Supplement, 1979, and in detail in *12-1-A*, an unpublished play set in one of the Relocation camps.

3. "' . . . I Still Carry It Around,'" RIKKA, 3:4 (Winter 1976), 11–19. The phrase comes from Lawson Inada.

4. "The Poetry of the Issei on the American Relocation Experience," *Calafia, The California Poetry*, ed. Ishmael Reed (Berkeley: Y'Bird Books, 1979), p. lxxi.

5. Letters from Wakako Yamauchi and Hisaye Yamamoto [DeSoto] to Dorothy Ritsuko Yashimuro McDonald in April 1979.

6. Yamamoto read this story at the Asian American Writers session at Beyond Baroque, Venice, California, 17 November 1979.

7. "The Brown House," rpt. in *Asian-American Authors*, ed. Kai-yu Hsu and Helen Palubinskas (Boston: Houghton Mifflin, 1972). Also rpt. in *Yardbird Reader No. 3*.

8. "Las Vegas Charley," rpt. in *The Third Woman, Minority Women Writers of the United States*, ed. Dexter Fisher (Boston: Houghton Mifflin, 1980) and in *Asian-American Heritage*, ed. David Hsin-Fu Wand (New York: Washington Square Press, 1974).

9. Rpt. in *Speaking for Ourselves*, ed. Lillian Faderman and Barbara Bradshaw (Glendale: Scott Foresman, 1969, 1975). Also in *Amerasia Journal*, Vol. 3, No. 2 (1976) and *The Ethnic American Woman, Problems, Protests and Lifestyle*, ed. Edith Blicksilver (Dubuque: Kendall/Hunt, 1978).

10. "Epithalamium," *Carleton Miscellany*, 1 (Fall 1960), 56–67. Although the setting is reminiscent of the Catholic Worker refuge on Staten Island, Yamamoto says that the protagonist's religious deliberations are not autobiographical.

11. *Rafu Shimpo*, Holiday Supplement, 1979.

12. "Survival," *Bridge Magazine*, Part II of special double issue on Asian American Women, Vol. 7, No. 1 (Spring 1979).

☐ STAN YOGI ■

Legacies Revealed: Uncovering Buried Plots in the Stories of Hisaye Yamamoto

Between 1948 and 1961 the Nisei woman Hisaye Yamamoto gained national attention as a short story writer.[1] She was awarded a John Hay Whitney Foundation Opportunity Fellowship in 1950, and her stories depicting the lives of Japanese immigrants and their children began appearing in national journals.[2] That Yamamoto would be the subject of interest in 1950 is intriguing given the general lack of enthusiasm for women writers and the lingering hostility towards Japanese Americans in the aftermath of World War II. As a minority woman writer, Yamamoto had to contend with both sexual and racial barriers. She not only faced sexism from the general society, she also confronted it in her immediate community. Japanese immigrants brought with them cultural beliefs that discounted the importance of women. In an autobiographical story, Yamamoto succinctly captures these sentiments when she comments, "I gathered that my father didn't see any necessity of higher education for women."[3] Besides this devaluation of women, Yamamoto also had to deal with a mainstream culture that still viewed Japanese Americans negatively.[4] In 1948, when Yamamoto's stories were first published, World War II was still a fresh memory, and the antagonistic attitudes

From *Studies in American Fiction* 17:2 (1989): 169–181.

towards Japanese Americans that landed them in internment camps during the war still remained.

Although the sexism and racism Yamamoto encountered could have discouraged her literary efforts, a vibrant group of Nisei writers emerged in the 1930s and 1940s to spur the development of a literary voice. Building on the tradition of their parents, who wrote *haiku, tanka,* and *senryu* (Japanese poetic forms) for Japanese language papers in America,[5] young Nisei began a literary culture of their own. During the early 1930s, the English-language section editors of Japanese American papers in Los Angeles, San Francisco, and Seattle encouraged young writers to submit poems and stories.[6] As Elaine Kim notes:

> Ironically, it was the segregation of the *nisei* that first encouraged their literary attempts. Among themselves, they did not need to fear being misconstrued according to some distorting stereotype or worry about having to preface each poem, story, or essay with an explanation of who they were, why they were writing in English, or how they differed from prevailing images of Japanese Americans. The existence of a small but concrete, palpable, and known audience of fellow *nisei* gave many writers a feeling of confidence.[7]

As Nisei writers became more organized, publishing such journals as *Reimei* in Salt Lake City and *Leaves* in Los Angeles, they received encouragement from progressive non-Japanese writers and artists, including Louis Adamic, Carey McWilliams, William Saroyan, and John Fante. In 1939 the League of Nisei Writers and Artists formed "for the purpose of promoting individual and collaborative creative activity, of stimulating a critical outlook on matters of life, art and broad problems of society."[8]

A peripheral associate of the League of Nisei Writers and Artists, Yamamoto was nonetheless one of the few Nisei to gain recognition beyond the Japanese American community.[9] This recognition is well deserved, for Yamamoto's stories are not only powerful portraits of Japanese American life, they are also technically fascinating. Through the use of narrators with limited perspectives, Yamamoto develops "buried plots,"

144

Thesis

veiled means of conveying stories that link her work with feminist critical theory as well as with Japanese American communication patterns.[10] Yamamoto crafts stories with surface meanings that hint at powerful undercurrents. In uncovering the buried plots of Yamamoto's stories, one can not only better understand the experiences of Japanese Americans but also explore the intersection of gender, culture, and language.[11]

Buried plots operate in different manners in Yamamoto's works. Two of her stories, "Seventeen Syllables" (1949) and "Yoneko's Earthquake" (1951), exemplify the varying ways that Yamamoto uses this device. "Yoneko's Earthquake" is deliciously ambiguous, containing hidden, often tragic, secrets. "Seventeen Syllables" begins with a focus on one plot but subtly shifts to disclose another that intertwines with the original action. The buried plots of each story reveal the experiences of Issei women and the troubling legacies they pass on to their daughters.

Ostensibly a story about the sexual awakening of an adolescent Nisei, "Seventeen Syllables" is as much a story about a young woman's mother as it is about her. Focused on a Japanese American farm family, the story deals with the initiation of a teen into the mysteries of adult life. Rosie Hayashi, the young central character, enters into a relationship with Jesus Carrasco, the teen-aged son of hired hands, and discovers the painful joy of sexual attraction. Through Rosie's perspective, Yamamoto reveals a plot concerning Rosie's mother. Mrs. Hayashi is deeply interested in writing haiku and spends increasing time pursuing this hobby, ultimately winning a haiku contest sponsored by a Japanese American newspaper. Her career as a poet, however, is aborted when her husband, who becomes increasingly intolerant of his wife's literary preoccupation, erupts in anger and violently destroys the prize she wins, a Hiroshige print. After witnessing this incident, Rosie listens to her mother confess the disturbing events that led to her immigration to the U.S. Yamamoto crafts the story to demonstrate constant links between the two women, and the parallels she develops underscore the legacy of disruption and pain that mother passes on to daughter.

"Seventeen Syllables" operates on a series of deceptions and opens with an innocent hoax. After Mrs. Hayashi recites a haiku she has composed in Japanese, Rosie pretends "to understand it thoroughly and appreciate it no end." Although Mrs. Hayashi seeks to convey the beauty of her hobby, an absence of genuine communication between the two women occurs because Rosie does not understand the Japanese her mother uses.[12] For Rosie, "it was so much easier to say, yes, yes even when one meant no, no," and she innocently attempts to deceive her mother by pretending to enjoy the poem.

Yamamoto links this initial and innocent deception to more calculated trickery. Jesus Carrasco, the son of seasonal workers, invites Rosie to meet him in a packing shed because, he tells Rosie, "I've got a secret I want to tell you." The two youths engage in adolescent teasing, and from this context it becomes apparent that Jesus' "secret" is a pretense to meet Rosie alone. Rosie, however, is blind to the import of Jesus' invitation. When she arrives at the shed at the appointed time she demands "now tell me the secret."

Jesus' claim of conveying a secret is not completely without merit, for he proceeds to disclose to Rosie what was, up to this point in her life, a secret: the complexity of sexual attraction. In her encounter with Jesus, Rosie echoes her earlier response to her mother:

> When he took hold of her empty hand, she could find no words to protest; her vocabulary had become distressingly constricted and she thought desperately that all that remained intact now was yes and no and oh, and even these few sounds would not easily out. Thus, kissed by Jesus, Rosie fell for the first time entirely victim to a helplessness delectable beyond speech.

This image of Rosie, utterly dumbfounded, strikingly resembles her struggle to hide her ignorance of the haiku's meaning. In her experience with Jesus, however, the limited vocabulary of "yes" and "no" reappears but cannot even be vocalized; Jesus has left her speechless. With the realization that "yes" and "no" are the basic words through which individuals express their will, one begins to recognize an important link between Rosie's encounter with Jesus and her earlier experience with her mother. For Mrs. Hayashi, writing haiku is a means of asserting herself and escaping the daily toil on the farm. Rosie's loss of will in this situation thus becomes an innocent analogue to the control Mrs. Hayashi lacks over her own life. Much like Rosie, who succumbs to Jesus' desires, Mrs. Hayashi is forced to cease writing by her husband.

Once establishing the plot concerning Rosie's relationship with Jesus, Yamamoto begins to develop the buried plot regarding Mrs. Hayashi. Jesus' deception of Rosie, resulting in her initiation into sexual knowledge, is in turn linked to the confession of deception that Rosie's mother makes. After serenely observing her husband chop up and burn the prize she won in a haiku contest, Mrs. Hayashi narrates the history behind her immigration to the U.S., a history hitherto kept secret:

> At eighteen she had been in love with the first son of one of the well-to-do families in her village. The two had met whenever and wherever they could, secretly, because it would not have done for his family to see him favor her—her father had no money; he was a drunkard and a gambler besides. She had learned she was with child; an excellent match had already been arranged for her lover. Despised by her family, she had given premature birth to a stillborn son, who would be seventeen now.

As an alternative to suicide, Mrs. Hayashi asks her sister in America to send for her. Her sister arranges a marriage with Rosie's father, who "was never told why his unseen betrothed was so eager to hasten the day of meeting."

Mrs. Hayashi's confession brings together many of the themes already introduced in the story. The constriction of communication explored in the opening has its more tragic parallel in the experiences of Rosie's mother: Mrs. Hayashi has no means of expressing her desires and feelings other than to kill herself or run away. She cannot, moreover, reveal her tarnished past to her husband. The theme of blossoming sexuality has its more dire consequences for Mrs. Hayashi. She consummates her affair but has no power to make it binding. Others dictate the termination of her relationship, and the stillborn child serves as a manifestation of her lost love.[13]

Although Mrs. Hayashi's arranged marriage is not too far from common practice, her case is burdened with complicating circumstances: her family ships her off in shame, and she hides the secret of her affair and dead child from her husband. The options open to her are few. Having severed family ties, she cannot return to Japan. She is trapped in America, where she works like a machine in the fields and packing sheds. Writing, one of the few escapes from her demanding life, is denied her. Just as her love affair is cut off, just as her son is born too soon, so too is her career as a poet prematurely halted.

Only after learning of Mrs. Hayashi's history are the implications of the title "Seventeen Syllables" fleshed out. The haikus that Rosie's mother writes become metaphors of both freedom and constraint. Writing allows Mrs. Hayashi to transcend her mundane and harsh existence and ponder higher ideas. The haiku form, in which "she must pack all her meaning into seventeen syllables," also becomes a metaphor for the constraints that force Mrs. Hayashi to find meaning in small ways. The number seventeen, in addition, has special meaning for both Rosie and her mother. For Mrs. Hayashi, the number recalls a tragic loss; her stillborn son would at the time of the story be seventeen years old.[14] For Rosie, however, the number carries tremendous hope. Jesus, soon to be a senior in high school and her guide to budding sexuality, is probably seventeen years old.

After learning of her painful past, one can recognize the irony of the pen name Mrs. Hayashi adopts. "Ume Hanazono" literally translates as "Plum Flowergarden." (Yamamoto also links mother and daughter through their names. "Rosie" echoes the flower imagery of "Flowergarden.") The pen name is inappropriate, however, because Ume Hanazono's career as a poet never blossoms as the images of plums and flower gardens imply. On the contrary, Mrs. Hayashi's identity as a poet is ended before it fully develops.

After telling Rosie of her past, Mrs. Hayashi kneels on the floor and takes her by the wrists, insisting that her daughter capitulate to her demand: "Promise me you will never marry!" The image and the request dovetail with Rosie's encounter with Jesus. Her mother's grip reminds Rosie of "Jesus's hand, how it had touched her and where," creating a story imagistic link between the two episodes and connecting Rosie's story with the buried plot concerning Mrs. Hayashi.[15] The "familiar glib agreement"—"Yes, yes, I promise"—which Rosie gives her mother recalls the constriction Rosie has vocalizing the words "yes" and "no" in her encounter with Jesus and her similar response in the beginning of the story. In this instance, however, the answer that Rosie gives her mother carries ominous weight. Her mother, as if seeing through this deception, looks at Rosie with "eyes and twisted mouth" that seem to say "you fool."

Rosie cannot understand, or perhaps does not want to recognize, the painful implications of her mother's story. She is about the same age her mother was when she had her affair. Before Mrs. Hayashi tells her story, Rosie, as if knowing the tale, thinks: "Don't tell me now . . . tell me tomorrow, tell me next week, don't tell me today." Rosie realizes, however, that her mother will continue regardless of protests. Rosie also feels that the "telling would combine with the other violence of the hot afternoon to level her life, her world to the very ground." Like an old weed strangling the stem of a supple flower, Mrs. Hayashi's history interweaves with and shadows Rosie's discovery of her sexuality. Rosie receives a complex legacy of subordination and thwarted pursuits, of resistance and containment. Mrs. Hayashi resists norms; she has an affair and writes poetry. These rebellions are squelched, and Mrs. Hayashi's warning not to marry is given out of concern that Rosie not follow in a path of disillusionment.

At the end of "Seventeen Syllables" it is unclear whether Rosie will accept the legacy of subordination her mother leaves her.[16] Although Rosie "glibly" agrees that she will not marry, the promise is not genuine; she agrees merely to please her mother. Rosie's exciting encounter with Jesus, however, is somewhat canceled out by the strife she witnesses between her parents and by her mother's confession of dashed love. As if a sign of her arrival into adulthood, Rosie receives an "embrace and consoling hand" from her mother much later than she expects. This image not only recalls the previous images of Jesus' embrace and Mrs. Hayashi's grip on Rosie's wrist, it also suggests the maturity that Mrs. Hayashi now expects of her daughter, who has been initiated into the excitement, pain, and disillusionment of adult life.

Included in *Best American Short Stories of 1952*, "Yoneko's Earthquake," like "Seventeen Syllables," focuses on a rural Japanese American family. The story chronicles the infatuation of a young Nisei girl, Yoneko Hosoume, with Marpo, a Filipino hired hand, in the context of emotional and psychological disturbances that occur within the family after an earthquake. "Yoneko's Earthquake" is spellbinding in its subtle conveyance of the buried story of Yoneko's mother. As the tale progresses, Yamamoto subtly suggests events unseen. Told through the prism of young Yoneko's eyes, the story seldom deals directly with the experiences of Mrs. Hosoume. Unlike Mrs. Hayashi's history, which is revealed explicitly, Mrs. Hosoume's actions are never directly conveyed. Her plot is buried within Yoneko's.

Yamamoto links the two plots, however, through Marpo, who is associated with the turbulent earthquake and, ironically, with Christ. Marpo and the fateful earthquake not only create physical havoc; much like Mrs. Hayashi's confession in "Seventeen Syllables," which threatens to level Rosie's life "to the very ground," they also serve as catalysts for domestic, generational, and ultimately spiritual upheavals.

As the story begins, Yamamoto introduces religion in conjunction with the idea of limited perspective. Yoneko is "impressed" by her cousins, "the Christians." She joins them at a church service; when she does not know the words to a hymn, she "open[s] her mouth and grimace[s] nonchalantly to the rhythm." This miming is paradigmatic of her actions throughout the story. Just as she mouths words without understanding their meaning, Yoneko observes and indeed participates in more ominous events without truly comprehending their significance.

Yoneko's cousins and the church service do not bring her closer to an understanding of God, so "it remained for Marpo to bring the word of God to Yoneko." After a "protracted discussion on religion" with Marpo, Yoneko unquestioningly accepts the tenets of Christianity and becomes "an ideal apostle, adoring Jesus, desiring Heaven, and fearing Hell."

150

Marpo's evangelical role is important because he becomes a Christ figure to Yoneko. Not only does he bring her to a recognition of God, he takes on the proportions of a miracle worker, for to Yoneko "there seemed to be nothing Marpo could not do." To prove this, Yoneko catalogues Marpo's talents as an athlete, musician, artist, and radio technician. In her feelings towards Marpo, Yoneko mixes religious awe with childish love. Through Yoneko's infatuation, however, Yamamoto establishes an innocent foil which mirrors the more serious relationship the mother develops with Marpo.

Yamamoto not only links Marpo with Christ, she also associates him with the fateful earthquake. Among Marpo's many possessions is a "muscle-builder sent him by Charles Atlas which, despite his unassuming size, he could stretch the length of his outspread arms; his teeth gritted then and his whole body became temporarily victim to a jerky vibration." Not only are the grimace and body contortion an ironic mirror of the crucified Christ, the "jerky vibration" to which Marpo is subject associates him with the earthquake that sparks events that alter the psychic landscape of the characters. Yamamoto furthers Marpo's imagistic link with the disturbances caused by the earthquake. He sings, for example, with "professional quavers and rolled r's when he applie[s] a slight pressure to his Adam's apple with thumb and forefinger," and he sings songs with exaggerated "r's" such as "The Rose of Tralee" and the "Londonderry Air." He also builds a radio that brings in "equal proportions of static and entertainment." The trills and static become aural equivalents of physical shaking.

Yamamoto also employs quaking imagery with Mr. Hosoume and thus connects him with the upheavals that follow the earthquake. She ironically uses sexual references to describe Mr. Hosoume's experiences during and immediately after the earthquake. Mr. Hosoume is driving home when the earthquake hits, and his car is "kissed by a broken live wire dangling from a suddenly leaning pole." The word "kissed" is especially ironic because this experience will leave Mr. Hosoume impotent in almost all senses of the word. Yamamoto continues with more sexual imagery: to save himself from electrocution, Mr. Hosoume begins to "writhe and kick" away from the "sputtering wire." Upon returning home after the

151

earthquake, he is "trembling." Through these images of shaking, Yamamoto not only bonds Mr. Hosoume with the alterations caused by the earthquake, she underscores his impotence through the orgasmic associations the images suggest.

Mr. Hosoume is incapacitated to such a degree that Marpo displaces him in almost every respect, and this displacement results in tragedy. Evidence of this displacement is seen as soon as the earth begins trembling. Yamamoto binds Marpo to Mrs. Hosoume through their respective reactions to the quake. As the earth rattles, Mrs. Hosoume screams "*Jishin, Jishin!*" while gathering her children and running into an open field. As if a translated echo, "Marpo, stumbling in from the fields, join[s] them, saying, 'Earthquake, earthquake!'" The incident blossoms into a powerful image of Marpo taking Mr. Hosoume's place in the family. Marpo hugs Mrs. Hosoume and her children "as much to protect them as to support himself." This image visually symbolize the "paternal" roles of supporter and comforter Marpo will take on in the family.

The displacement of Mr. Hosoume continues when Marpo takes over his employer's labor responsibilities. Mrs. Hosoume and Marpo now do all the field work. Marpo, in addition, does most of the driving, and he and Mrs. Hosoume go into town for weekly shopping trips. Mr. Hosoume, in contrast, stays "at home most of the time. Sometimes, if he had a relatively painless day, he would have supper on the stove when Mrs. Hosoume came in from the fields." This reversal of roles is significant when seen in context of Issei history. Issei families were usually strictly patriarchal. In addition to working beside their husbands in the fields. Issei women living on farms also had domestic duties. Issei divided daily activities and responsibilities along the lines of "inside" and "outside": "wives took care of everything 'inside' the house, home or family, and men took care of 'everything else.'"[17] Cooking would be considered an "inside" responsibility, while interaction with merchants might be considered an "outside" activity. For Mr. Hosoume to perform domestic duties and for Mrs. Hosoume to take on traditionally masculine responsibilities is in itself a major upheaval.

After establishing Marpo as an integral part of the

family, Yamamoto begins to develop more fully the buried plot. She provides a clue to this plot when Mrs. Hosoume, "breathless from the fields one day," presents Yoneko with a gold-colored ring with a glasslike stone. She tells Yoneko, "I'm going to give you this ring. If your father asks where you got it, say you found it on the street." Yoneko, oblivious to the origins of the ring, does not even question her mother. After Mrs. Hosoume returns to the fields, Yoneko puts "the pretty ring on her middle finger." This ambiguous incident initiates an investigation into the buried plot. Although it is never explicitly stated, one can gather from the events of the story that Mrs. Hosoume receives the ring from Marpo. The ring obviously is not from Mr. Hosoume, and Mrs. Hosoume interacts with Marpo on a daily basis, whether working in the fields or traveling into town. This constant contact blooms into a serious relationship.

The ring establishes a complex link between Yoneko and her mother. It not only symbolizes Marpo's feelings for Mrs. Hosoume, but also connects Mrs. Hosoume and Yoneko. The ring manifests the feelings they both share for Marpo. Mrs. Hosoume's acceptance of the ring and her subsequent relay of it to her daughter further illustrates upheaval in the family. Yoneko does not see the significance of the ring in the context of her mother's relationship with Marpo; she is too young to understand its importance. She participates, however, in deceiving her father about her mother's affair. Not only is Mrs. Hosoume's adultery a direct violation of patriarchal dominance in the family, Yoneko's unknowing compliance in hiding the affair suggests generational defiance of the patriarchy. Yoneko, who is already upset with her father for an annoying display in front of her friends, is delighted for the "chance to have some secret revenge on her father."

Further evidence of Mrs. Hosoume's affair and the erosion of Mr. Hosoume's power in the family is evident in a fight that erupts between Mr. and Mrs. Hosoume. After discussing with Mrs. Hosoume the merits of Yoneko's wearing nail polish, Mr. Hosoume, believing that his wife openly contradicts him, casts an insulting epithet at her. When Mrs. Hosoume resists this insult, her husband slaps her. That an Issei woman would stand up to her husband in this way would, indeed, be seen by an Issei male as insolent. The various reactions to the incident are also telling: "Mrs. Hosoume was immobile for an instant . . . although she glanced over at Marpo, who happened to be in the room reading a newspaper." That Marpo is present is important in itself because it demonstrates the extent to which he has displaced Mr. Hosoume. Although Mrs. Hosoume's glance can be interpreted as reflecting her concern that a family squabble takes place in front of a hired hand, it can also represent silent communication between lovers Mrs. Hosoume and Marpo. This interpretation gains credence when Marpo comes to Mrs. Hosoume's defense and stops Mr. Hosoume from slapping his wife again. This action is particularly powerful when one remembers that before the earthquake Marpo was "a rather shy young man meek to the point of speechlessness in the presence of Mr. and Mrs. Hosoume."

After this incident, Yamamoto fully develops the clues which hint at a buried plot. Marpo mysteriously leaves the family, and on the day of his disappearance the Hosoume family takes an enigmatic trip to the hospital. Yoneko and her brother, Seigo, do not comprehend why their parents make this trip. After her visit with the doctor, Mrs. Hosoume is obviously in pain, but when she responds to Yoneko's query as to the "source of her distress," she answers that "she was feeling a little under the weather and that the doctor had administered some necessarily astringent treatment." Only after the family returns home does Yamamoto offer evidence of untold actions.

This evidence, however, is not presented in a straightforward manner; it develops from a series of cryptic events, the most significant of which is the death of Yoneko's younger brother, Seigo. If Marpo is somehow linked to Christ, it is Seigo who is sacrificed, and his death subsequently instills Mrs. Hosoume's fervent faith in God. At the end, Mrs. Hosoume tells the innocent Yoneko, "Never kill a person, Yoneko, because if you do, God will take from you someone you love." This statement becomes the key to uncovering previous events in the story. Through this warning, Yamamoto fleshes out Mrs. Hosoume's psychology. She feels that the death of Seigo is God's means of punishing her for killing another: it becomes apparent that the "killing" Mrs. Hosoume refers to is the abortion of a child.

This would explain the mysterious trip to the hospital. The purpose of the trip, of which Mr. Hosoume tells Yoneko and Seigo they must never speak, is to abort the unborn child of Marpo, the result of his affair with Mrs. Hosoume. Yamamoto offers a symbolic representation of the abortion through the images that frame the event. While driving to the hospital, Mr. Hosoume strikes "a beautiful collie which had dashed out barking from someone's yard. The car jerked with the impact, but Mr. Hosoume drove right on and Yoneko, wanting suddenly to vomit, looked back and saw the collie lying very still at the side of the road." Later, "on the way home they passed the place of the encounter with the collie, and Yoneko looked up and down the stretch of road but the dog was nowhere to be seen." Through this incident, Yamamoto hints at Mrs. Hosoume's "buried" action.[18]

After the abortion and the death of Seigo, the void once filled by Marpo is filled by God. Struck with guilt over the abortion and Seigo's death, Mrs. Hosoume finds comfort in Christianity. In a twisted sense, Marpo serves as an agent bringing Mrs. Hosoume to God. Just as Christ initiated spiritual upheavals, Marpo is a catalyst who spiritually transforms characters in the story. He brings Yoneko to a recognition of God, although her faith is shattered during the earthquake. When she hears her mother talk of God, she is quick to respond, "I don't believe in that, I don't believe in God." Her rejection of God parallels her rejection of Marpo after he abruptly leaves the family. Yoneko lacks the faith in things unseen to which her mother now clings. Yoneko's experience with Marpo leaves her void of faith, while Mrs. Hosoume's relationship with him ultimately results in her conversion.

Like "Seventeen Syllables," "Yoneko's Earthquake" ends ambiguously. It is unclear whether Yoneko will inherit the legacy of subjugation her mother offers. Yamamoto hints that this may not occur; Yoneko does not understand her mother's advice: "Never kill a person, Yoneko, because if you do, God will take from you someone you love." As Charles L. Crow notes, "Yoneko does not pause to ponder the ambiguities of this statement—was the person taken Seigo or Marpo?"[19] As if confirming that the daughter will not accept her mother's legacy, Yoneko loses the ring her mother gave her, a loss which symbolizes not only a lapse between Yoneko and Marpo but also a severed link between Yoneko and her mother.

Although both "Seventeen Syllables" and "Yoneko's Earthquake" end with Issei women surrendering to patriarchal systems, Yamamoto does not depict these choices as weak or simplistic. On the contrary, by layering her stories and developing buried plots, Yamamoto fully explores the tremendous psychological and emotional costs to Issei women who attempt to pursue their desires in a context hostile to their wishes. Unlike Rosie in "Seventeen Syllables," who can only feign understanding of her mother's haiku, readers who dig through to the buried plots of "Seventeen Syllables" and "Yoneko's Earthquake" will be rewarded with masterful storytelling by an author who has captured the complexities of Japanese American experiences.[20]

☐ Notes ■

1. The term "Nisei," a combination of the Japanese words for "two" and "generation," refers to second generation, America-born Japanese Americans. The term "Issei" refers to Japanese immigrants, parents of the Nisei.

2. Yamamoto was also encouraged by Elizabeth Bishop and by Stanford professor and poet Yvor Winters, who had wanted her to accept a Stanford Writing Fellowship. Charles L. Crow, "A MELUS Interview: Hisaye Yamamoto," *MELUS* 14, No. 1 (1987), 77–78.

3. Hisaye Yamamoto, "Eju-kei-shung! Eju-kei-shung!" *Rafu Shimpo* (Dec. 20, 1980), p. 11. The Japanese American woman Mitsuye Yamada also captures the sexism of Issei when she recounts an argument she had with her father regarding her pacifist beliefs. She recalls, "My father reassured me that it was 'all right' for me to be a pacifist because as a . . . 'girl' *it didn't make any difference to anyone*." Mitsuye Yamada, "Invisibility is an Unnatural Disaster: Reflections of an Asian American Woman," in *This Bridge Called My Back: Writings by Radical Women of Color,* ed. Cherríe Moraga and Gloria Anzaldúa (New York: Kitchen Table: Women of Color Press, 1983), p. 38.

4. G. M. Gilbert noted in 1951 that Japanese were still characterized as immature, sly, treacherous, and nationalistic. G. M. Gil-

bert, "Stereotype Persistence and Change among College Students," *Journal of Abnormal and Social Psychology* 46 (1951), 245–54.

5. Yamamoto's mother wrote *senryu* for these papers.

6. Iwao Kawakami, English-language section editor of the San Francisco paper *The New World,* inaugurated a story and essay club on January 13, 1930.

7. Elaine H. Kim, *Asian American Literature: An Introduction to the Writings and Their Social Context* (Philadelphia: Temple University Press, 1982), p. 141.

8. League of Nisei Writers and Artists, typescript, 1939.

9. Others who received national attention were Toyo Suyemoto, whose poetry was published in *Yale Review,* and the short story writer Toshio Mori, whose works appeared in national journals such as *New Directions in Poetry and Prose* and *Common Ground.* A collection of his stories, *Yokohama, California,* was slated for publication prior to the war. Because of wartime hostilities towards Japanese, it did not appear until 1949.

10. "Buried plots" are related to the common literary idea of the "double plot." Whereas double plots involve an explicit presentation of a secondary, albeit related, plot in a story or play (for example, the Glouscester plot in *King Lear*), buried plots in Yamamoto's stories are not always clearly delineated. Often the reader must piece together a buried plot from clues garnered in the "main" or "surface plot." Buried plots are also related to the feminist literary theories of Elaine Showalter and Annette Kolodny. Showalter has developed the idea of "muted stories" and asserts that "in the purest feminist literary criticism we are . . . presented with a radical alteration of our vision, a demand that we see meaning in what has previously been empty space. The orthodox plot recedes, and another plot, hitherto submerged in the anonymity of the background, stands out in bold relief like a thumbprint." See Elaine Showalter, "Feminist Criticism in the Wilderness," in *The New Feminist Criticism: Essays on Women, Literature and Theory,* ed. Elaine Showalter (New York: Pantheon, 1985), p. 266. Showalter suggests a stylistic interpretation or reinterpretation of explicit actions or events in a surface plot to uncover the muted rebellion of women. Although related to Showalter's muted stories, the concept of buried plots is somewhat different. Often in Yamamoto's works, we need not reinterpret the "surface" plot but rather look to what is only alluded to, what remains unstated. In addition, the term "buried" is flexible; in some cases, a plot is

buried in the sense that it does not appear, or is not fully developed, until well into the story. These buried plots often focus on a character who is defined through the actions of others. This elliptical character development in Yamamoto's stories relates to Annette Kolodny's identification of "reflexive perception" in works by women writers. Kolodny argues that reflexive perception is a typical stylistic feature of female fiction and occurs when a character "discover[s] herself or find[s] some part of herself in activities she has not planned or in situations she cannot fully comprehend." See Annette Kolodny, "Some Notes on Defining a 'Feminist Literary Criticism,'" *Critical Inquiry* 2 (1975), 79. Yamamoto employs variations of this device. Although characters in her stories are often involved in situations they cannot fully understand, this does not always result in self-discovery.

11. Buried plots have forceful analogues in Japanese American culture. The behavior associated with the idea of *enryo* among Japanese Americans provides a cogent parallel. *Enryo* is difficult to define since it involves several different types of behavior including the denial of something proffered even though that item is wanted, the acceptance of a less desired object even if given a choice, and the hesitancy to ask questions or to make demands. The actions associated with *enryo* originated with norms in Japan that governed the ways in which "inferiors" were to behave towards "superiors." Transferred to and altered in America, *enryo* now encompasses a whole range of behaviors from "what to do in ambiguous situations, to how to cover moments of confusion, embarrassment, and anxiety." See Harry H. L. Kitano, *Japanese Americans: The Evolution of a Subculture* (Englewood Cliffs: Prentice-Hall, 1976), p. 24. Linking the diverse behaviors associated with *enryo* is the idea that manifest actions do not always accurately reflect inner feelings. Those unfamiliar with Japanese American culture might not be sensitive to the subtleties underlying behavior and consequently misinterpret actions associated with *enryo*. The *enryo* dynamic is a potential cultural equivalent to a literary buried plot.

12. Robert Rolf argues that the haiku form "functions as a symbol of the incomplete communication between the Issei parent and Nisei child." Robert Rolf, "The Short Stories of Hisaye Yamamoto, Japanese American Writer," *Bulletin of Fukuoka University of Education* 31 (1982), 81.

13. That Rosie's mother would immigrate to the U.S. under

these circumstances may strike readers unfamiliar with Japanese American history as odd. In fact, the type of marriage in which Mrs. Hayashi is involved was not too deviant from the prevalent practice of "picture marriages" among Issei. Arranged marriages were traditional in Japan. As Yuji Ichioka explains:

> Heads of household selected marriage partners for family members through intermediaries or go-betweens. An exchange of photographs sometimes occurred in the screening process, with family genealogy, wealth, education, and health figuring heavily in the selection criteria. Go-betweens arranged parleys between families at which proposed unions were discussed and negotiated. Although at such meetings prospective spouses normally met each other for the first time, it would be unusual for them to talk to each other. After all, the meetings were for the benefit of heads of family, and not designed for future couples to become acquainted with each other. If the families mutually consented, engagement and marriage ensued. See Yuji Ichioka, *The Issei: The World of the First Generation Japanese Immigrants, 1885–1924* (New York: Free Press, 1988), p. 164.

When Japanese men in the U.S. sought to marry, this traditional practice was altered to suit the needs of Issei. Men forwarded their relatives photographs of themselves along with information about their situation in America. Relatives would then negotiate a marriage, and an Issei man would in turn receive a picture of his new spouse. Women would be sent off to America where they would meet their husbands for the first time. Anti-Japanese forces cited picture-marriages as proof of Japanese unassimilability. Although the exact number of picture-brides is unknown, "the majority of wives who entered [Japanese] immigrant society between 1910 and 1920 came as picture-brides." Ichioka, p. 165.

14. Charles L. Crow also notes this in his essay, "The *Issei* Father in the Fiction of Hisaye Yamamoto," in *Opening Up Literary Criticism: Essays on American Prose and Poetry,* ed. Leo Truchlar (Salzburg: Verlag Wolfgang Neugebauer, 1986), p. 35. Crow considers Yamamoto's portrayal of the father in "Seventeen Syllables" as unflattering. Yamamoto has responded that Mr. Hayashi "was only acting in the way he'd been brought up to act, the way men were supposed to be." Crow, "A MELUS Interview," p. 80.

15. Yamamoto suggests the patriarchy of Christianity when Rosie, after her mother demands that she never marry, calls out

silently to Jesus, "not certain whether she was invoking the help of the son of the Carrascos or of God." Rosie is searching for a male savior to help her escape the troubling request her mother makes. The mixture of romantic and religious associations is intriguing and is repeated in "Yoneko's Earthquake." Jesus, the son of the Carrascos, could "save" Rosie by proving to her that romance is not always doomed as it was in Mrs. Hayashi's experience. Jesus, the son of God, on the other hand, could "save" Rosie by healing the psychological and emotional wounds from which the family suffers.

16. Elaine Kim suggests that Rosie will learn from her mother's experience. Kim, p. 163.

17. Sylvia Junko Yanagisako, *Transforming the Past: Tradition and Kinship Among Japanese Americans* (Stanford: Stanford University Press, 1985), p. 101. Yanagisako's study deals with urban Issei. Since no comparable study focuses on rural Issei, I generalize her findings to rural Issei.

18. Yuri Kageyama also notes the symbolic nature of the collie's death. Yuri Kageyama, "Hisaye Yamamoto—Nisei Writer," *Sunbury* 10, p. 36. King-Kok Cheung observes, "the unblinking killing of the animal enables us not only to perceive the father's intense anger and his total indifference to the life about to be destroyed but also to imagine the mother's contrasting psychological state. She must cringe inwardly as she witnesses the act that foreshadows the fate of her unborn child." King-Kok Cheung, "Introduction," *Seventeen Syllables and Other Stories* (Latham, N.Y.: Kitchen Table: Women of Color Press, 1988), p. xix.

19. Charles L. Crow, "Home and Transcendence in Los Angeles Fiction," in *Los Angeles Fiction,* ed. David Fine (Albuquerque: University of New Mexico Press, 1984), p. 202.

20. The author thanks Susan Schweik, King-Kok Cheung, Eric Sundquist, Genaro Padilla, and Gayle Fujita-Sato for their helpful comments on earlier versions of this essay.

Double-Telling: Intertextual Silence in Hisaye Yamamoto's Fiction

Feminist scholars Joan Radner and Susan Lanser have demonstrated how women writers use "strategies of coding" to express "ideas and attitudes proscribed by the dominant culture" (412). Elaine Showalter, taking off from anthropologists Shirley and Edwin Ardener's model of women's culture, argues that women's fiction can be read as a "double-voiced discourse": "The orthodox plot recedes, and another plot, hitherto submerged in the anonymity of the background, stands out in bold relief like a thumbprint" (34). And Susan Stanford Friedman proposes a "psycho-political hermeneutic" for reading women's narratives as the "return of the repressed" (142). While borrowing these interpretive strategies in my own textual analysis, I feel also a strong need to go beyond the critics' theories to account for the multiple levels of silence embedded in the fiction of Hisaye Yamamoto, a nisei (second-generation Japanese American) writer. The critics acknowledge that a woman of a racial minority may be twice muted, but they make no allowances for differences in cultural manifestations and evaluations of speech and silence. What some American linguists (e.g. Lakoff, O'Barr and Atkins) regard as "women's language" or "powerless language" is shown, for instance, to be the communicative norm in Japan (Wetzel 555–58). Nonverbal communication and indirectness of speech remain

From *American Literary History* 3:2 (1991): 277–293.

pervasive in traditional Japanese American families, at least among the first two generations (Fujita 34, Miyamoto 35). Hence the use of indirection by a nisei woman writer must not be attributed to gender alone. Furthermore, in focusing exclusively on female silence under patriarchy, feminist scholars generally overlook the degree to which men, too, must repress their emotions because of conventional definitions of manhood, especially in cultures that associate silence with fortitude. This article contextualizes Yamamoto's method of what I call "double-telling" within Japanese American culture and illustrates her artful deployment of thematic and rhetorical silences. I hope also to stretch the bounds of prevailing feminist analysis by showing how Yamamoto uses muted plots and bicultural codes to reveal the repression of both women *and* men.

I

Yamamoto's literary acclaim derives in part from her consummate narrative strategies. Her technique of double-telling—conveying two tales in the guise of one—involves an intertextual use of a familiar device. In two of her most haunting stories, "Seventeen Syllables" and "Yoneko's Earthquake," the overt "action" is presented through a naive narrator who reflects the mind of a young girl, while the covert drama concerns the conflict between the girl's issei (first-generation) parents. Though undoubtedly influenced by modernist experimentation with limited point of view, Yamamoto tailors the method to the Japanese American context. Her two stories capitalize not only on the infrequent verbal communication between issei spouses (Yanagisako 105, 122) but also on the peculiar interaction between issei parents and nisei children. Issei parents (especially fathers) tend to be authoritative and protective toward the young, so that free verbal exchange between parents and children is frequently suppressed (Kikumura 98). By playing the naive nisei point of view against the pregnant silence of the issei, Yamamoto constructs hidden plots and deflects attention from unsettling messages. Suspense develops in both stories in part because the parents refrain from disclosing their problems to their children; only through the ingenuous telling of the nisei daughters do we catch the dark nuances of adult reticence.

The elliptical style more than captures the interaction between the two generations; it also provides an escape valve from other pressures. As a woman writing at a time when feminist sensibilities were scarcely publishable, Yamamoto couches her sympathy in a disarming style that keeps alarming subtexts below the surface. We may infer her self-consciousness as a woman writer and her awareness of her verbal power from the telling pseudonym—Napoleon—she once adopted, purportedly "as an apology for [her] little madness" (Yamamoto, "Writing"). Belonging to a racial minority undoubtedly heightens her "anxiety of authorship," especially in face of the anti-Japanese sentiment that came to a head after the bombing of Pearl Harbor. Though the incarceration of over 110,000 people of Japanese ancestry ended with the war, political and social constrictions imposed by the dominant culture necessitated textual constraints beyond the duration of the physical confinement (cf. Schweik 89). Finally, as a nisei brought up to observe Japanese etiquette, Yamamoto may remain influenced by the "interpersonal style" (Miyamoto's term) of her own ethnic community, one which discourages verbal confrontation and open protest. If American women in general have been brought up to be more polite than men in their speech and writing (Lakoff), Japanese American women whose feminine reserve is reinforced by the cultural decorum of yet another tradition are likely to be even more circumspect in expressing themselves—at least on the surface.[1]

The last explanation may accentuate the stereotype of the "inscrutable Oriental" and blur the distinction between Japanese and Japanese Americans. My intention is quite the reverse: I wish to explode the stereotype by demystifying rather than denying the Japanese American preference for nonverbal or indirect communication. Important as it is to distinguish between Japanese and Japanese Americans, continuities between ancestral and ethnic cultures—especially in the first two generations—must also be acknowledged.[2]

Yamamoto herself replies indirectly to the question of cultural influence: "Since I was brought up like most Nisei, with Japanese ideas of *gaman* and *enryo* and that whole etiquette structure, I imagine my writing has been influenced by such behavior patterns—it would be strange if it wasn't" (Letter, 9 June 1988). *Enryo* and *gaman* are Japanese terms associated with proper behavior. The interaction rules related to *enryo* (often translated as "reserve," "deference," or "diffidence") are learned early in a Japanese family: "A child quickly learns the importance of reticence, modesty, indirection, and humility and is punished for boastful, aggressive, loud, and self-centered behavior" (Kikumura and Kitano 54). In the interaction between Japanese subordinates and their superiors or between Japanese Americans and whites, "One of the main manifestations of *enryo* was the conscious use of silence as a safe or neutral response to an embarrassing or ambiguous situation" (53). *Gaman*, meaning "internalization . . . and suppression of anger and emotion" (Kitano 136), is further associated with dogged perseverance: "The *Issei's* ability to *gaman* (stick things out at all costs) was often what carried them through times of hardship, disillusionment, and loneliness" (Kikumura and Kitano 55)

Yamamoto thus parlays cultural precepts into literary gambits. She makes strategic use, for instance, of a particular conversational technique that Stanford Lyman attributes to the nisei. Lyman argues that their conversations "almost always partake of the elements of an information game between persons maintaining decorum by seemingly mystifying one another." The listener must "ascertain the context of the speech he hears and . . . glean from his knowledge of the speaker and the context just what is the important point" (53). Both "Seventeen Syllables" and "Yoneko's Earthquake" engage us in decoding messages scripted into the seemingly random observations of two young girls. Each girl confides to us matters of utmost concern to *her*—events that constitute the manifest plot—while observing in passing her family's "routine." Between the lines lurks another plot that focuses on the child's parents, whose repressed emotions grip us as in an undertow.

164

II

The opening of "Seventeen Syllables" is deceptively merry and straightforward:

> The first Rosie knew that her mother had taken to writing poems was one evening when she finished one and read it aloud for her daughter's approval. . . . Rosie pretended to understand it thoroughly and appreciate it no end, partly because she hesitated to disillusion her mother about the quantity and quality of Japanese she had learned. . . . Even so, her mother must have been skeptical about the depth of Rosie's understanding, because she explained afterwards about the kind of poem she was trying to write.

Right from the start we witness and participate in an "information game." The anecdote introduces us to both the motif and the technique of indirection. Mother and daughter relate to each other tactfully and evasively, and they refrain from acknowledging or confronting the problem of communication: Rosie conceals her limited knowledge of Japanese; her mother avoids embarrassing her daughter by not challenging her understanding.

The author likewise grants us the daughter's impressions while teasing us with the mother's unknown thoughts. We know that although Rosie responds enthusiastically to her mother's literary effort by saying "Yes, yes, I understand," she feigns her appreciation to gloss over her linguistic deficiency. She herself has read a haiku written in English and would like to share it with her mother, but she finds the task of translation daunting: "It was much more possible to say yes, yes." The mother's thoughts, by contrast, are presented only in speculative terms. We are told that she "must have been skeptical" about Rosie's comprehension and that (after Rosie's halfhearted compliment) she resumes composing, "either satisfied or seeing through the deception and resigned." Along with the daughter, we share the uncertainty implied by "must have been" and the either-or phrase. But the daughter's quandary prompts us to imagine the mother's parallel predicament:

Rosie's inability to share what she reads (in English) points to her mother's even greater frustration of being unable to share what she writes (in Japanese). The mother's creative activity must be largely a lone venture, for she cannot discuss her writing with either her daughter or, as we soon learn, her husband. Rosie's explicit responses will continue to serve as oblique analogues to her mother's hidden thoughts.

The daughter's immediate perspective and the mother's removed one set in motion two parallel plots. One recounts Rosie's adolescent experiences, particularly the joys and fears of incipient sexuality. The other describes the mother's increasing impulse to write and discuss haiku—a drive almost as insistent as sex. While we know from the beginning that the mother (Tome Hayashi), under the pseudonym Ume Hanazono, has become "an extravagant contributor" to a Japanese American newspaper, the narrator's tone, which reflects the "rosy" temperament of the daughter, diffuses the gravity of the suspended plot. (There is little distance between the breezy discourse of Rosie and that of the narrator.) Tome Hayashi and Ume Hanazono apparently lead a peaceful coexistence: the formidable amount of housework and fieldwork Hayashi performs does not deter Hanazono from writing. Only in retrospect do we register innuendoes. Use of a pseudonym is common among Japanese poets, yet the pen name also gives Hayashi a separate personality: she can write only when she assumes an identity independent of her husband's. The adjective "extravagant" further hints that even her daughter considers her poetic contribution to be a luxury incompatible with the exigencies in the "sweltering fields" where the mother picks tomatoes (cf. Wong). Finally, the narrator portrays Hanazono as a "muttering stranger," suggesting that the mother's poetic self is alien to both father and daughter, both of whom feel excluded from her creative life, which we learn was "very brief—perhaps three months at most." The reader is then left wondering about the cause of the mother's aborted creativity, but is "distracted" by Rosie's adolescent concerns. For instance, when the Hayashis visit the Hayanos, the new coat of one of the teenage daughters becomes the center of the discursive attention. The adults remain very much in the background, with Mr. Hayano and Mrs. Hayashi discussing haiku, Mr. Hayashi reading a magazine, and Mrs. Hayano sitting by herself. We share Rosie's puzzlement when Mr. Hayashi leaves abruptly, without even telling his wife. The episode exemplifies what Radner and Lanser call "distraction"—the muffling of a "feminist message [by] some kind of 'noise,' interference, or obscurity that will keep the message from being heard except by those who listen very carefully" (417–18). In this instance the "noise" is the girls' hoopla over clothing, a fittingly feminine preoccupation to provide an unspoken contrast to Mrs. Hayashi's "abnormal" obsession, one which incurs her husband's displeasure.

Although the minds of the couple remain closed, the author guides our response indirectly through the daughter's reaction. When Mrs. Hayashi rejoins her husband, she apologizes: "You know how I get when it's haiku . . . I forget what time it is." Watching her parents, Rosie feels "a rush of hate for both—for her mother for begging, for her father for denying her mother." Yamamoto suggests that unspeakable feelings similar to Rosie's may lurk beneath her mother's abject excuse and apparent contrition. Furthermore, when Rosie, in her anger, fantasizes a car collision leaving "three contorted, bleeding bodies, one of them hers," we are given a sidelong glance at the subdued conflict between her parents that will culminate in a real act of violence in which the three lives will indeed be enmeshed. Rosie, for all her internal agitation, remains quiet and demure on the surface. Like her parents, who refrain from speaking their minds in the child's presence, she has learned to contain her emotions.

No sooner has the parental conflict been intimated than it is upstaged by Rosie's first brush with the opposite sex, the focus of the next two sections. During a rendezvous in which Rosie meets Jesus Carrasco (the son of a Mexican couple who work for her family), she swoons by the book: "Kissed by Jesus, Rosie fell, for the first time, entirely victim to a helplessness delectable beyond speech." In itself the meeting between the youngsters heralds the beginning of love, but seen in retrospect against the adult plot, Rosie's budding romance is foreboding, even foredoomed (cf. Radner and Lanser on "juxtaposition" 416).

Rosie herself makes no connections. Returning to the

house after her newfound experience, she finds her mother talking with her relatives about a haiku competition. When she runs into her father, his gruffness makes her assume that he is cross with her. We suspect that he is upset instead at his wife's continuing interest in haiku, though we do not know the extent of his unstated disapproval, since Rosie—our source of information—is too dazed herself at this point to discern any parental discord. Daughter and mother alike are absorbed in self-discovery; preoccupied with love or art, they pay little, if any, attention to Mr. Hayashi's moodiness.

The two plots do not come together until the final section, in which again the focus falls initially on Rosie, who has been daydreaming about Jesus and feeling "grave and giddy by turns." When her father tells her that she must help sort tomatoes after school—"This heat's not doing them any good. And we've got no time for a break today"—it is the only time we hear Mr. Hayashi speak more than one sentence. Unremarkable as his words are, they prove portentous. The pressing tomato harvest is interrupted by the arrival of Mr. Kuroda, a newspaper editor who comes to inform Rosie's mother that she has won a haiku contest and who brings her the award—a *Hiroshige* print "sketched with delicate quickness." When Mrs. Hayashi invites him into the house for tea, the father utters his first explicit comment about his wife, or rather, about her artistic fervor, "Ha, your mother's crazy!" and soon asks Rosie to remind Mrs. Hayashi about the tomatoes. Finding her mother absorbed in the editor's exposition of a haiku theory, Rosie merely relays the message and returns to the field, where she and her father work on in silence. "But suddenly, her father uttered an incredible noise, exactly like the cork of a bottle popping, and the next Rosie knew, he was stalking angrily toward the house."

The hitherto muted plot explodes in a wrenching epiphany when Mr. Hayashi emerges with the picture, which he proceeds to destroy with an axe: "Smashing the picture, glass and all . . . he reached over the kerosene that was used to encourage the bath fire and poured it over the wreckage." Rosie rushes to the house and finds her mother, who appears "very calm," watching the fire through the window. Her frightening calm reveals the depths of her misery. Though her reaction to her husband's outrage is not told, the incinerated picture speaks for the way rage and despair consume her. The word "cremation" links object and person: the burning of the art object mirrors the expiring artist. We now understand why the mother's "life span" as a poet is so brief. In keeping with a tale spare in dialogue, the climax consists not in verbal confrontation but in a devastating action: the reader, like the daughter, is made to gaze in horror at the husband's wrath and the wife's desolation.

The two plots are then deftly conjoined. As mother and daughter watch the dying fire together, their lives are intertwined. Rosie, who has newly experienced the thrills of romance, must look squarely at her mother's chastening marriage and re-view her adolescent world through the darkening lens of Mrs. Hayashi's hindsight. When the mother asks, "Do you know why I married your father?" Rosie has a premonition that "the *telling* would combine with the other violence of the hot afternoon to level her life, her world to the very ground" (emphasis added). No longer condensing her private thoughts into a haiku, the mother reveals her secret past to the reluctant listener in a torrent of words. Her outpouring, like the father's reckless act, deviates from the code of emotional and verbal restraint observed thus far in the story.

Mrs. Hayashi's confession traces her endless heartaches back to a dire romance and spells a cautionary tale for Rosie. Pregnant by her lover in Japan, she could not marry because of their unequal social status (a factor also potentially dividing Rosie and Jesus, whose parents work for the Hayashis). Spurned by her family, she wed Mr. Hayashi as an alternative to suicide. Her child, had it not been stillborn, would have been seventeen. The number connects past bereavement with present loss. She may have tried to distill her grief into her nightly scribbles. But her creativity—poetry within seventeen syllables—is also prematurely doomed.

The mother's regrets run counter to the daughter's dreams and desires. The contesting emotions are superimposed in the dramatic last paragraph of the story:

> Suddenly, her mother knelt on the floor and took [Rosie] by the wrists. "Rosie," she said urgently, "Promise me you will

never marry!" Shocked more by the request than the revelation, Rosie stared at her mother's face. Jesus, Jesus, she called silently. . . . Promise, her mother whispered fiercely, promise. Yes, yes, I promise, Rosie said. But for an instant she turned away, and her mother, hearing the familiar glib agreement, released her. Oh, you, you, you, her eyes and twisted mouth said, you fool. Rosie, covering her face, began at last to cry, and the embrace and consoling hand came much later than she expected.

The passage poignantly double-tells. The mother's request, so unexpected in light of the Japanese conception of marriage as *giri* (obligation) and as "a natural stage in the course of one's life" (Yanagisako 95), underscores her thorough disillusionment with men. Deserted and stifled, Mrs. Hayashi tries to prevent her daughter from meeting the same fate. Yet her sudden kneeling, anxious clutching, and reiteration of "promise" oddly and ironically correspond to the posture, gesture, and entreaty of an ardent suitor proposing marriage.

Though not deaf to her mother's appeal, Rosie drifts into a romantic reverie at the very moment Mrs. Hayashi implores her to remain single. Rosie's reaction to the demand is couched in words that recall her recent sexual awakening. "Jesus" here is both a spontaneous exclamation and a conscious invocation of her beau, whose arousing grip contrasts with Mrs. Hayashi's tenacious clutch. "Yes, yes" recalls not only the double affirmative at the beginning of the story, when Rosie pretends to understand the workings of haiku, but also her first kiss with Jesus: "When he took hold of her empty hand . . . her vocabulary had become distressingly constricted and . . . all that remained intact now was yes and no and oh." The affirmative answer—albeit a hollow acquiescence extorted by the mother—also extends the proposal analogy (cf. Molly Bloom's famous response). As an earnest plea against marriage and as a travesty of a proposal, the passage pits Mrs. Hayashi's cynical wisdom against Rosie's dampened but inextinguishable hopes. Through Yamamoto's sleight of "hand," Mrs. Hayashi's embitterment and Rosie's initiation are together encapsulated in the delicate understatement that concludes the story. The tactile images—"the embrace and consoling hand"—once

170

more recall Rosie's encounter with Jesus, but the timing here tells much more. The disconsolate mother, taking umbrage at Rosie's insincere reply, cannot bring herself to hug her sobbing daughter immediately. The image of delayed embrace, as Stan Yogi observes, also "suggests the maturity that Mrs. Hayashi now expects of her daughter, who has been initiated into the excitement, pain, and disillusionment of adult life." Yamamoto condenses meaning at once through verbal echoes and by dramatizing nonverbal interaction.

III

In "Yoneko's Earthquake," the manifest plot describes a young girl's passing crush on a farmhand and her contingent, short-lived, Christian faith. The latent plot hints at her mother's secret love affair with the same man and her eventual conversion to Christianity. But unlike the submerged plot of "Seventeen Syllables," which flows along with the story and swells up at the end, the second plot in "Yoneko's Earthquake" is completely and persistently masked.

A third-person limited point of view makes the opaqueness possible: we see the story through the eyes of ten-year-old Yoneko Hosoume, the eponymous protagonist. By imitating the haphazard manner of the child, the narrator drops telling hints as though they were random digressions. For instance, the seemingly trivial anecdote at the opening of the story, in which Yoneko's brother, Seigo, mistakes her sister's praying posture for an outburst of grief, reminds us that perception often falls short. Just as Seigo misreads his older sister's religious posture, Yoneko fails to understand a series of adult gestures.

Through Yoneko's evaluations of Marpo (the Filipino farmhand who works for her family) and her mother, we learn that both adults are remarkably attractive. Yoneko idolizes Marpo and enumerates at length his multiple accomplishments as Christian, farmworker, athlete, musician, artist, and radio technician. We suspect that such a versatile man charms not only little Yoneko but older members of her sex as well. Through Yoneko we also learn that Mrs. Hosoume is a rare beauty: "she had once heard someone comparing her mother to 'a dewy, half-opened rosebud.'" The seductive

Mrs. Hosoume surely has other admirers besides her daughter. We infer the likelihood of mutual attraction between the two adults from Yoneko's adoration for both. An affair between the two presumably begins around the time when there is an earthquake and also a car accident in which Mr. Hosoume is apparently rendered impotent in a car accident. Unable to farm since the accident, he is confined to the house while Marpo and Mrs. Hosoume work in the field and run errands together. We get our first hint of intimacy between the two when Mrs. Hosoume gives Yoneko a ring, saying, "If your father asks where you got it, say you found it on the street."

Neither the affair nor Mr. Hosoume's impotence is openly told, since Yoneko cannot fathom the sexual dynamics in the adult world. For Yoneko, whom Marpo has converted to Christianity, the greatest consequence of the earthquake is her loss of faith in God: her belief is permanently shaken when her fervent prayers seem unheeded during the prolonged heavings. Because of her highstrung reaction, the whole household refers to the disaster as "Yoneko's Earthquake." Only toward the end do we discover that the earthquake also has had physical and emotional aftershocks for Yoneko's parents and Marpo.

We can see the key events that follow only darkly, as through an ill-lit scrim, by connecting the isolated details furnished by the naive narrator. One day Marpo disappears abruptly "without even saying good-bye to Yoneko and Seigo." On that day the Hosoumes, quite out of their weekday routine, go to the city. Driving at top speed, Mr. Hosoume hits a collie: "The car jerked with the impact, but Mr. Hosoume drove right on." When the parents emerge from the hospital, the mother is "obviously in pain," which she attributes to "some necessarily astringent treatment." The father admonishes the children to keep the excursion a secret.

The description of the trip to the hospital resonates with the parents' untold agitations. The unblinking killing of the collie, which symbolizes the life to be disposed of at the hospital, evinces the father's indignation at the liaison between Marpo and Mrs. Hosoume and his indifference to the life about to be destroyed. By contrast, Yoneko's unspoken pity for the animal reflects her mother's unspeakable grief. Mrs. Hosoume must have cringed inwardly while witnessing the act that foreshadows the fate of her unborn child. As in the picture-burning scene, extreme emotions are conveyed by remarkable verbal economy: we are made to react to what has not been said.

The "pregnant" silence remains unbroken. Yoneko never learns about the abortion; nor can she connect Marpo's departure with the visit to the hospital. Like Rosie, who has been too absorbed in her own romance to notice the discord between her parents, Yoneko is too hurt herself by Marpo's "abrupt desertion" to discern her mother's heartbreak. Only after Seigo has suddenly died of illness does Yoneko notice that her mother, who has "swollen eyes in the morning for weeks afterwards," is "inconsolable." Yoneko attributes her mother's distress to Seigo's death, but the author has intimated additional causes. The mother is mourning for not one but two lives and perhaps also for her absent lover.

At the end Mrs. Hosoume, seeking to teach Yoneko a lesson, adumbrates a causal link between the two premature deaths, but her cryptic moral is lost on her daughter:

> "Never kill a person, Yoneko, because if you do, God will take from you someone you love."
>
> "Oh, that," said Yoneko quickly, "I don't believe in that, I don't believe in God." . . . She had believed for a moment that her mother was going to ask about the ring (which, alas, she had lost already, somewhere in the flumes along the cantaloupe patch).

Both Mrs. Hosoume's "Never kill a person" and Mrs. Hayashi's "Promise me you will never marry" are at once direct imperatives to the daughters and oblique indictments of the husbands. The verbal constructions fall under the category of "hedging," or strategies "for equivocating about or weakening a message" (Radner and Lanser 420). But while Mrs. Hayashi and Mrs. Hosoume avoid explicitly referring to their husbands, they also heighten the blame, the one by denouncing men categorically if circuitously, the other by viewing her presumably involuntary abortion as an act of "killing" by the husband.

Like the conclusion of "Seventeen Syllables," this ending adroitly welds together the juvenile and adult plots. Yoneko has been converted by Marpo to Christianity, though she loses her faith soon enough; her mother, a nonbeliever at the beginning, has become a devout Christian since Seigo's death. That the latter conversion, too, may be brought about by Marpo is left implicit. Marpo's departure affects both mother and daughter, but Mrs. Hosoume's sorrow far exceeds Yoneko's fleeting sadness, no more lasting than her religious belief. The ring, to the daughter a mere trinket, must signify for the mother an inner tumult as intense as the earthquake that shattered Yoneko's faith.

IV

What Showalter calls "double-voiced discourse" certainly informs these two stories, in which the muted sufferings of the mothers emerge belatedly. But Yamamoto's plots also monitor male silences. If mothers and daughters in the two stories often talk at cross-purposes, communication between fathers and daughters is altogether restricted. In the few instances in which the fathers do speak, the tone is generally peremptory or critical. Interaction between the spouses is scarcely better. Yet the tight-lipped husbands, ostensibly "guardians of the prison doors" (Kim 99), are themselves bound by patriarchal conventions.

Since Japanese American patriarchy, no less than Japanese American silence, is inflected by both history and culture, framing the two stories within historical and cultural contexts brings out the paternal contour of each muted plot. The first waves of Japanese immigrants (1885–1910) consisted mainly of single men who, after establishing themselves in the new country, sought wives either by returning to Japan or by exchanging photos across the Pacific.[3] The "picture brides" who came to America by the latter means (mostly between 1910 and 1920) were generally ten to fifteen years younger than their husbands. Trickery through long-distance marriage was not uncommon: men often "forwarded photographs taken in their youth or touched up ones that concealed their real age" (Ichioka 347). Judging from Mrs. Hayashi's confession at the end of "Seventeen Syllables," we can suppose that Mr. Hayashi, "who was never told why his unseen betrothed was so eager to hasten the day of meeting," was himself deceived.

We can also see that while the husbands strictly abide by the Confucian code demanding implicit respect from children to parents, and from wife to husband, their young wives and children have begun to demand greater independence. The difference may be due to disparity in age and temperament; but it may also be traced to the altered status of Japanese males in America, which was intensely anti-Oriental at the time.[4] As farmers preoccupied with survival in a hostile environment, Mr. Hayashi and Mr. Hosoume are understandably earthbound, as reflected in Mr. Hayashi's overwhelming concern for the tomatoes and Mr. Hosoume's humorless refusal to let Yoneko make fudge because "sugar was not a plaything" (51–52). They can find the writing of poetry only "extravagant" and the application of cosmetics "gaudy."

Governed by a code of masculinity that calls for rigorous self-restraint, the two men mostly keep their disquiet to themselves. While reticence is traditionally inculcated in both Japanese men and women, men in particular have been taught that any "outward appearance that is boisterous, excessively emotional, visibly passionate, obviously fearful . . . is distasteful and itself shameful, fit perhaps only for children." (Lyman 52; see also Miyamoto 31–32, 40–42). Wakako Yamauchi, a contemporary of Yamamoto, alludes to this masculine code when she illustrates the socialization of Benji, the nine-year-old nisei protagonist in "Handkerchief": "It had occurred to Benji to talk to Papa about . . . his unhappiness, his loneliness . . . no, not that. Loneliness was a weakness, a man didn't expose that soft underside. Papa was a man, airtight, strong . . . a man of few words, fewer emotions. . . . And if you said, 'I hurt,' it had to be something Papa could see—a ragged wound" (146–47). While this notion of manhood is not specific to Japanese and Japanese Americans, cultural rules reinforce the taciturn manners of Mr. Hayashi and Mr. Hosoume.[5] The fathers' stories are told even more indirectly than the mothers'. Whereas the subjective responses of the daughters reflect the mothers' hidden passions, only the daughters' off-hand observations suggest the fathers' woes. Nevertheless, both narratives are punctuated with sufficient hints to indicate that mounting masculine anxiety, not habitual insensitivity, sparks violence. The seemingly impassive Mr. Hayashi may in fact be plagued by loneliness, inadequacy, and jealousy, though none of these feelings have been openly admitted by the character or noted by the narrator. The narrator does mention, however, that Mr. Hayashi and his wife used to play cards together before retiring jointly and that as a result of Mrs. Hayashi's new interest, he has to "resort to solitaire." Since Mrs. Hayashi composes late into the night, we may further assume that her husband now goes to bed alone. His annoyance during the visit to the Hayanos obviously emanates from his feeling of exclusion from the intellectual discussion. But the reader may deduce jealousy as an additional provocation. Mr. Hayano, whose wife has already lost both health and beauty, is himself "handsome, tall, and strong," at least in Rosie's eyes. Buzzing through the elisions is the suggestion that not fatigue (the reason voiced by Mrs. Hayashi) but jealousy drives Mr. Hayashi away. Mrs. Hayashi's former lover was a man of a higher social class than she; Mr. Hayashi—a farmer—is of a lower class than his wife's family. He may feel troubled by Mrs. Hayashi's verbal sophistication—itself a reminder of their disparate class origins. Above all, he may have sensed a compatibility or suspected a bond—physical and intellectual—between his wife and Mr. Hayano which is absent from both of the marriages.

Mr. Hosoume's behavior also suggests that his male pride is chafed by an unspeakable failure—his sexual impotence. Out of his sense of injured manhood he grumbles about his children's disrespect, slaps his wife for contradicting him, and threatens to fire Marpo for interfering. Furthermore, he links everyone's "impudent" behavior to his "illness," betraying an obsessive anxiety. Given that he thinks his family is turning against him out of scorn, his wife's love affair and ensuing pregnancy must be an ultimate affront to his masculine image. His aggression on the way to the hospital can be better understood in the light of his mortification: the fetus is an irksome reminder at once of cuckoldry and impotence.

Mr. Hosoume's manner softens noticeably after the abor-

176

tion, for he is able to resume, literally, his role as the "supporter" of his now feeble wife. He even becomes "very gentle" toward her during her long bout of dejection after Seigo's death. Sadly enough, these tender moments can take place only when she is falling apart physically and emotionally, and when Mr. Hosoume is no longer threatened by her insubordination. But that does not mean that his own suffering has diminished. Seigo's death is no less a blow to the father than to the mother and is perhaps another ironic turn in the muted drama of masculine anxiety. The warning of divine retribution that Mrs. Hosoume gives to her daughter applies to her husband with withering vengeance: he has lost his only male heir and can never have another.

To mitigate the initial negative impressions of Mr. Hayashi and Mr. Hosoume is not to condone their actions but to show that their behavior deserves more sympathetic analysis than dismissal as the general "failure of the [issei] fathers," (Crow, "*Issei* Father" 34). Had the fathers been able to reveal their vulnerability, the tragic endings might have been averted; instead they *gaman* till their escalated anger erupts in violence. Meanwhile, their taciturnity may have widened the gap between themselves and their spouses, who not surprisingly become drawn to the likes of Mr. Hayano, Mr. Kuroda, and Marpo; physical and intellectual attractions aside, these men communicate verbally with the women.

The two stories may have encoded Yamamoto's own ambivalence toward her cultural inheritance. Her naive narrators, embodying the free spirits of the young nisei, highlight the rigid conventions that riddle the lives of issei women and men. Seen through the startled or uncomprehending eyes of bicultural daughters who must soon come to grips with their maternal legacies, the mothers' private sorrow and the fathers' brooding rage reverberate ominously. At the same time, Yamamoto's stylistic restraint pays a tacit tribute to those cultural forerunners who can say more in less, who can funnel vast meaning and feeling into seventeen syllables.[6] Her strategy of double-telling is especially suited to evoking suppressed feelings, revealing the anxieties and hurts that lie beneath the surface of language. The hushed climax of each story is captured in a verbal snapshot. By zooming in on the deliberate destruction of the Hiroshige and on the steady crushing of the collie, she transmits and transmutes the characters' unspoken emotions through her own articulate silence.

 Notes ■

This article is adapted from King-Kok Cheung, *Articulate Silences: Hisaye Yamamoto, Maxine Hong Kingston, Joy Kogawa* (Ithaca, N.Y.: Cornell University Press, 1993).

1. Yamamoto believes that "there is something in the nature of the Nisei" which checks the impulse to write: "For a writer proceeds from a compulsion to communicate a vision and he cannot afford to bother with what people in general think of him. We Nisei, discreet, circumspect, care very much what others think of us" ("Writing").

2. Yanagisako observes that "at the same time that Japanese American families were formed through Issei marriage, Japanese family relationships were transported. . . . Issei marriages were from the beginning embedded in families that crossed national boundaries" (29).

3. The practice, an extension of social customs in Japan, was denounced as immoral by American Exclusionists and was terminated in 1921 (Ichioka 342–43).

4. Discriminatory laws such as the Alien Land Acts of 1913 and 1920 in California made Japanese and other Asians "aliens ineligible for citizenship" and prevented them from owning lands. Some bought lands under the names of their American-born children.

5. Speaking of Mr. Hayashi in an interview, Yamamoto said that "he was only acting the way he'd been brought up to act, the way men were supposed to be" (Crow, "MELUS Interview" 80).

6. Yamamoto reveals that although all the details in "Seventeen Syllables" are invented, it is based on the story of her own mother, a writer of *senryo,* a form of satirical verse that contains seventeen syllables (Koppelman 162).

 Works Cited ■

Crow, Charles L. "The *Issei* Father in the Fiction of Hisaye Yamamoto." *Opening Up Literary Criticism: Essays on American*

Prose and Poetry. Edited by Leo Truchlar. Salzburg, Austria: Verlag Wolfgang Neugebauer, 1986. 34–40.

———. "A MELUS Interview: Hisaye Yamamoto." *MELUS* 14:1 (1987): 73–84.

Friedman, Susan Stanford. "The Return of the Repressed in Women's Narratives." *Journal of Narrative Technique* 19:1 (1989): 141–156.

Fujita, Gayle K. "To Attend the Sound of Stone: The Sensibility of Silence in *Obasan.*" *MELUS* 12:3 (1985): 33–42.

Ichioka, Yuji. "*Amerika Nadeshiko*: Japanese Immigrant Women in the United States, 1900–1924." *Pacific Historical Review* 59:2 (1980): 339–357.

Kikumura, Akemi. *Through Harsh Winters: The Life of a Japanese Immigrant Woman.* Novato, California: Chandler & Sharp, 1981.

Kikumura, Akemi, and Harry H. L. Kitano. "The Japanese American Family." *Ethnic Families in America: Patterns and Variations.* 2nd ed. Edited by Charles H. Mindel and Robert W. Habenstein. New York: Elsevier, 1981. 49–60.

Kim, Elaine H. "Defining Asian American Realities Through Literature," *Cultural Critique* 6 (Spring 1987): 87–111.

Kitano, Harry H. *Japanese Americans: The Evolution of a Subculture.* Englewood Cliffs, N.J.: Prentice-Hall, 1969.

Koppelman, Susan, ed. *Between Mothers and Daughters: Stories across a Generation.* Old Westbury, N.Y.: Feminist Press, 1985.

Lakoff, Robin. *Language and Woman's Place.* New York: Harper, 1975.

Lyman, Stanford M. "Generation and Character: the Case of the Japanese Americans." *Roots: An Asian American Reader.* Edited by Amy Tachiki et al. Los Angeles: UCLA Asian American Studies Center, 1971. 48–71.

Miyamoto, S. Frank. "Problems of Interpersonal Style among the Nisei." *Amerasia Journal* 13:2 (1986–1987): 29–45.

O'Barr, William M., and Bowman K. Atkins. "'Women's Language' or 'Powerless Language'?" *Women and Language in Literature and Society.* Edited by Sally McConnell-Ginet, Ruth Borker, and Nelly Furman. New York: Praeger, 1980. 93–110.

Radner, Joan and Susan Lanser, "The Feminist Voice: Coding in Women's Folklore and Literature," *Journal of American Folklore* 100 (October–December 1987): 412–425.

Schweik, Susan. "The 'Pre-Poetics' of Internment: The Example of Toyo Suyemoto." *American Literary History* (Spring 1989): 89–109.

Showalter, Elaine. "Feminist Criticism in the Wilderness." *Writing and Sexual Difference*. Edited by Elizabeth Abel. Chicago: University of Chicago Press, 1982. 9–35.

Wetzel, Patricia J. "Are 'Powerless' Communication Strategies the Japanese Norm?" *Language in Society* 17:4 (1988): 555–564.

Wong, Sau-ling Cynthia. "Necessity and Extravagance in Maxine Hong Kingston's *The Woman Warrior*: Art and the Ethnic Experience." MELUS 15:1 (1988): 3–26.

Yamamoto, Hisaye. Letter to the author, 9 June 1988.

———. *Seventeen Syllables and Other Stories*. Latham, N.Y.: Kitchen Table Press, 1988.

———. "Writing." *Amerasia Journal* 3:2 (1976): 126–133.

Yamauchi, Wakako. "Handkerchief." *Amerasia Journal* 4:1 (1977): 143–150.

Yanagisako, Sylvia Junko. *Transforming the Past: Tradition and Kinship among Japanese Americans*. Stanford: Stanford University Press, 1985.

Yogi, Stan. "Legacies Revealed: Uncovering Buried Plots in the Stories of Hisaye Yamamoto." *Studies in American Fiction* 17:2 (1989): 169—181.

☐ DONALD C. GOELLNICHT ■

Transplanted Discourse in Yamamoto's "Seventeen Syllables"

I'm sure the Japanese tradition has had a great influence
on my writing since my parents brought it with them
from Japan and how could they not help but transmit it
to us? I even wonder if I would have been a writer at all
without this tradition to go by, since most of my stories
seem to deal with this interaction of the Japanese
tradition with the American experience.
(YAMAMOTO, quoted in McDonald and Newman)

Criticism of Hisaye Yamamoto's short stories often focuses on gender and generational differences within Japanese American families (see, for example, Kim 157–163). Conflicts based on class that may impinge on or intertwine with gender and generational conflicts have tended to pass unnoticed, perhaps because they are usually embedded in the subtext of the Issei narratives rather than appearing on the surface of the Nisei center of consciousness. "Seventeen Syllables" provides a valuable case in point, as Yamamoto skillfully weaves issues and motifs of class and gender that originate in the Old World/ Mother Culture with generational issues of cross-cultural conflict that are unique to the immigrants' New World/America.[1] Scholarship which has focused on this text, however, has not usually picked up the nuances of subtle overlapping. Susan Koppelman, for example, treats the story as a feminist tract in her collection *Between Mothers and Daughters: Stories Across a Generation,* where she discusses it under the heading "Mothers and Daughters Up Against the Patriarchy":

> Where there is no true freedom, there can be no true love. Mothers know that, especially mothers who are the victims of multiple oppressions. Daughters feeling the first stirrings of the flesh in their early adolescence, and befuddled by the myth of romantic love, often do not. Because the choice between loyalty to oneself and loyalty to a beloved is not one a free person should have to make, and because the daughters do not yet understand that in the patriarchy women are not free persons, they often resent their mothers for whatever choices are urged on them (as in . . . "Seventeen Syllables"). (xvii)

Although I do not wish to take issue with the general sentiments expressed here, I do want to emphasize that the story is much more complex in its treatment of gender conflict than this critical comment implies, and much of that complexity originates in class conflict that is almost invisible to the story's center of consciousness, the teenage Rosie, but which the subtlety of Yamamoto's art allows us, as readers, to see.[2] We gain a clear vision of the cultural specificity grounding this story, however, only if we appreciate the traditional Japanese culture *and* the historical conditions of Japanese Americans depicted in the story's present.

Yamamoto introduces class difference into the story through different discourse levels among the Japanese speakers and writers. The title itself signals this theme by evoking the poetic discourse of *haiku,* a motif which is then (re)presented as the voice of the urbane, upper-class, educated, artistic Japanese. Unbeknownst to either her husband or her daughter, the writing of *haiku* connects Tome Hayashi to her long-hidden love affair in Japan with a young man from a higher class. Class differences prevented her from marrying this lover, as she finally tells her daughter, Rosie, at the end. The narrator reports the story as if it were a series of facts from a teen magazine:

> At eighteen she had been in love with the first son of one of
> the well-to-do families in her village. The two had met when-
> ever and wherever they could, secretly, because it would not
> have done for his family to see him favor her—her father had
> no money; he was a drunkard and a gambler besides. She had
> learned she was with child; an excellent match had already
> been arranged for her lover. Despised by her family, she had
> given premature birth to a stillborn son, who would be sev-
> enteen now.

The emotional flatness in this description, which masks the
horror of Tome's situation, testifies to Tome's resigned despair
and to Rosie's attempted refusal to let this narrative "level her
life" as she holds open the cultural gap between her "American" self and her "Japanese" mother. Although this explanation of the mother's ambition figures strategically at the end of
the story, flooding us, the readers, with knowledge, her desire
for a better, higher-class life is marked from the outset by her
writing *haiku* under "the blossoming pen name, Ume Hanazono." The term "blossoming" links this persona to pregnancy,
and the fact that the stillborn child she had for her lover in
Japan would now be seventeen years old if he had lived welds
the child to the *haiku* poems of seventeen syllables Tome Hayashi writes in America. Writing *haiku* in the language of
the artistic, leisured class represents a displaced desire for the
child, lover, and life she lost years before. The fact that the
mother's writing career "was very brief," aborted after "three
months at most" strengthens the connection between her poetry and her stillborn child. The imaginary world of *haiku*,
which she enters by means of her expensive "pale green Parker" pen, separates Tome from her strenuous life as a housewife and laborer on a vegetable farm in southern California, a
life shared with a husband of simple mind who obviously
comes from a lower standing than herself.

The stillborn son in Japan may also signal the
death(liness) of traditional Japanese culture based on rigid
class and language differences; a striking example of such
closed mores is the rule of primogeniture, which dictates that
the first-born son uphold family and class traditions as he will
inherit the family property. Subsequent sons, virtually disin-

183

herited under this system, could escape its entrapment by emigrating to America, but Tome was unfortunately involved with a "first son," and she is the one forced to flee because her class does not make her an acceptable match for the family of her lover. The constriction of this traditional system becomes represented in the rigidity of the *haiku* form itself, with its three-line, five-seven-five syllable structure—patiently explained by Tome to her daughter at the start of the story—to which the freedom-seeking, American-born Rosie cannot relate except with giggles and deception. Tome's temporary devotion to *haiku* is clearly an attempt to adopt a veneer of sophisticated, urbane speech in order to prove herself good enough for the wealthy Japanese family of her lover, by whom she was originally rejected; but it is also an attempt to cover the deeply repressed emotions of her early passion and the intense feelings of loss for her stillborn child.

To appreciate fully Yamamoto's brilliant use of *haiku* as a structuring device in the story it is necessary to detour momentarily to explore the background of this literary form. Begun in the sixteenth century as the opening part (*hokku*) of a longer, group-composed poetic form called *haikai renga,* *haiku* had during the sixteenth century gained respect as a literary form on its own; by the late nineteenth century it was a revered but rule-bound poetic structure. As Makoto Ueda observes: "The poets . . . were not only restricted by the rules, but also wanted to increase the number of restrictive rules. This was in a way a necessity under the circumstances, because the number of people who wrote *hokku* ["starting verse," as *haiku* was still called until the late nineteenth century] as a pastime had greatly increased, and these amateurs wanted to have sophisticated rules to play what they considered an urbane game" (4). The Japanese government appointed certain contemporary *haiku* masters to posts "as National Preceptors, a rank normally allotted to Shinto and Buddhist priests" (6); they in turn pronounced particular *haiku* schools and lineages to be legitimate, so that the link between *haiku* and the biological blood-lines that dictate social class are strong. To be sure, great debate surged at the end of the nineteenth and start of the twentieth centuries about modern approaches to *haiku* that advocated breaking the rules, even abandoning the 5-7-5 syllabic structure in favor of free verse; but the result, by 1920, was the triumph of a new conservatism, presided over by Takahama Kyoshi, the dictatorial editor of the highly influential literary magazine *Cuckoo (Hototogisu)*. "In his view anyone who chooses to write in the haiku form has chosen to put himself against the background of the classical haiku poets and their works. 'Haiku is a type of literature in which form is a pre-determined factor,' Kyoshi observed. 'Its life depends on its classical flavour'" (Ueda 11) or its inherited legitimacy that is guaranteed by obedience to the rules. These "rules" require that *haiku* should contain a "season word" (*kigo*);[3] as Harold G. Henderson observes, it should also include some reference to nature and should deal with a particular occurrence that is in the act of happening (Henderson, quoted in Cohen 19).

This background casts Tome Hayashi's attempted "rebellion" through writing poetry into new relief. First, it is well known that immigrant cultures, like the Japanese American, tend for reasons of preservation and nostalgia to be even more conservative than the mother culture they have left, or at least to cling to the traditional elements of that transplanted culture. I believe that Tome Hayashi does precisely this, a point that Yamamoto emphasizes by having the narrator observe that Rosie's "mother was writing the *haiku* for a daily newspaper, the *Mainichi Shimbun*, that was published in San Francisco. Los Angeles, to be sure, was closer to the farming community in which the Hayashi family lived and several Japanese vernaculars were printed there, but Rosie's parents said they preferred the tone of the northern paper." Tome is attracted to the conservative, urbane "Japanese" tradition and sophistication represented by San Francisco rather than to the free-wheeling "American" vulgarity of nearby Los Angeles.

Further, Rosie knows that because of her mother's artistic and linguistic conservatism—her mother hardly speaks any English and no French—she would not find amusing the irreverent and avant garde *haiku* in English and French that Rosie discovers in the back of one of her mother's literary magazines from Japan—a sign that the mother culture forges ahead of the immigrant one. This *haiku* delights Rosie, at least in part because of its multicultural nature, but she knows she cannot share it with her mother. The poem reads:

> It is morning, and lo!
> I lie awake, comme il faut,
> sighing for some dough.

The absence of a season word, the concern with material conditions rather than with a moment of insight into nature, the use of colloquialism and humor, all help to cast this poem as closer to *senryu*, which uses the same 5-7-5 syllabic form, than to traditional *haiku*, a fact that registers class distinctions of which Rosie is unaware, although she seems to intuit such distinctions when she withholds the poem from her mother. As Yagi Kametaro explains:

> Haiku was a bourgeois literature but it required some depth of learning and used refined language so it was considered to belong to "people of taste" (*furyujin*). On the other hand, *senryu*, which used colloquial Japanese and often vulgarisms and was classified as humorous—intended to make one smile or even burst into laughter—spread among the general populace. As a result, *senryu* has been regarded as inferior and has been neglected by devotees of haiku.
>
> (72)

In obvious contrast to Rosie's favorite, the *haiku* her mother is writing at the start of the story tries "to capture the charm of a kitten, as well as comment on the superstition that owning a cat of three colors meant good luck." Tome's artistic and social conservatism are depicted in layers of depth: her use of Japanese, of traditional subject matter, and even of superstition as she attempts to give a legitimacy to her present creativity that was denied to her former one, her illegitimate, stillborn child. Tome's *haiku*—which the narrator describes but never reproduces for us—acts, then, as a synecdoche for the absent presence of the traditional mother culture of Japan which, Yamamoto suggests, continues to circulate in the form

186

of cultural artifacts, but which, like the lost child, can never be genuinely reproduced or re-presented in the new immigrant culture. *Haiku* can, of course, be written, but it will of necessity be Japanese American rather than Japanese. The impossibility of re-presencing the "pure," "originary" culture both heightens and renders futile Tome's sense of loss and nostalgia.

I do not stress these elements of the narrative, however, to belittle the hardship and abuse Tome Hayashi suffers. Her story of tragic love does expose the Japanese system of patriarchy that dictates her worth in the commodity exchange that is traditional marriage. According to this system, she was not a valuable enough commodity for exchange with the high-class family of her lover, which sought to cement an alliance with a family of its own class, thus securing its social standing; at the same time, her lover tragically robbed her of the one commodity that is of value to a woman in the marriage market of any class: Tome's virginity. Thus, romantic love failed Tome in a marriage system that places very little value on individual desire, and she was left with the terrifying choices of suicide or marriage (as a picture bride) to a man in America she had never seen, but whose lower-class standing as a farmer guaranteed he would accept her devalued worth.[4]

This traditional system of marriage embedded within a rigid structure of class and gender divisions is the subtext of her mother's plea to Rosie never to marry, but Rosie, born and raised in America and thus cut off from the nuances of Japanese culture and discourse, fails at the outset to understand either her mother's oppression or her father's rage and sense of helplessness at her mother's pretension. Rosie does have some vague sense of her mother's desire for a more cultured life: she recognizes that Mr. Kuroda, the *haiku* editor for the *Mainichi Shimbun* who visits their farm to deliver Tome's prize, speaks "a more elegant Japanese than she [Rosie] was used to," and that when the editor arrives her mother begins to speak "the language of Mr. Kuroda." But Rosie cannot comprehend the effect of this class difference on her father, his feelings of helplessness, inferiority, and rage that result in his violent burning of Tome's *haiku* prize, the Hiroshige print which is itself a synecdoche for the cultivated life of the edu-

187

cated Japanese. Although he does not know the details of his wife's tragic love story, the print acts a reminder of everything he is not. As someone who is himself occupying a "feminine" subject position in relation to white America, oppressed by a racism that is never overtly depicted in the story, he feels particularly threatened by his wife's class-conscious pretensions, which he interprets as an attempt to undermine his masculine authority.[5] The subtlety of Yamamoto's art allows us to see beyond Rosie's naive perspective to appreciate the father's feeling of helplessness and defeat, while still sympathizing with the mother for the psychological and physical violence inflicted on her.[6]

It is ironic—even contradictory—then, that Tome's aspirations to authorship should find expression in her writing *haiku*. The contradiction emerges from the discrepancy between her desire for authority over some part of her life, an unconscious act of rebellion against the control of her husband by moving outside his domain and class, away from his sphere of patriarchal influence in an attempt to author(ize) her own narrative—or so her artistic life can be interpreted—and the very traditional form that desire takes: *haiku*, which, as she practices it, is a highly constricted, rule-bound structure that imposes discipline and authority that might be seen as parallel to, rather than swerving away from, the domination of her husband. A second level of irony can be remarked in the disjunction between *haiku* as the public symbol of *culture* in the story and *haiku* as the vehicle for an intimate, spontaneous relationship of the individual to *nature*. Writing haiku may be, in part, Tome's private attempt to view nature as less dreary and less tied to the material means of production—the tomato farm—by framing it in the literary conventions that are closely linked to Zen Buddhism's notions of *satori* or sudden awakening through an appreciation of the mystery and wonder of the natural world (Cohen 28). Perhaps most ironic of all, the appeal of *haiku* for someone like Tome may be revealed in Kyoshi's belief "that haiku, with its traditional form and rules, presupposed a certain specific attitude toward life on the part of the poet. Haiku poets, he thought, look at life with 'a detachment of mind,' which makes it possible for them to bear with, or even enjoy, sad moments of life" (Ueda 11).

Tome could be taking refuge in a literary form the very ideology of which reaffirms her entrapment through its predilection toward melancholia and stoic acceptance.[7]

It is interesting, then, that critics have noted similarities between Tome's bid for liberty and independence through *haiku* and Mrs. Hosoume's rebellion against her husband through her love affair with Marpo, the Filipino farmhand employed by her husband, in Yamamoto's equally compelling and subtle story "Yoneko's Earthquake" (see McDonald and Newman 28; Kim 162). Far from being similar, the two attempts at liberation appear to me to be diametrically opposed. Tome Hayashi's "rebellion" is in fact an attempt to return to the mother culture—albeit at a station above her present one—a desire to be absorbed into, even praised by, the elite and traditional world of Japanese prints, poetry magazines, literary pen-names, and cultured conversation on the theories of writing seventeen-syllable poems. Mrs. Hosoume's bid for freedom, on the other hand, involves travelling beyond her culture into the arms of a Filipino laborer; it involves rejection of a passionless marriage and the embrace of sensual pleasure and risk in a cross-cultural relationship that could be seen as quintessentially American, and which bears a closer resemblance to Rosie Hayashi's infatuation with Jesus, the Mexican American son of farm laborers, than to her mother's pretensions to artistic liberty. On another level, Tome Hayashi's desire to transcend her husband's narrow world of field labor implicitly carries with it a rejection of the very means of production that afford her some leisure to write (the narrator labels her "an extravagant contributor" to magazines), while Mrs. Hosoume's uniting with Marpo to run her husband's farm reveals her sense of solidarity with the working class, the alliance of two oppressed groups—women and landless labor—in an attempt to undermine the hegemony of the patriarchy.[8] Tome Hayashi aspires/retreats to the discourse of elitist tradition, swapping the authority of her husband for that of the urbane Mr. Kuroda—she "fall[s] easily into his style"; Mrs. Hosoume, on the other hand, advances to a new discourse of the body, of American multiculturalism that at least holds the promise of racial, class, and gender equality, although she fails to hold this bold new position when challenged by Japanese patriarchy. Mrs. Hosoume is horrified at her husband's accusation that she is *nama-iki,* insolent—a term "used only with women and children, to indicate that they are out of line" (Yogi 148)—and so she succumbs to his demand that she abort Marpo's child. Mr. Hosoume thus reasserts his patriarchal authority over his wife's body through language; his invoking of Japanese discourse to combat her potential "Americanness" is especially significant. He must demand the abortion for, just as the stillborn child in "Seventeen Syllables" would have signalled the failure of the traditional Japanese class system, a child of Mrs. Hosoume's and Marpo's would represent a challenge to the traditional race and class distinctions on which Mr. Hosoume's power is based. Comparison of these two stories brings us to the recognition that in "Seventeen Syllables" Yamamoto skillfully weaves a web of dialectical contradictions in which apparently "feminist" desires for liberation reveal themselves to be in alliance with bourgeois power.

Although the polite constriction of Tome's poetic discourse encourages the sublimation of repressed emotion into artistic form, I should remark that the silent rage and wordless explosions of Mr. Hayashi—"her father uttered an incredible noise, exactly like the cork of a bottle popping" before he "smash[ed] the [Hiroshige] picture, glass and all (she heard the explosion faintly)"—do not seem any more successful at dealing with passionate feelings. Paradoxically, the language-lessness of Rosie's and Jesus's youthful passion *does* appear to be the most healthy expression of emotion in the story: "she could find no words to protest; her vocabulary had become distressingly constricted. . . . Thus, kissed by Jesus, Rosie fell for the first time entirely victim to a helplessness delectable beyond speech." It is only the discourse of the body that manages momentarily to subvert the repressive order of symbolic language. "But the terrible, beautiful sensation lasted no more than a second" before Rosie too retreats behind the gender, race, and class taboos that forbid a Japanese American girl whose father owns a farm from becoming romantically involved with a Mexican American boy whose parents are farm laborers, an inverted repetition of the class distinctions suffered by her mother as a young woman in Japan. An American multicultural emotion that transcends the barriers of traditional discourse is glimpsed for a moment—and even returns briefly to Rosie as a sweet memory at the end—but is ultimately snatched away. In her subtle paralleling and reversal of the class differences between Rosie and Jesus with those between her mother and her first lover in Japan, Yamamoto not only critiques the restrictive Japanese system, she also complicates and interrogates the promise of "America" as a more egalitarian society by demonstrating the negative effects of traditional discourse systems on the emergent immigrant culture.

☐ *Notes* ■

I wish to thank King-Kok Cheung, whose enabling criticisms helped improve this paper.

1. By "class" I mean a subtle and complex interplay of such factors as family standing, wealth, occupation, and education. As Elaine Kim points out, the Japanese men who came to America between 1885 and 1907 "were not the most impoverished persons in their homelands and were also relatively well educated" (112); within this group, however, there were differences between merchants, intellectuals, farmers, manual workers, etc.

2. For an analysis of Yamamoto's brilliant "technique of double-telling," of "playing the naive nisei point of view against the pregnant silence of the issei," see Cheung. Yogi also deals with the different levels of consciousness of Rosie and her mother; he also places the story in a much more culturally specific context than a critic like Koppelman does, but he still reads the conflict as almost exclusively gender-based.

3. Joan Giroux points out that words indicating a specific season—common in the Japanese language—are "[a]n integral element of most haiku . . . [and] relates to a Zen interest in nature" (94); "[t]he season word provides a brief reference to the time of year and suggests a whole background of imagery which greatly broadens the scope of the poem" (97). Yagi Kametaro observes that the season word "was a principal ingredient of the haiku when it was differenti-

ated from linked verse (*renga*) and gained independent stature, and it has remained an essential ever since" (80).

4. "According to the Gentlemen's Agreement of 1907, Japanese immigrants were able to bring in wives as non-laborers and to establish families in America. . . . By 1924, when all Japanese immigration was finally halted by law, over 14,000 Japanese women had come, mostly as 'picture brides,' to join husbands they had seen only in photographs" (Kim 124). Tome would have been one of this group.

5. The 1913 California Alien Land Law allowed only U.S. citizens and persons eligible for citizenship to own land. Japanese immigrants like Mr. Hayashi could not own land, but their American-born children, who were citizens, could. Thus many Issei were forced to register their lands in their children's names, or sometimes in the names of American neighbors. This is a submerged but additional level of conflict in Yamamoto's stories. On the stereotyping of Asian men as "feminine," "passive," "submissive," see Chin and Chan; Kim 18–22.

6. When questioned, in "A MELUS Interview" with Charles Crow, about her treatment of Mr. Hayashi, Yamamoto responds: "I didn't think I was being *vicious* toward the husband, because he was only acting the way he'd been brought up to act, the way men were supposed to be" (80). Her point is that gender roles also trap and victimize men.

7. Yamamoto herself implies a connection between *haiku* and psychological displacement/repression when she suggests that Nisei *haiku* poets in the internment camps during World War II rarely depicted camp experience (see "'. . . I Still Carry It Around'").

8. Yet even here Yamamoto does not resort to single binary oppositions of the villainous husband versus the virtuous wife. Instead, she deconstructs the oppositions by forcing us to recognize that Mr. Hosoume's authority is only relative: he has power over his Issei wife and the Filipino farmhand, but in relation to the racist dominant culture he, like Mr. Hayashi, occupies a "feminine" subject position, one symbolized in the story when the accident leaves him impotent and weak, unable to manage the farm and thus forced to do the "women's work" of cooking and housekeeping. Mr. Hosoume's relations of power are further complicated by the fact that, although he is a *de facto* landowner, he too is legally landless (see note 5 above). Gender and class positions are extremely complex in these stories.

☐ *Works Cited* ■

Cheung, King-Kok. "Double-Telling: Intertextual Silence in Hisaye Yamamoto's Fiction." *American Literary History* 3:2 (1991): 277–293.

Chin, Frank, and Jeffery Paul Chan. "Racist Love." *Seeing Through Shuck,* edited by Richard Kostelanetz: 65–79. New York: Ballantine, 1972.

Cohen, William Howard. *To Walk in Seasons: An Introduction to Haiku.* Rutland and Tokyo: Charles E. Tuttle, 1972.

Crow, Charles L. "A MELUS Interview: Hisaye Yamamoto." *MELUS* 14:1 (1987): 73–84.

Giroux, Joan. *The Haiku Form.* Rutland and Tokyo: Charles E. Tuttle, 1974.

Henderson, Harold G. *Haiku in English.* Rutland and Tokyo. Charles E. Tuttle, 1967.

Kim, Elaine H. *Asian American Literature: An Introduction to the Writings and Their Social Context.* Philadelphia: Temple University Press, 1982.

Koppelman, Susan, ed. *Between Mothers and Daughters.* New York: Feminist Press, 1985.

McDonald, Dorothy Ritsuko, and Katharine Newman. "Relocation and Dislocation: The Writings of Hisaye Yamamoto and Wakako Yamauchi." *MELUS* 7:3 (1980): 21–38.

Ueda, Makoto, ed. and trans. *Modern Japanese Haiku: An Anthology.* Toronto: University of Toronto Press, 1976.

Yagi Kametaro. *Haiku: Messages from Matsuyama.* Edited by Oliver Statler. Rochester, Michigan: Katydid Books, 1991.

Yamamoto, Hisaye. "' . . . I Still Carry It Around.'" *RIKKA* 3:4 (1976): 11–14.

———. *Seventeen Syllables and Other Stories.* Introduction by King-Kok Cheung. Latham, N.Y.: Kitchen Table: Women of Color Press, 1988.

Yogi, Stan. "Rebels and Heroines: Subversive Narratives in the Stories of Wakako Yamauchi and Hisaye Yamamoto." In *Reading the Literatures of Asian America,* edited by Shirley Geok-lin Lim and Amy Ling: 131–150. Philadelphia: Temple University Press, 1992.

"Seventeen Syllables":
A Symbolic Haiku

In 1942, the Japanese Relocation Act incarcerated 110,000
Japanese. Born in 1921 of Japanese immigrant parents, Hisaye Yamamoto is a Nisei and one of those who watched
closely the effects of that tragic internment.[1] Although there
are books, taped reminiscences bound into collections, and a
slender handful of films, there is little criticism available that
examines the experience of fiction writers who may have been
marked by concentration camps like Manzanar, which was
the first of ten such camps. The saga of the people who suffered this indignity has been documented by writers. Michi
Weglyn, for example, gives a detailed account of this experience in *Years of Infamy: The Untold Story of America's Concentration Camps.*

In the brief biographical information on Hisaye Yamamoto that she provides in *Between Mothers and Daughters*
preceding Yamamoto's short story "Seventeen Syllables," Susan Koppelman writes: "She, along with 110,000 other Japanese Americans, was subjected to relocation and imprisonment. . . . During the war, she moved to Massachusetts for
a summer, but returned to camp, and then to California in
1945 where she was employed by the *Los Angeles Tribune*"
(161). Confinement seems to have sensitized Yamamoto to
the devastating results of a loss of control. In almost all
her short stories, her central characters battle overwhelming
odds. In "Relocation and Dislocation: The Writings of Hisaye
Yamamoto and Wakako Yamauchi," McDonald and Newman

From *Studies in Short Fiction* 27:2 (1990): 197–202.

accurately assess that she selects characters who are "hurt, who have deviated from the norm, who are grasping for some bits of beauty in their desperation. . . . All who seek but lose are of interest to Yamamoto" (28). This assessment also applies to Yamamoto's much anthologized "Seventeen Syllables." However, despite its popularity, the artistic levels in the tale, as in the others, remain unexplored. Koppelman draws attention to the fact that Yamamoto's stories have been reprinted at least twenty times in one or more of twelve anthologies since 1969. Yet Yamamoto still has not received the critical attention she merits.

Typical of a Yamamoto story, "Seventeen Syllables" offers multiple perspectives which need to be peeled back layer upon layer, for this tale simultaneously records a daughter's—Rosie's—awakening sensuality, and depicts a mother's—Tome Hayashi's—devastating annihilation. The tale's power lies in the vortex created by the mother's stepping outside her traditional Japanese Issei role of farm worker, cook, housekeeper, and wife. The narrative tensions arise out of a seemingly simple interest that Tome develops, haiku. At one level, the story depicts the cultural barrier that haiku creates and reveals among Tome, her husband, and her daughter; at another level, the tale unravels the destruction of a woman who creates independently.

To neglect Yamamoto's artistic achievement in using haiku is to bypass the deeper metaphor for separation which it suggests. To understand the subtle symbolism of haiku, one must understand the complexity of this art form: its simplicity is deceptive in depth of content and in origin. In the Introduction to the first of his four volumes entitled *Haiku,* R. H. Blyth explains that this type of poetry needs to be understood from the Zen point of view. He describes haiku as "a spiritual state of mind in which individuals are not separated from other things, instead remain identical with them while yet retaining their individuality and defining peculiarities" (iii). Obviously, neither Rosie nor Mr. Hayashi is able to understand haiku or the meaning it has for Tome. Both father and daughter lack the undiluted, intuitive understanding necessary, for haiku represents the Eastern world of religious and poetic experience. Japanese traditional roles and the American world seem

196

to have stripped Mr. Hayashi and Rosie of the innate ability to be one and yet separate. Blyth compares the haiku experience to a kind of enlightenment in which the reader sees into the life of things.

During the three months that Tome contributes haiku to *Mainichi Shimbun,* "The Daily Newspaper," she takes the "blossoming name" of Ume Hanazono. In Japanese, the name *Ume* stands for an exquisite flowering tree which blossoms in early spring and bears fruit by the end of spring—that is, in three months. *Hanazono* means "a flower garden." Both names enfold one of the central experiences described in the story: Tome Hayashi's brief awakening into a creative independence which does not include her Japanese husband of "simple mind" or her Nisei daughter who pretends to understand Japanese because she doesn't want to disillusion her mother about the "quantity and quality" of the Japanese she knows. On the other hand, *Tome* ironically signifies "good fortune," or "luck," while *Hayashi* means "woods." In the names, one sees some of the subtle shades of meaning implied in this Nisei, second generation Japanese American, story.

The number three plays a subtle role in "Seventeen Syllables." Tome's/Ume's brief awakening lasts for *"perhaps three months"* (italics mine)—*a season*—as does her name-sake tree, Ume, which blossoms and bears fruit in *three* months. The brief three months are echoed by the *three* line scheme—five, seven, and five syllables—used for haiku when it is translated or written in English. Haiku becomes the metaphor for Tome's separateness. After she works in the fields, keeps house, cooks, washes, and serves dinner, she becomes a significant other person; she transforms into Ume Hanazone—a poet.

The creative pull Ume feels assumes threatening dimensions as she discusses haiku with other males. Tome steps outside her role as an insignificant other and strives for intellectual stimulation and challenges in the process of composing poetry. Essentially, haiku transforms her from a quiet wife into one who becomes in a sense a true Japanese, an "earnest muttering stranger, who often neglected speaking when spoken to and stayed busy at the parlor table as late as midnight scribbling with pencil on scratch paper . . ." Mr. Hayashi now must play solitaire. The gulf between the Hayashis widens each time the family goes visiting. Her haiku makes her forget her traditional role—the submissive, passive working person—for Tome engages in comparing ecstatic notes with visiting poets while her husband entertains "the nonliterary members" or looks at *Life* magazine instead of intuiting *life* through his wife's poetry as would a true lover of haiku or ukiyo-e.

Rosie's emerging womanhood parallels the three months of Tome's poetry writing. Rosie secretly meets with Jesus Carrasco, the son of the Mexican family hired for the harvest. With the first stolen kiss, he awakens her sensuality: "Once he had made her screech hideously by crossing over, while her back was turned, to place atop the tomatoes in her green-stained basket a truly monstrous, pale green worm (it had looked more like an infant snake)." The phallic innuendo is hard to ignore.

Rosie is so wrapped in herself that she fails to see her mother's need for identity, creativity, and approval. Each time Ume reads a poem for approval, Rosie's response is a refrain: "It was so much easier to say yes, yes, even when one meant no, no." The "yes, yes" she says to placate her mother reflects the cultural vacuum that exists between the mother and daughter as it reflects Rosie's inability to become one with the haiku that Ume writes. However, the language barrier between the mother and daughter pales besides the growing haiku barrier between the parents.

One hot afternoon, "the hottest day of the year," when the creative pull seems to have reached breaking point, the haiku editor of the *Mainichi Shimbun* personally delivers the first-prize award that Ume wins. The Hiroshige Mr. Kuroda brings subtly echoes the spiritual chasm between the Hayashis, as it affirms the deep relationship of oriental art to haiku. Blyth explains:

> A haiku poet may express his understanding pictorially as well as verbally. . . . It is indirect, in that the pictures he sees teach him how to look at and feel and listen to the world of nature. . . . They show him where the value and meaning of

things [are], so he may say in words what the pictures say in
lines, concerning that mysterious interplay of the simple and
the complicated, the general and the particular. . . . The
ukiyo-e of Hiroshige would have no significance, were the
scenery of Japan as plain and clear in outline as they.

(86)

Like haiku, Hiroshige's famous landscapes evoke emersion
and must be intuited. The viewer must feel her feet in the pink
clouds he paints and become one of the individuals in the sampans that float near the pines. The gap in understanding is
reflected in Rosie's cold, literal description of the Hiroshige:

> Rosie thought it was a pleasant picture, which looked to
> have been sketched with delicate quickness. There were pink
> clouds, containing some graceful calligraphy, and a sea that
> was a pale blue except at the edges, containing four sampans
> with indications of people in them.

The entire description reflects the failure to see the mysterious interplay among life, the painting and the self. Rosie's inability to imagine the floating world of ukiyo-e or to intuit
what the picture suggests reaffirms the barriers between her
mother and herself as well as between the Japanese culture
and herself.

In the excitement of receiving the prize, Ume takes
over from Tome—the subservient tomato packer—and entertains the illustrious Japanese visitor at tea. Once more cut out
from a true understanding, Mr. Hayashi storms in, seizes the
prize, takes it outside, and proceeds to smash and burn it.

After the mother and daughter watch the fire die, Tome
tells her story to her daughter. "It was like a story out of the
magazines. . . . Her mother, at nineteen, had come to America
and married her father as an alternative to suicide." At this
point, the title "Seventeen Syllables" becomes meaningful. It
seems to stand not only for the number of syllables in a haiku
but also for the stillborn illegitimate child Tome bore *seventeen years* ago in Japan, a syllable for each silent year she lives
in America. The reader then recalls the patience with which

Ume had explained haiku: "See Rosie, . . . it was a *haiku,* a poem in which she must pack all her meaning into seventeen syllables only . . ."

The power of this seemingly simple Nisei tale comes from several interwoven themes. The primary one reveals a cultural straitjacket in which a male dominates and destroys a gentle woman who is consumed by an urgent need to create and express herself. Moreover, the narrative suggests another possible female tragedy in Rosie's future. Rosie and Jesus' relationship harbors a potential intercultural conflict, for Jesus is not of her ethnic group or station. Rosie's romance recalls her mother's unfortunate love affair with the young Japanese who was above her social position.

The conclusion of the story echoes the cultural chasm between the mother and daughter also, for Tome asks Rosie, "Promise me you will never marry." Tome receives the same glib agreement Rosie used for haiku—the old lie—"Yes, yes, I promise." Ironically, just as Tome barely understands English, Rosie scarcely understands the mother's suffocating plea. Each is a prisoner, isolated in solitary confinement. Tragically, Tome loses her second child also, this time to an alien culture which does not have an artistic spiritual intuitiveness or the same gender restrictions as the Japanese. Rejected by both husband and daughter, Ume Hanazone is destroyed, no more to be a flowering garden.

Tome's fate is played in counterpoint, as it were, in the story of Mrs. Hayano, who we are told bore four lovely daughters, each named after *one season* (again, *three months*) of the year. Haru, *spring,* is her first-born. The reader is told "something had been wrong with Mrs. Hayano ever since the birth of her first child." Mrs. Hayano, who was reputed to have been the belle of her native village, moves stooped and shuffling, violently trembling, always. Mr. Hayano, we are told, is "handsome, tall, and strong." So Mrs. Hayano has her brief spring like Ume/Tome and is destroyed.

What is the reader to intuit about the female role in this culture? These women blossom/create and pay the price—intense personal jeopardy or annihilation. The duration of their flowering shrinks to the length of almost a season; confined and compressed, their existences recall a sparse seventeen-syllable ephemeral haiku.

"Seventeen Syllables" remains irrevocably a woman's story. The flavor and anguish which lace it and make it powerful come from the collision of Eastern and Western values. Tome steps outside her place as child bearer, housekeeper, and farmworker when she attempts to gain control and carve an independent artistic territory for herself, and she is smothered. Rosie identifies with her American background and culture. Ironically, even in Japanese class, she entertains her friend by mimicking a series of British and American movie stars. Rosie doesn't understand Tome, nor does she understand her own roots or the Japanese language and culture.

Both the Japanese and American cultures makes demands which by themselves can create intense disequilibrium. In close juxtaposition, they seem to destroy the occupants or at best leave them in the middle of the *woods* (Hayashi). Perhaps a letter written by Yamamoto, which Koppelman quotes in her introduction to the story, throws additional light on the power of this tale; Yamamoto speaks of the pain she feels when she thinks of her mother, who could have used a more understanding daughter. Yamamoto goes on to say that "Seventeen Syllables" is her mother's story, even though the details are not true. Although the Japanese and American cultures do not fuse in this tale, art and the artist do, for "Seventeen Syllables" becomes the daughter's symbolic haiku for the mother—the "yes, yes" said finally, packed with all the intuitive meaning and understanding in Zen fashion.

☐ *Note* ■

1. Weglyn explains that the Japanese were usually lumped together into one derogatory group—"Japs"—during the war years, but needed to be seen as four groups, for they had experienced different formative backgrounds. The Issei were first generation Japanese who had an entire Japanese cultural background. The Nisei were second generation Japanese who had received their entire education in the United States. The Kibei were Nisei who were divided

into two groups. The Japanese used this term to refer to those American-born Japanese who received their education in Japan till they were seventeen, and also to those who received their early formative education in America and then went to Japan for four or fives years of education (41).

◻ Works Cited ■

Blyth, R. H. *Haiku,* 4 vols. Japan: Hokuseido, 1966. Vol. 1.

Koppelman, Susan, ed. *Between Mothers and Daughters.* New York: Feminist Press, 1985.

McDonald, Dorothy Ritsuko, and Katharine Newman. "Relocation and Dislocation: The Writings of Hisaye Yamamoto and Wakako Yamauchi." *MELUS* (1980): 21–38.

Weglyn, Michi. *Years of Infamy: The Untold Story of America's Concentration Camps.* New York: Morrow Quill, 1976.

Yamamoto, Hisaye. "Seventeen Syllables." *Partisan Review,* November 1949.

———. "Writing." *Amerasia Journal* 3:2 (1976): 126–133.

☐ ROBERT M. PAYNE ■

Adapting (to) the Margins: *Hot Summer Winds* and the Stories of Hisaye Yamamoto

First broadcast in May 1991 as part of PBS's *American Playhouse* series, Emiko Omori's television film *Hot Summer Winds* marks a significant step for Asian American cinema. A drama about a Japanese American woman, written and directed by a Japanese American woman, based on the writings of a Japanese American woman, has finally found the opportunity to reach a wide viewing public. Because of its singularity, *Hot Summer Winds* claims an accessible space of integrity and dignity for the Asian American image in a medium which has done much to marginalize that image.[1] The film was well-received by its diverse audience and by the Asian American community. And given the infrequency of popularly available Japanese American dramas, the co-producing PBS station created a curriculum guide for the high-school classroom to emphasize what students can learn from *Hot Summer Winds*'s presentation of Japanese American life (Nakamura 3). But while the film's skillful execution merits this praise and attention, no one has yet raised questions of narrative differences between the film and the adapted stories. The absence of this discussion, even in the curriculum guide, is especially puzzling because the differences are so striking, differences which intriguingly illuminate issues of ethnic representation in American media.

From *East-West Film Journal* 7:2 (1993): 39–53.

Hot Summer Winds melds two short stories by Japanese American author Hisaye Yamamoto into a single, hour-long drama. The two fascinating stories, "Seventeen Syllables" (1949) and "Yoneko's Earthquake" (1951), were published with little fanfare, but they gathered a loyal following in the early 1970s, when Asian Americans sought to reclaim their own cultural and literary history.[2] Yamamoto published some of her earliest short stories during the late forties and early fifties, a time when few Asian American writers were reaching beyond their specific communities and into a broader readership. Although Jade Snow Wong and Monica Sone distinguished themselves during this period as non-fiction writers, an Asian American woman's name was as hard to find on the fiction shelves as it is now on the director's chair.[3] Yamamoto's presence, then, as a female Japanese American fiction writer in these post-internment years instantly signalled an identity different from the overwhelmingly white, male American literary world.

However, Yamamoto's writing goes further: it encourages the reader to delve beyond the surface content of plot and story. Ostensibly, both "Seventeen Syllables" and "Yoneko's Earthquake" are slice-of-life stories observing a young *nisei* (second-generation Japanese American) girl's day-to-day preoccupations with farm life and with her *issei* (immigrant) parents in the 1930s. But both the stories' youthful protagonists are blind to turbulent tragedies that rage beyond the page. The stories' most pressing concerns lurk between the lines, within the nebulous space of misunderstanding between a naive American daughter and her world-weary Japanese mother. Elaine Kim describes this generational tension as a continuing concern throughout Yamamoto's writing:

> Most of Yamamoto's stories have something to say about the relationship between the *issei* and *nisei* generations, who are brought together in stories essentially addressed to fellow *nisei* almost as a warning to them not to lose the experiences of their parents, which they (and she) can only partially understand. . . . Generally, the stories are told from the viewpoint of a *nisei* narrator who sees the *issei* as through a glass

darkly, without ever fully comprehending the feelings and actions of the older persons. (Kim 158)

"Yoneko's Earthquake," for example, follows Yoneko Hosoume, a ten-year-old *nisei* girl, as she observes her uneventful life on a California farm. Yoneko plays with her younger brother, Seigo, and gets a crush on Marpo, the handsome Filipino farmhand. But the story's third-person narrator drops tiny clues that things beyond Yoneko's comprehension loom beyond the scope of the narrative:

> [Yoneko's] mother came home breathless from the fields one day and pushed a ring at her, a gold-colored ring with a tiny glasslike stone in it, saying, "Look, Yoneko, I'm going to give you this ring. If your father asks where you got it, say you found it on the street." Yoneko was perplexed but delighted . . . and she said, certainly, she was willing to comply with her mother's request. Her mother went back to the fields then and Yoneko put the pretty ring on her middle finger, taking up the loose space with a bit of newspaper. It was similar to the rings found occasionally in boxes of Crackerjacks, except that it appeared a bit more substantial.
>
> Mr. Hosoume never asked about the ring; in fact, he never noticed she was wearing one.

Yoneko is hurt by Marpo's sudden disappearance and bewildered by a strange trip the family takes into town: Yoneko and Seigo have to wait patiently in the family pick-up while their parents visit the town's Japanese hospital. The parents eventually return, the father helping the mother to walk. Yoneko never learns what happened inside the hospital.

Seigo's sudden death not long afterwards makes Mrs. Hosoume inconsolable. Yoneko tries to hide her hurt feelings now that both Seigo and Marpo are gone. The story ends on a haunting note, as Yoneko awkwardly announces her new intellectual independence in front of her mother.

> One evening . . . Yoneko was helping her mother with the dishes when she found herself being examined with such

peculiarly intent eyes that, with a start of guilt, she began searching in her mind for a possible crime she had lately committed. But Mrs. Hosoume only said, "Never kill a person, Yoneko, because if you do, God will take from you someone you love."

"Oh, that," said Yoneko quickly, "I don't believe in that, I don't believe in God." And her words tumbling pell-mell over one another, she went on eagerly to explain a few of her reasons why. . . . She had believed for a moment that her mother was going to ask about the ring (which, alas, she had lost already, somewhere in the flumes along the cantaloupe patch).

At first, it seems clumsy to end a story with parentheses. But upon closer inspection, the reader realizes that the entire story is parenthetical, incidental to the real drama beyond Yoneko's youthful comprehension. The attentive audience has gradually pieced together the "off-stage" story: Mrs. Hosoume has had an affair with Marpo, and the trip into town was for her to get an abortion. The vague insinuation of an absent narrative leaves chilling gaps in Yoneko's perception of events. What, for example, does Mrs. Hosoume mean by "never kill a person"? Is she referring to the aborted fetus? Or is she implying that Marpo's unseen departure was equally violent and irreversible? Unable to interpret her mother's odd behavior, Yoneko receives her first disturbing inkling of the cruel world that awaits her as an adult, a world ominous in its imperceptibility.

Because Yamamoto's young main characters are not aware of all the important events influencing their lives, the reader of both "Yoneko's Earthquake" and "Seventeen Syllables" must peer beyond the girls' limited purview to discern the narratives' crucial hidden content. Abandoning seamless narrative closure, Yamamoto crafts a writerly text that demands the participation of her audience to complement the written story with their own construction of the absent narrative.

Perhaps inspired by the evocative understatement of haiku, Yamamoto's narrative strategy calls attention to the ethnic issues inherent in her stories.[4] Her characters' status as so-called ethnic minorities suggests a problematic relationship to her own Americanness: straddling but separated from the signifiers of two cultures, Japanese and American, the *issei* and *nisei* characters are crucibles of a new identity which must discover its own meaning and purpose. As personified by Yoneko, a Japanese American identity already exists, but it is still unfinished, growing, maturing. However, rather than unproblematically defining such a "Japanese American" identity, Yamamoto's synthesis of disparate cultural signifiers ultimately turns in on itself: the constant exchange of culturally distinctive ideas and activities among the diverse characters implicitly questions the narrow idea of culture as a collection of fixed, insular ethnic groups. Furthermore, the possibility, however deferred, of intercultural/inter-ethnic unions in Yamamoto's stories also indicates—and perhaps celebrates—the constantly fluctuating cultural and ethnic makeup of America's human landscape. Yoneko may exemplify a synthesis of Japanese and American cultures, but she can't contain the boundless fluidity of cultural interaction.[5]

In this context, Yamamoto's narrative ellipses take on an added resonance. Discussing the ambivalence of both narration and the national self-image, Homi K. Bhabha connects the loose-ended narrative to resistance against a nation's narrative authority and its construction of an unquestioned, seemingly homogeneous national identity:

> [Narrative openness] investigates the nation-space in the *process* of the articulation of elements: where meanings may be partial because they are *in medias res;* and history may be half-made because it is in the process of being made; and the image of cultural authority may be ambivalent because it is caught, uncertainly, in the act of composing its powerful image.
>
> (Bhabha 3)

The reader, then, may easily interpret Yamamoto's crucial narrative absences as a correlation to the relative absence of Japanese Americans—and people of color in general—in the discourse of American history as it has traditionally been taught in mainstream education. In particular, the pedagogical absence of the Japanese American internment, only recently remedied, has long elided this crucial event in the history of the U.S. Constitution. Also, Yamamoto's narrative lacunae are associable to invisibly oppressive power relations among the characters in her stories: the absence of important narrative information marks the missing alternative voice of the underling. Just as they suggest the amorphous space of an alternate literary discourse, the rupturous gaps in Yamamoto's stories suggest the contours of a perceptually radical history denied by patriarchy, hierarchy, and racism. By drawing the reader to the silences *within* the open-ended narrative, Yamamoto's stories quietly question what remains to be said *beyond* the narrative, and beyond the construct of American culture as fundamentally immutable and Eurocentric. By nurturing narrative openness, Yamamoto's writing incarnates Bhabha's concept of "minority discourse":

> The minority [discourse] does not simply confront the pedagogical, or powerful master-discourse with a contradictory or negating referent. It does not turn contradiction into a dialectical process. It interrogates its object by initially withholding its objective. Insinuating itself into the terms of the reference of the dominant discourse, the supplementary [discourse] antagonizes the implicit power to generalize, to produce the sociological solidity. The questioning of the supplement is not a repetitive rhetoric of the "end" of society but a meditation on the disposition of space and time from which the narrative of the nation must *begin*.
>
> (Bhabha 306)

Emiko Omori's *Hot Summer Winds* establishes its own identity by skillfully combining "Seventeen Syllables" and "Yoneko's Earthquake" into a single story, and by its change of title (even though the film's working title alternately used those of the short stories). Because Omori entered into the film industry as a documentary cinematographer, it's no surprise that her film pays meticulous attention to visual detail. Great care is taken to naturalistically re-create rural California in 1934. Some scenes ease the progression of plot so the camera may dwell on the visual intricacies of Japanese American family life: the appearance of the family's tomato fields, bottles hanging from a string, the family quietly enjoying a hard-earned meal, the mother enjoying a bath in the Japanese *furo*, a fallen tomato floating in a pond, among other fascinating and absorbing images. In this way, *Hot Summer Winds* forges an awareness of Japanese American culture through the visual presence of the non-white characters within the cinematic frame.[6] Simply by allowing these characters to positively inhabit a visual space, Omori, like Yamamoto, implicitly criticizes the creative organizations, both textual and institutional, which so frequently obscure Asian American life and thereby foster greater Eurocentrism among film and television audiences. Thus, the film crafts its own Japanese American discourse within the institution of Public Television. But a closer look at Omori's adaptation reveals a discourse in sharp contrast to Yamamoto's.

Simply put, *Hot Summer Winds* grafts the narrative of "Yoneko's Earthquake" onto the end of "Seventeen Syllables," so the mother's affair with the hired hand is spurred by her husband's oppression of her identity as a haiku poet. However, the film employs the characters of "Yoneko's Earthquake," therefore many issues central to "Seventeen Syllables" are never touched upon. Some of the film's changes preserve certain aspects of the stories: for example, Yamamoto's concern for non-Asian ethnic groups (more evident in "Seventeen Syllables") is maintained by changing Marpo to a Chicano. But the film veers sharply from the stories in two significant ways. First, the absent narratives only implied by Yamamoto are unambiguously dramatized on the screen by Omori. Second, the film elides Yamamoto's urgent pessimism when, after the mother's abortion, the father has a change of heart and allows her to continue writing haiku. And since Seigo doesn't die, everybody appears to live happily ever after.

On one level, Omori's optimistic ending may be seen as part of a feminist discourse. In the film, the mother's identity as a haiku poet challenges, disrupts, and finally alters the patriarchal *issei* household. The act of writing puts into motion an expressive means of self-definition which may subvert—however minimally—the prescriptive and restrictive gender roles of this nuclear family. Unlike the end of "Seventeen Syllables," where the mother's identity as a poet is ultimately crushed and obliterated by the father, the endurance of the mother's writing at the end of *Hot Summer Winds* affirms the resilience of the female discourse. Furthermore, when Yoneko's mother turns to Marpo for sexual consolation, and when she is finally reconciled with her husband, she goes against the long Eurocentric tradition of fictional Asian women— from Madame Butterfly and Suzie Wong to the female leads of *Miss Saigon* and *Come See the Paradise*—who seek romantic completion in the arms of white men.

However, by bringing Yamamoto's ominous absent narratives to the unambiguous center of its story, *Hot Summer Winds* removes the dreadful unspoken menace of these events. Omori abandons the fascinatingly interrogative perspective of the youngster, the intriguing quality that makes the stories so outstanding, to convey something less impressive: an adult's sympathetic perspective of adultery. The film thereby deprives the material of its distinctiveness and relegates Yoneko to an uncompelling supporting character in a drama focused upon her mother.

Although the mother's abortion is still kept off-screen, it functions in a completely different manner than in "Yoneko's Earthquake." In the short story, the abortion was implicitly a patriarchal act of violence against the mother's yearning for a more fulfilling life outside her loveless marriage. Even though the abortion was never explicitly acknowledged within the story, its brutality was displaced onto a collie killed by the father's pick-up truck on its way to the doctor. In *Hot Summer Winds*, the family travels to the doctor without incident, and after the off-screen abortion, the father shows his wife open affection for the first time in the film. The parents' reconciliation follows the mother's recovery, when her husband gives her a fancy new writing pen, tacitly encouraging her to write more haiku. So, the film portrays the abortion not as an act of patriarchal violence, but as a healing force rendered benign by its invisibility.[7]

Hot Summer Winds views the Japanese American family as a flexible institution, rather than a bastion of patriarchal intransigence, as in the stories. In the film, the father's willingness to let his wife write again, as well as his preparing food for the children while she is recovering from the abortion, signifies an equal willingness on his part to relax the usually stringent gender roles of the *issei* household. By the film's conclusion, a stratified Japanese American family has been transformed into a liberal field of activity that may accommodate romantic love, domestic work-sharing, creativity, and reproductive freedom. The parents' reconciliation, then, redeems the patriarchal, ethnically homogeneous, nuclear family that the stories' narrative openness implicitly interrogated.

The film's cohesive story structure and the omniscient voice-over narration by the adult Yoneko (in place of the stories' circumscribed third-person narrator) continuously fill in the events of the plot, so there is no need to question the daughter's awareness of what is happening. The viewer comes to believe that young Yoneko knows and understands everything concerning her parents' relationship, which is plainly detailed on the screen. The film resolves the conflict between the parents with the finality of a happy ending. And Yoneko's adult voice-over, echoing her opening words in the film's conclusion, neatly brings itself full circle. If the young Yoneko of the short story represents a discourse still in development, Yoneko's adult voice on the film's soundtrack signifies a discourse which has reached maturity and completion. The dramatization of the stories' "off-stage" events, as well as the film's more-or-less classical structure, enclose the diegesis within a contained, unquestioning narrative realm. Where Yamamoto stresses a rupturous narrative absence, Omori stresses a seamless visual presence. Where the stories work toward narrative openness, *Hot Summer Winds* works toward narrative closure.

Still, the closure doesn't entirely succeed. The neat resolution utterly depends on the father's miraculous transformation from a household autocrat to a more flexible, more giving marriage partner. The film never allows insight into how and why this character makes such a sudden and drastic shift in personality. Earlier, the father slapped his wife merely for talking back to him, but when she tells him that she is pregnant by another man, the husband only storms out of the house to quietly contemplate the rural landscape. The father in the film, as in the stories, is a man of few words, so it would be characteristic of him to keep his feelings hidden. But the film's vision of how to transform this *issei* household from a conservative patriarchal domain to a liberal site of sharing remains lost within the father's unexplained change of heart. *Hot Summer Winds*'s elision of how this change comes about elides, in turn, the perpetuation of patriarchy: the film seems oblivious to the fact that this reformed, seemingly non-patriarchal Japanese American household exists only at the father's mercurial whim. But unlike Yamamoto's stories, this sort of textual openness appears completely inadvertent.

A more intriguing narrative openness within the film is suggested by the mother's poetry. In joining Yamamoto's two stories, the film omits the mother's explanation of her past and how she came to America. The viewer never learns exactly why Yoneko's well-educated mother married a barely literate farmer. However, the mother's bittersweet poems subtly suggest a painful past. For example:

> A long picture scroll
> Humorous and pathetic
> Both, this past of mine.

After her husband destroys her writing materials, Yoneko's mother begins her affair with Marpo, which functions as both an act of defiance against her husband's cruelty and an outlet for the emotions she is now forbidden to channel through poetry. In its most intriguing and anomalous scene, the film suggests the affair as a substitute for the creativity of writing: as she baths in the *furo*, the mother fantasizes about Marpo seducing her after her bath. In rhythmic cross-fades, her *mind-screen* (to use Bruce Kawin's term) alternates with images of her slow, sensual bathing.[8] When her bath is over, she approaches Marpo, who invites her into his shack for tea: this shot matches exactly the opening image of her fantasy. The scene fades out, letting the viewer assume that the mother's fantasy will be consummated.

In this scene, for the only time in the film, the chronological flow of time is disrupted to suggest a female discourse which correspondingly disrupts the monogamous marriage and the ethnically homogeneous, patriarchal family. Just as the monogamous marriage can't contain the mother's sexual desire, the seamless, linear narrative can't contain her desire for self-expression. Still, the perceptual issues raised by the bathing scene are eventually subsumed within the film's closed ending. The mother's female discourse is finally appropriated and rendered unthreatening by patriarchal approval of her poetry. The disruptive potential of the bathing scene is thus reduced to the readerly: it freezes into a self-reflexive stroke by the filmmaker to display her command of the medium. Such a readerly flourish doesn't correspond to the writerly ruptures of Yamamoto's literary narratives.[9]

Ultimately, Yamamoto's discourse of literary absence and Omori's discourse of visual presence are at odds. By leaving her stories open-ended, prodding her readers to extrapolate the reasons why the narratives refuse to completely account for themselves, Yamamoto compellingly questions the marginalizing dominant. Omori, on the other hand, seeks a place of integrity for the Asian American image within the closed confines of the dominant discourse.

Both the film and the stories, then, embody the liminality of a minority presence in American media: the film marks one threshold of possibilities for the Asian image as part of a dominant discourse, while the stories suggest another threshold beyond which an alternate Asian American discourse must be imagined. In both cases, the possibilities of transcending marginalization remain themselves marginalized—relegated to the quiet, unspoken, unrealized corners of the text—despite the fact that marginalized people command the center of the fiction. Nevertheless, while Yamamoto's stories urge the reader to cross their discursive threshold, Omori's film appears content to remain within the discursive limits of dominant cinema. The film thereby affirms these limits—as it affirms the ethnically homogeneous, patriarchal family—as a site of liberal accommodation. Because *Hot Summer Winds* redeems these dominant authorities, it's no wonder that the film actively seeks a place within the high-school classroom, within the pedagogical, Bhabha's "powerful master-discourse."

But *Hot Summer Winds* can't envision how or why a dominant ideology would willingly cede its power and accept a potentially disruptive alternative discourse, as represented by the mother's poetry. The film can only imagine a dominant figure's sudden and inexplicable transformation from an intolerant patriarch to a tolerant patriarch. This isn't to say that the film is closed to alternate readings (for example, the father's status as both a household authority and a national subaltern makes him an ambiguous and multi-faceted figure), but in valorizing the dominant discourse as a site of liberal accommodation, Omori rejects the rich discursive interrogation at the heart of Yamamoto's stories.

Moreover, dominant cinema developed its discourse of closure through many racially reductionistic narratives—with D. W. Griffith's *The Birth of a Nation* (1915) standing as the best-known and most blatantly racist paradigm. So, the viewer may still ask whether Omori's efforts to locate an equitable space for Asian Americans within the dominant might be misplaced. After all, if the dominant discourse is so accommodating, why is an Asian American film like *Hot Summer Winds* relegated to PBS, while the dominant entertainment industry grants higher profiles to projects that actively marginalize the presence of Asian Americans? The 1990 controversies surrounding both the Broadway production of *Miss Saigon* and the Hollywood movie *Come See the Paradise* have recently exemplified the industry's insistence on Asian marginalization, even in the face of outspoken criticism.[10] Can Asian American filmmakers absorb the standards of dominant cinema without compromising the distinctiveness of their voices? Or in the words of documentarian Renee Tajima: "Asian American films have gained in technical standards, narrative cohesion, and basic watchability. We have learned the master's language, but have we sacrificed our own?" (Tajima 30).

In the same article, Tajima asserts that Asian American cinema will realize its fullest power in concert with other oppressed and marginalized voices searching for their own distinctive accent. One may then assume that Tajima is searching not for a cinematic discourse that presumes to define Asian Americanness for all time to come, but for one that breaks down arbitrary, Eurocentric racial classifications and frees people from thinking of themselves primarily in terms of race. Just as Yamamoto's stories provide a perceptually inquisitive space to contemplate patriarchy as an oppressive force that

214

transcends racial and cultural "boundaries," so an alternate cinematic discourse might illuminate positive commonalities shared between cultures and ethnicities. Although it would work against racism and the lingering legacy of white colonial domination, such a prospective discourse would be severely limiting if it excluded marginalized voices emerging from white America and Europe.

In this spirit, it's worth noting that the feature films which best correspond to Yamamoto's alternate discourse weren't made by an Asian American. Two of Spanish director Víctor Erice's films, *The Spirit of the Beehive (El Espíritu de la colmena,* 1973) and *El Sur* (1983), seem to be discursive companions to "Yoneko's Earthquake" and "Seventeen Syllables": both of Erice's films employ adolescent or pre-adolescent female protagonists; his camera adopts a visual and narrative field which approximates the inquisitive curiosity of the young girls, creating an investigative diegetic space; and most importantly, Erice, too, leaves intriguing structuring absences in his narratives, elliptical ruptures which (in this case) provoke the viewer to question the films in the context of fascist Spain. Because Erice, like Yamamoto, locates his own alternate, elliptical, anti-fascist discourse in the eyes of children, his films give us some idea of the non-dominant cinematic strategies that were available to Omori's adaptation. And although such strategies are more than commensurate with Yamamoto's stories, *Hot Summer Winds,* in shifting emphasis from the child characters to the adults, chose not to utilize them.

Hisaye Yamamoto's stories remind the audience of the power of imagination. By leaving crucial details to the reader or viewer, the open narrative acknowledges its indebtedness to the active mind on the other side of the page, the other side of the screen. Narrative "incompletion" may also signify a societal incompletion, a nation's inability to realize an identity for all of its people outside racism and other forms of marginalization. The gaps in the text, as Bhabha has said, suggest where the culture's future remains to be written, as they simultaneously suggest that the writing must be done by the audience.

Ethnic visibility, as represented by *Hot Summer Winds,* is an important and valuable part of forging a national and cultural identity beyond racism. And audiences of all colors should continue to insist on increasing the well-rounded representation of non-white people in popular media. But such an identity can't be forged by visibility alone: Hollywood has too often appropriated images of minorities to encourage greater demographic support for films which implicitly sustain the racial status quo. More attention must be given to what kinds of discourses may be created through greater cultural diversity in the media, and how these discourses might create new ways of thinking about—and beyond—race and ethnicity.

☐ Notes ■

A shorter version of this essay was presented at "Dangerous Liaisons? A Conference on Literature, Film, and Video," held at the University of Southern California, on February 15, 1992. I would like to thank David James and Marsha Kinder for their insightful comments during this article's preparation.

1. I use the term "Asian American" with the knowledge that it is an externally assigned racial category which arbitrarily groups together people of widely divergent cultures and histories. The term's use in this essay is not intended to reify this racial construct. However, given the history of American racism, culturally specific Japanese American issues are unavoidably linked to larger, more general Asian American issues.

2. "Seventeen Syllables" was first published in the November 1949 issue of *Partisan Review.* pp. 1122–34. "Yoneko's Earthquake" first appeared in *Furioso,* vol. 6, no. 1 (1951), pp. 5–16. Both stories are reprinted in Yamamoto, *Seventeen Syllables* (8–19, 46–56).

3. For a history of Asian American writing at this time, see Kim (140–41). See also Yamamoto's "Writing."

4. Cf. King-Kok Cheung, Introduction to *Seventeen Syllables and Other Stories,* xxiii. The centrality of haiku to the plot—even to the title—of "Seventeen Syllables" supports readings of this poetic form as a stylistic influence upon Yamamoto.

5. Here, I'm drawing upon James Clifford's heterogeneous concept of culture. See Clifford (46).

6. *Hot Summer Winds* also boasts a very talented cast, with

Natsuko Ohama as the mother, Sab Shimono as the father, Pepe Serena as Marpo, Tricia Joe as Yoneko, and Rand Takeuchi as Seigo.

7. Although "Yoneko's Earthquake" carries an implicitly negative view of Mrs. Hosoume's abortion, I'd like to make it clear that I'm not lauding the story to argue against reproductive freedom. In the current debate over abortion, the paramount concern of the pro-choice position is a woman's right to decide for herself whether or not to bring a pregnancy to term. In "Yoneko's Earthquake," Mr. Hosoume appears to be the abortion's greatest beneficiary, because he can selfishly maintain the appearance of a monogamous marriage. Nothing in the story suggests that Yoneko's mother had any choice in the matter.

8. Bruce Kawin: "There are . . . three familiar ways of signifying subjectivity within the first-person narrative field: to present what a character says (voice over), sees (subjective focus, imitative angle of vision), or thinks. The term I propose for this final category is *mindscreen,* by which I mean simply the field of the mind's eye." See Kawin (10).

9. The bathing scene also begs the question of the voice-over's omniscience: how did the adult Yoneko, supposedly the film's narrator, get inside her mother's head—especially in a scene where the child Yoneko isn't present on-screen? The viewer may conclude that Yoneko ultimately isn't the film's controlling perspective. Rather, Yoneko's split points of view (as a child and as an adult) are only two of many perspectives (including the mother's) sewn together by the film to create its omniscient visual field. This narrative strategy reinforces the film's adherence to dominant cinema.

10. For more about the *Miss Saigon* controversy as "part of a broader conservative assault on progressive attempts to alter the patterns of [white] racial privilege," see Omi. For details about the controversy over *Come See the Paradise,* see Aoki.

☐ Works Cited ■

Aoki, Guy. "Another Look at *Paradise.*" *Tozai Times* (Los Angeles), April, 8–9, 1991.

Bhabha, Homi K., ed. *Nation and Narration.* New York: Routledge, 1990.

Clifford, James. *The Predicament of Culture: Twentieth-Century*

Ethnography, Literature, and Art. Cambridge: Harvard University Press, 1988.

Kawin, Bruce F. *Mindscreen: Bergman, Godard, and First-Person Film.* Princeton: Princeton University Press, 1978.

Kim, Elaine H. *Asian American Literature: An Introduction to the Writings and Their Social Context.* Philadelphia: Temple University Press, 1982.

Nakamura, Cayleen. *Seventeen Syllables: A Curriculum Guide for High School Classroom Use.* Los Angeles: KCET Television, 1991.

Omi, Michael. "The Issue Is About Race and Racism." *Hokubei Mainichi* (San Francisco), 25 September, 1990:2.

Tajima, Renee. "Moving the Image: Asian American Independent Filmmaking, 1970–1990," in *Moving the Image: Independent Asian Pacific American Media Arts.* edited by Russell Leong: 10–33. Los Angeles: UCLA Asian American Studies Center, 1991.

Yamamoto, Hisaye. "Writing." *Rafu Shimpo* (Los Angeles), 20 December, 1968: 14 ff.

———. *Seventeen Syllables and Other Stories.* Introduction by King-Kok Cheung. Latham, N.Y.: Kitchen Table: Women of Color Press, 1988.

Selected Bibliography

Works by Hisaye Yamamoto

"An Abandoned Pot of Rice." *Rafu Shimpo* 22 December 1984:6–7, 14.

"Appointment in Japan." *Rafu Shimpo* 21 December 1954: 12.

"Bettina." *Rafu Shimpo* 21 December 1955: 6, 14.

"The Boy from Nebraska." *Crossroads* 23 December 1949.

"Broccoli and Spinach." *Hokubei Mainichi* 1 January 1991 Supplement: 2.

"The Brown House." *Harper's Bazaar* October 1951: 166, 283–84. Reprinted in *Seventeen Syllables and Other Stories.*

"Christmas Eve on South Boyle." *Rafu Shimpo* 20 December 1957: 9, 18.

"A Day in Little Tokyo." *Amerasia Journal* 13:2 (1986–87): 21–28. Reprinted in *Seventeen Syllables and Other Stories.*

"Dried Snakeskins." *Rafu Shimpo* 22 December 1952: 15.

"Educational Opportunities." *Hokubei Mainichi* 1 January 1989: 6–7.

"Eju-kei-shung! Eju-kei-shung!" *Rafu Shimpo* 20 December 1980: 11–12, 16.

"The Enormous Piano." *Rafu Shimpo* 20 December 1977: 6, 31.

"Epithalamium." *Carleton Miscellany* 1:4 (1960): 56–67. Reprinted in *Seventeen Syllables and Other Stories.*

"The Eskimo Connection." *Rafu Shimpo* 21 December 1983: 9, 17, 22, 38. Reprinted in *Seventeen Syllables and Other Stories.*

"Eucalyptus," *Gidra* [20th Anniversary Issue] (1990): 34–36.

"A Fire in Fontana." *Rafu Shimpo* 21 December 1985: 8–9, 16–17, 19. Reprinted in *Rereading America: Cultural Contexts for Critical Thinking and Writing,* 2nd Ed. Edited by Gary Columbo, Robert Cullen and Bonnie Lisle. Boston: Bedford Books, 1992: 366–373.

"Florentine Gardens." *Asian America: Journal of Culture and the Arts* 1 (Winter 1992): 10—25.

"Gang Aft a-Gley." *Rafu Shimpo* 21 December 1953: 13–14.

"God Sees the Truth But Waits." *Catholic Worker* February 1957: 6.

"Having Babies." *Rafu Shimpo* 20 December 1962: 21.

"The High-Heeled Shoes, A Memoir." *Partisan Review* October 1948: 1079–1085. Reprinted in *Seventeen Syllables and Other Stories.*

"'. . . I Still Carry It Around.'" *RIKKA* 3:4 (1976): 11–19.

"In Search of a Happy Ending." *Pacific Citizen* 22 December 1951: 17–24.

"Ingurishi Tsuransureishan." *Rafu Shimpo* 20 December 1958: 9.

"Japanese in American Literature." *Rafu Shimpo* 20 December 1971: 13, 28, 36.

"Kichi Harada." *Pacific Citizen* 20 December 1957: B11.

"Las Vegas Charley." *Arizona Quarterly* 17 (1961): 303–322. Reprinted in *Seventeen Syllables and Other Stories.*

"The Legend of Miss Sasagawara." *Kenyon Review* 12:1 (1950): 99–114. Reprinted in *Seventeen Syllables and Other Stories.*

"Life Among the Oil Fields, A Memoir." *Rafu Shimpo* 20 December 1979: 13, 24–25. Reprinted in *Seventeen Syllables and Other Stories.*

"Life and Death of a Nisei GI: After Johnny Died." *Pacific Citizen* 1 December 1945: 5. Originally published in the column "Small Talk" in the *Los Angeles Tribune* 26 November 1945: 20–21.

"The Losing of a Language." *Rafu Shimpo* 20 December 1963: 7.

"A Man from Hiroshima." *Rafu Shimpo* 20 December 1956: 9.

"Miyoko O'Brien (Or, Everybody's Turning Japanese)." *Pacific Citizen* 20–27 December 1985: A46.

"Morning Rain." *Pacific Citizen* 19 December 1952: 46, 50. Reprinted in *Seventeen Syllables and Other Stories.*

"My Father Can Beat Muhammad Ali." *Echoes* 4 (1986): 14–15. Reprinted in *Seventeen Syllables and Other Stories.*

"The Nature of Things." *Rafu Shimpo* 20 December 1965: 7, 9–10, 12.

"Nip in the Bud." *Rafu Shimpo* 20 December 1961: 9–10.

"The Other Cheek." *Rafu Shimpo* 19 December 1959: 9.

"Peter Maurin Farm." *Catholic Worker* June 1953: 3, December 1954: 3, 8; January 1955: 3, 7; February 1955: 3, 5; July–August 1955: 6.

"Pleasure of Plain Rice." *Rafu Shimpo* 20 December 1960: 9, 10, 14. Reprinted in *Southwest: A Contemporary Anthology.* Albuquerque: Red Earth Press, 1977: 295–301.

"Reading and Writing." *Hokubei Mainichi* 1 January 1988: 5–6. Reprinted in *Seventeen Syllables and Other Stories.*

"A Really Good Bus Stop." *Hokubei Mainichi* 21 January 1990: 1.

"Reunion," *Rafu Shimpo* 12 December 1992: A14–15.

"Seabrook Farms—20 Years Later." *Catholic Worker* June 1954: 3, 6.

"Seventeen Syllables." *Partisan Review* November 1949: 1122–1134. Reprinted in *Seventeen Syllables and Other Stories.*

Seventeen Syllables: 5 Stories of Japanese American Life. Edited by Robert Rolf and Norimitsu Ayuzawa. Tokyo: Kirihara Shoten, 1985.

Seventeen Syllables and Other Stories. Latham, N.Y.: Kitchen Table: Women of Color Press, 1988.

"Sidney, the Flying Turtle." *Rafu Shimpo* 18 December 1967: 15, 27.

"A Slight Case of Mistaken Identity." *Rafu Shimpo* 19 December 1964: 6.

"The Streaming Tears." *Rafu Shimpo* 20 December 1951: 22, 24. Reprinted in *Six Short Stories by Japanese American Writers.* Edited by Iwao Yamamoto, Mie Hihara, and Shigeru Kobayashi. Tsurumi Shoten, 1991: 25–30.

"Surely I Must be Dreaming." *Poston Notes and Activities* April 1943.

"La tante de ma plume." *Rafu Shimpo* 31 December 1982: 11, 19, 25, 33.

"Tomato Surprise." *Rafu Shimpo* 19 December 1966: 26, 31.

"Underground Lady." *Pacific Citizen* 19–26 December 1986: A15, A20. Reprinted in *Seventeen Syllables and Other Stories.*

"Wilshire Bus." *Pacific Citizen* 23 December 1950: 17, 22. Reprinted in *Seventeen Syllables and Other Stories.*

"Writing." *Rafu Shimpo* 20 December 1968: 14ff. Reprinted in *Amerasia Journal* 3:2 (1976): 126–133.

"Yellow Leaves." *Rafu Shimpo* 20 December 1986: 36, 38–39.

"Yoneko's Earthquake." *Furioso* 6:1 (1951): 5–16. Reprinted in *Seventeen Syllables and Other Stories.*

Suggested Further Reading

Chan, Jeffery Paul, Frank Chin, Lawson Fusao Inada, and Shawn Wong, eds. *The Big Aiiieeeee! An Anthology of Asian American Writers.* New York: New American Library-Meridian, 1991.

Chan, Sucheng. *Asian Americans: An Interpretive History.* Boston: Twayne-Hall, 1991.

Cheung, King-Kok. *Articulate Silences: Hisaye Yamamoto, Maxine Hong Kingston, Joy Kogawa.* Ithaca: Cornell University Press, 1993.

———. "The Dream in Flames: Hisaye Yamamoto, Multiculturalism, and the Los Angeles Uprising." *Bucknell Review* 39.1 (1995). In press.

———. "Thrice Muted Tale: Interplay of Art and Politics in Hisaye Yamamoto's 'The Legend of Miss Sasagawara.'" *MELUS* 17:3 (1991–92). 109–125.

———, and Stan Yogi, eds. *Asian American Literature: An Annotated Bibliography.* New York: Modern Language Association, 1988.

Chin, Frank, Jeffery Paul Chan, Lawson Fusao Inada, and Shawn Wong, Eds. *Aiiieeeee! An Anthology of Asian-American Writers.* 1974. Washington, D.C.: Howard University Press, 1983.

Crow, Charles L. "Home and Transcendence in Los Angeles Fiction." *Los Angeles in Fiction: A Collection of Original Essays.* Edited by David Fine. Albuquerque: University of New Mexico Press, 1984: 189–205.

———. "A MELUS Interview: Hisaye Yamamoto." *MELUS* 14:1 (1987): 73–84.

Daniels, Roger. *Concentration Camps, North America: Japanese in the U.S. and Canada during World War II.* Malabar, Florida: R. E. Krieger, 1981.

Hsu, Kai-yu and Helen Palubinskas, eds. *Asian-American Authors.* 1972. Boston: Houghton, Mifflin, 1976.

Ichioka, Yuji. "*Amerika Nadeshiko:* Japanese Immigrant Women in the United States, 1900–1924." *Pacific Historical Review* 59:2 (1980): 339–357.

————. *The Issei: The World of the First Generation Japanese Immigrants, 1885–1924.* New York: Free Press, 1988.

Kageyama, Yuri. "Hisaye Yamamoto: Nisei Writer." *Sunbury* 10 (1981): 32–42.

Kim, Elaine H. *Asian American Literature: An Introduction to the Writings and Their Social Context.* Philadelphia: Temple University Press, 1982.

Koppelman, Susan, ed. *Between Mothers and Daughters.* New York: Feminist Press, 1985.

Matsumoto, Valerie. "Desperately Seeking 'Deirdre': Gender Roles, Multicultural Relations, and Nisei Women Writers of the 1930s." *Frontiers* 12:1 (1991): 19–32.

Nakamura, Cayleen. *"Seventeen Syllables": A Curriculum Guide for High School Classroom Use in Conjunction with "Hot Summer Winds."* Los Angeles: Community Television of Southern California, 1991.

Schweik, Susan. *A Gulf So Deeply Cut: American Women Poets and the Second World War.* Madison: University of Wisconsin Press, 1991.

Takaki, Ronald. *Strangers from a Different Shore: A History of Asian Americans.* Boston: Little, Brown, 1989.

Weglyn, Michi. *Years of Infamy: The Untold Story of America's Concentration Camps.* New York: William Morrow, 1976.

Yanagisako, Sylvia Junko. *Transforming the Past: Tradition and Kinship among Japanese Americans.* Stanford: Stanford University Press, 1985.

Yogi, Stan. "Legacies Revealed: Uncovering Buried Plots in the Stories of Hisaye Yamamoto and Wakako Yamauchi." M.A. Thesis, University of California, Berkeley, 1988.

————. "Rebels and Heroines: Subversive Narratives in the Stories of Wakako Yamauchi and Hisaye Yamamoto." In *Reading the Literature of Asian America.* Edited by Shirley Geok-lin Lim and Amy Ling. Philadelphia: Temple University Press, 1992. 131–150.

❑ Permissions ■

CPSIA information can be obtained at www.ICGtesting.com
Printed in the USA
BVOW040831010713

324558BV00005B/17/A